Philosophy of Psychology

For Keiko Miyazono and Kenichi Miyazono
For Ennia Scarduelli and Adalberto Bortolotti

Philosophy of Psychology

An Introduction

**Kengo Miyazono and
Lisa Bortolotti**

polity

First published in 2021 by Polity Press

Reprinted 2022

Polity Press
65 Bridge Street
Cambridge CB2 1UR, UK

Polity Press
101 Station Landing
Suite 300
Medford, MA 02155, USA

ISBN-13: 978-1-5095-1547-9
ISBN-13: 978-1-5095-1548-6 (pb)

A catalogue record for this book is available from the British Library.

Typeset in 10.5 on 13 pt Sabon
by Fakenham Prepress Solutions, Fakenham, Norfolk NR21 8NL
Printed and bound in Great Britain by TJ Books Limited, Padstow

The publisher has used its best endeavours to ensure that the URLs for external websites referred to in this book are correct and active at the time of going to press. However, the publisher has no responsibility for the websites and can make no guarantee that a site will remain live or that the content is or will remain appropriate.

Every effort has been made to trace all copyright holders, but if any have been overlooked the publisher will be pleased to include any necessary credits in any subsequent reprint or edition.

For further information on Polity, visit our website:
politybooks.com

Contents

Detailed Contents

Acknowledgements

Our greatest debt is to Yukihiro Nobuhara: if he had not invited Lisa to present her work on delusions at the University of Tokyo in October 2010, then Kengo and Lisa wouldn't have met and discovered common interests and potential areas of collaboration.

Next, we are grateful to the Japan Society for the Promotion of Science: Kengo was funded by one of their international fellowships to visit Lisa at the University of Birmingham. There, he completed his research on delusions and actively participated in Lisa's projects. Being colleagues enabled Lisa and Kengo to talk about belief, delusion, and rationality together, and also become friends. Lisa's European Research Council project, PERFECT, made it possible for the collaboration to continue, at a distance. Kengo made significant contributions to the project outputs, and in particular to the notion of epistemic innocence that was developed as part of that project.

We thank anonymous reviewers for helpful and insightful suggestions. We are also grateful to Uku Tooming for detailed comments on the final manuscript, and to Benjamin Costello for his excellent proofreading. This work was supported by JSPS KAKENHI (16H06998, 18H00605).

This book project started in 2015, and it took us five years to complete the manuscript. We thank Pascal Porcheron, Ellen MacDonald-Kramer, and Stephanie Homer at Polity Press for their extraordinary patience and encouragement during this time.

Our project took time because we aimed to do something novel with it. Although there are good introductions to the philosophy of psychology or to the philosophy of the cognitive sciences, they tend to focus on what we call 'foundational philosophy of psychology', where the foundational issues in psychology (such as the nature of representation, or the language of thought hypothesis) are prioritized. In contrast, this book focuses on 'implicational philosophy of psychology', where the philosophical implications of psychological studies (such as the study of reasoning biases by Daniel Kahneman and Amos Tversky [discussed in Chapter 1], or the study of altruistic behaviour by Daniel Batson [discussed in Chapter 5]) take centre-stage.

The present book is an attempt to put together the issues we find interesting and stimulating at the intersection of philosophy and psychology, and share them with our students in an accessible and engaging way. We have had excellent role models as lecturers of Philosophy of Psychology over the years, including John Campbell, Martin Davies, David Papineau, Kim Sterelny, Helen Steward, ... to mention only a few.

We hope we have learnt something from them.

Introduction

An Overview

This book introduces and explains some central issues in the philosophy of psychology. It is important to note that it is not a neutral introduction to the topic. It is an opinionated introduction to the philosophy of psychology in which we defend a particular view of human cognition and agency. The view that we defend is that human cognition and agency are *imperfect*, in the sense that humans fail to meet some ideal standards of cognition and agency, such as the ideal of rationality, self-knowledge, and free and responsible agency.

Imagine that Lucy wants to pass her ballet exam tomorrow and she knows that she needs to rehearse the opening routine to make sure she remembers all the steps. Passing the exam is important to her, and she would be very disappointed if she failed. Yet she sits on the sofa to watch a movie instead of practising her routine. Given Lucy's goal (passing the ballet exam tomorrow), her behaviour (watching a movie instead of practising) may be considered *irrational* since she does not take the appropriate steps to fulfil her goal. Chapter 1 discusses various notions of rationality and some ways in which human agents might fall short of the standards of rationality.

Now imagine that Giorgio describes himself as an exceptionally generous child, always willing to support his friends. However, that is not how his friends describe him. On a number of occasions, they have observed that Giorgio has put his own needs before theirs and has refrained from sharing snacks or helping them with their homework. They think of him as mean and selfish. If Giorgio's friends are right, then we can say that Giorgio *lacks self-knowledge*. In other words, he does not have an accurate representation of himself. In particular, he attributes to himself qualities (such as generosity) that he does not have. Chapter 2 discusses several ways in which self-knowledge can fail.

Finally, imagine that Elsa, who is a white US citizen, thinks of herself as a very egalitarian person who respects everybody and considers them all equal, independently of ethnic origin or skin colour. However, when she goes to work, she avoids sitting next to Asian passengers on the bus and, when she talks to her colleagues at work, she tends to ignore her Nigerian secretary. Elsa does not have explicit beliefs that are prejudiced against people who look different from her but behaves in ways that are inconsistent with her explicit beliefs and values. She *is vulnerable to implicit biases* for which she *may or may not be responsible*. Chapter 3 deals with the duality of states and attitudes and Chapter 6 with the question whether people are responsible for their implicit biases.

You may have experienced similar failures of rationality and self-knowledge and have encountered biases in yourselves and others – you can come up with your own examples of how human agents are imperfect. Indeed, the view that human cognition and agency are imperfect is not surprising. Not many philosophers are convinced that humans are perfect agents who are ideally rational, have complete self-knowledge, and behave in unbiased ways. However, this book does not just claim that human cognition and agency are limited; on the basis of relevant psychological studies, it also makes some potentially surprising and controversial claims about *the extent to which* and *the reasons why* human cognition and agency are limited.

In this context, 'imperfect' does not mean 'stupid' or 'dumb'. It means that performance falls short of the ideal standards that apply to it. This book does not advocate an overly *pessimistic* conception of human cognition and agency. For instance, we do not endorse what John Kihlstrom (2004) calls the 'People are Stupid' school of psychology, which says that humans are fundamentally irrational, that their behaviour is automatic and inflexible, and that they are ignorant of what they are doing. Rather, we advocate a *realistic* conception that is informed by psychological findings and is defended by philosophical arguments. We resist two extreme views of human cognition and agency. On the one hand, we resist an overly optimistic view according to which human cognition and agency are perfect (or near-perfect) with respect to ideal standards such as rationality, self-knowledge, and free and responsible agency. On the other hand, we resist an overly pessimistic view according to which human cognition and agency are hopeless with respect to these ideal standards. Our cognition and agency are certainly not perfect. However, by learning about the nature of, extent of, and reasons for their limitations, human agents can improve their performance. That is one of the reasons why philosophy of psychology is important. It does not simply provide information about what human agents can or cannot do. It offers human agents the resources to enhance their performance (in reasoning, decision-making, problem-solving, etc.) so that they can get closer to the ideal standards.

There is another sense of 'imperfection' that is addressed in this book: human cognition and agency can be 'imperfect' in the sense that they are vulnerable to *disorders of the mind* (broadly construed, including psychiatric disorders, behavioural anomalies caused by brain damage, developmental disorders, etc.). Disorders of the mind are usually identified by behaviours that appear unusual. While it is common to be weak-willed like Lucy, blind to one's own character flaws like Giorgio, or unconsciously biased like Elsa, endorsing wildly implausible beliefs or seeing things that other people cannot see is less common and might lead to the person being diagnosed with a mental disorder. For instance, the mathematician John Nash experienced hallucinations and delusions, coming to believe that aliens were publishing messages in newspapers (which was described in the biographical movie *A Beautiful Mind*). This book will discuss 'abnormalities' of the mind, including delusion and confabulation (in Chapter 7) and autism and psychopathy (in Chapter 8). Thinking about unusual cognitions and behaviours helps us understand how the mind works and how vulnerability to disorders of the mind relates to the failure to meet ideal standards.

Here are the central questions discussed in the following chapters:

* *Rationality* (Chapter 1): Are we rational or irrational? How good are we at reasoning in accordance with the rules of logic and mathematics? How do we reason or make judgments? Do we rely on unreliable heuristics or shortcuts?

- *Self-Knowledge* (Chapter 2): How well do we know our own mind? How do we know our mental states? Is the process of knowing our own mental states different in kind from the process of knowing somebody else's mental states?
- *Duality* (Chapter 3): Is human reasoning determined by the inter-action between two distinct kinds of processes? If so, how are these processes different and how do they interact? Why are there only *two* kinds of processes, rather than *three* or *four*?
- *Moral Judgment* (Chapter 4): Are moral judgments based on reasoning or emotion? Or perhaps both? How do moral reasoning and moral emotion interact with one another to produce moral judgments?
- *Moral Motivation and Behaviour* (Chapter 5): Can we be genuinely altruistic? Or are we inevitably selfish? Does empathy cause genuinely altruistic behaviour? Does empathy-induced behaviour have morally desirable consequences?
- *Free Will and Responsibility* (Chapter 6): Are we free and respon-sible agents? Is the idea of free will compatible with the empirical findings in psychology and neuroscience? Are we responsible for our implicit biases?
- *Delusion and Confabulation* (Chapter 7): How are clinical delusions and confabulations different from everyday irrational beliefs? Are delusions more irrational than everyday irrational beliefs? Is the irrationality of delusions different in kind from the irrationality of everyday beliefs?
- *Autism and Psychopathy* (Chapter 8): What does autism tell us about mind-reading capacity and its role in social and communi-cative activities? What does psychopathy tell us about empathy and its role in moral behaviour?

Philosophy of Psychology

What is Philosophy of Psychology?

We use the term 'psychology' broadly. 'Psychology' in our sense of the word includes both psychological disciplines in the narrow sense – such as cognitive psychology, social psychology, developmental psychology, and evolutionary psychology – and research areas in neuroscience and psychiatry. (We also use phrases such as 'psychology and neuroscience' or 'psychology and psychiatry' in some contexts to emphasize the relevance of neuroscience or psychiatry.) 'Psychology' in our sense of the word is somewhat similar to 'cognitive science', but the latter typically includes not only psychology and neuroscience but also artificial intelligence research, linguistics, and anthropology, which will not be discussed in this book.

What is philosophy of psychology? Providing a clear definition of philosophy of psychology is challenging and perhaps not very helpful. One thing we can do at this stage, and perhaps a useful thing to do, is to introduce the field of philosophy of psychology with some examples of the questions it asks. Philosophy of psychology is the discipline in philosophy that asks the questions we mentioned above concerning rationality, self-knowledge, free will and responsibility, moral judgment, moral motivation and behaviour, and so on.

Below, we clarify what philosophy of psychology is by contrasting philosophy of psychology with two related areas of philosophy, philosophy of mind and philosophy of science, and then distinguishing two approaches to the philosophy of psychology: the first approach is mainly concerned with the theoretical and conceptual foundations of psychology and the second approach is mainly concerned with the implications of psychological studies for philosophically relevant issues.

Philosophy of Psychology and Philosophy of Mind

Philosophy of psychology can be thought of as a sub-area of philosophy of mind, where 'philosophy of mind' is understood very broadly as the philosophical exploration of the mind. The focus of mainstream philosophy of mind, which is sometimes called 'metaphysics of mind', has been on metaphysical issues of the mind, including the mind–body problem, mental causation, physicalism, and the nature of consciousness. Philosophy of psychology, in contrast, focuses on the kind of issues that are closely related to empirical studies of the mind or the kind of issues on which we cannot make progress without relevant empirical input. When philosophy of psychology addresses human rationality, for example, it examines the available empirical data to find out whether humans actually reason in accordance with the norms of rationality.

Philosophy of Psychology and Philosophy of Science

Philosophy of psychology can also be thought of as a sub-area of philosophy of science, where 'philosophy of science' is understood very broadly as the philosophical exploration of science. Philosophers of science study what a theory is, investigate applications of scientific method, and ask whether scientists make progress. Central issues in philosophy of science, or 'general philosophy of science', are not essentially connected to a particular scientific field (although many of the traditional issues in philosophy of science are explicitly or implicitly associated with the physical sciences). A recent trend in philosophy of science, however, is the growth and development of those sub-areas that deal with issues that are specific to a particular scientific field. For example, philosophy of biology discusses philosophical issues that emerge from biological studies (e.g., the issues related to adaptationism, the concept of 'function' in biology, the level of selection, etc.). Philosophy of psychology is another sub-area that discusses philosophical issues that emerge from psychological studies.

Foundational and Implicational

We find it useful to divide philosophy of psychology into two sub-areas: 'foundational philosophy of psychology' and 'implicational philosophy of psychology'.

Foundational philosophy of psychology is concerned with core concepts in psychology (e.g., 'representation', 'computation', or 'concept') and general hypotheses in psychology that can make sense of a series of relevant studies as interconnected, including: the massive modularity hypothesis, which roughly says that our mind is composed of 'modular' systems that are dedicated to some specific tasks (Fodor 1983); the language of thought hypothesis, which roughly says that our cognition is based upon processing language-like representations (Fodor 1975); and the adaptive unconsciousness hypothesis, which roughly says that a part of our mind has evolved via natural selection and we do not and cannot have direct access to it (Wilson 2002). Questions in foundational philosophy of psychology include: 'What are representations?', 'How does computation work?', 'Is the massive modularity hypothesis plausible?', 'Is the language of thought hypothesis needed to explain cognition?', and so on.

In contrast, implicational philosophy of psychology focuses on the results of particular psychological studies (rather than their theoretical foundations) and investigates their implications for issues that are philosophically relevant. For example, Chapter 1 will focus on a series of influential studies on reasoning biases (Kahneman, Slovic, & Tversky 1982; Tversky & Kahneman 1974) exploring the implications of such studies for questions concerning human rationality. It will ask, for example, whether these studies show that humans are irrational after all. Chapter 7 will discuss studies on the limitations of memory (Loftus 2003; Schacter & Addis 2007), which show that human agents can easily misremember even important details of past events and thus might have important implications for eye-witness testimony in forensic settings. One might subsequently ask whether these studies show that eye-witness testimony is fundamentally unreliable.

Although we think that the distinction between foundations and implications is useful, we do not assume that it is clear-cut. The difference between them is probably a matter of degree: for example, some issues are more foundational and less implicational than others. There will be some borderline cases. For example, the dual-process theory (the theory according to which there are two distinct types of cognitive processes: Type-1 processes that are fast, unconscious, and automatic, and Type-2 processes that are slow, conscious, and controlled), which is discussed in Chapter 3, might be a borderline case.

Both dimensions of philosophy of psychology are equally important, but this book is more focused on implicational philosophy of psychology than foundational philosophy of psychology. There are two reasons for this. First, implicational issues have recently stimulated very lively discussions in philosophy of psychology research (which used to be dominated by foundational issues). We wanted this book to reflect this recent trend. Second, existing philosophy of psychology textbooks mainly focus on foundational issues, leaving the implications largely unexplored. This book is motivated by our frustration with the lack of accessible resources for discussing implicational issues. Hereafter, 'philosophy of psychology' means implicational philosophy of psychology.

This book will focus on implicational issues rather than foundational issues; however, strictly speaking, its focus is even narrower. There are so many interesting implicational issues and one book is not able to cover them all. As hinted previously, we will prioritize topics related to the 'imperfection' of human cognition and agency. Our central topics will include reasoning, judgment, belief, emotion, behaviour, and agency. For this reason, unfortunately, we will largely ignore the issues concerning consciousness, perception, attention, and so on. (See Further Resources for some material on the issues that we do not discuss in this book.)

Why Do We Need Philosophy of Psychology?

Why do we need philosophy of psychology, in addition to metaphysical philosophy of mind and psychology as distinct disciplines? Why can't philosophers confine themselves to purely metaphysical issues? Why can't psychologists confine themselves to purely empirical investigations?

There has been no sharp distinction between philosophy and psychology in Western intellectual history. Many philosophers who talk about mind and cognition in the history of philosophy go beyond the field of philosophy of mind in a narrow sense and touch on issues that now belong to the field of psychology, for example: Plato's tripartite theory of soul (according to which the soul is divided into reason, spirit, and appetite) in *The Republic*; Descartes' physiological analysis of various emotions in *Passions of the Soul*; Hume's associationist psychology in *A Treatise of Human Nature*; Kant's classification of mental disorders in *Essay on the Maladies of the Head*, and so on. The sharp distinction between philosophy and psychology is a modern development, mainly due to the specialization of each field. The advancement of research in each field obliged some researchers to focus on the metaphysical issues of the mind, and other researchers to dedicate themselves to empirical investigations instead. This is an inevitable and perhaps good development overall, but it invites a potential problem: many of the fundamental questions about human nature require philosophical argumentation as well as empirical inputs.

Suppose that you are interested in whether humans have some property X, such as the property of being rational or the property of being altruistic. To answer this, you need to investigate two sets of questions: (1) 'What does it mean to have X?', 'What is necessary for a person to have X?', and 'What is sufficient for a person to have X?'; and (2) 'Do humans satisfy a sufficient condition for having X?', 'Do humans fail to satisfy a necessary condition for having X?', and 'What do empirical studies say about these issues?' Let us call the former the 'philosophical questions' about X, and the latter the 'psychological questions' about X.

Addressing the philosophical questions requires the articulation and justification of certain (controversial) claims, such as *'being rational' means reasoning in accordance with the rules of logic and mathematics*, or *'being altruistic' means being motivated to increase somebody else's well-being for its own sake*. Addressing the psychological questions requires setting up laboratory experiments and observations *in the wild*, where human behaviour is assessed on the basis of the criteria for rationality or altruism, such as measuring how many people out of 100 commit a logical fallacy in a simple test or how many people out of 100 act in a selfless way given the chance.

The reason you can't just let philosophers do what they do is that although a purely philosophical investigation is useful for addressing the philosophical questions, it does not say much about the psychological questions. For instance, a philosophical argument does not say anything about whether as a matter of fact humans can be motivated to increase somebody else's well-being for its own sake. In contrast, the reason you can't just let psychologists do what they do is that although a purely psychological investigation is useful for addressing the psychological questions, it does not say much about the philosophical questions. For example, a psychological experiment does not say anything about whether 'rationality' should be regarded as the capacity for reasoning in accordance with the rules of logic and mathematics.

Let us think about a further example (which we discuss in detail in Chapter 6). Suppose that you want to know whether humans have free will and responsibility, according to relevant psychological findings. To know this, you need to investigate both the philosophical and the psychological questions: (1) 'What does it mean to have free will?', 'What is necessary for a person to have free will?', 'What is sufficient for a person to have free will?'; (2) 'Do humans satisfy a sufficient condition for having free will?', 'Or, do humans fail to satisfy a necessary condition for having free will?', 'What do empirical studies say about these issues?'

A purely philosophical investigation can address the philosophical questions, but not the psychological questions. For example, one might argue, for some philosophical reasons, that it is necessary for person *A* to have free will that *A*'s conscious mental states and processes play some significant causal role in producing or controlling *A*'s behaviour. This is certainly a possible answer to a philosophical question, but we need to know more to ascertain whether humans have free will. In particular, the psychological questions have not been answered yet. It is still unclear whether, according to relevant empirical studies, conscious states and processes in human cognition play the right kind of causal roles. As we shall see in Chapter 6, this is the topic of a recent interdisciplinary debate on free will.

A purely psychological investigation can address the psychological questions, but not the philosophical questions. For example, psychological studies might suggest that Elsa's discriminatory behaviour is generated by her implicit biases, which can only be detected by psychological tests. Elsa is not introspectively aware of her biases. This is certainly an interesting finding, but we need to know more to judge whether she is responsible for her discriminatory behaviour. In particular, the philosophical questions have not yet been addressed. It is still unclear whether Elsa's lack of introspective awareness of her implicit biases is incompatible with her being responsible for her discriminatory behaviour. As we shall see in Chapter 6, this is the topic of a recent discussion about whether people are responsible for their implicit biases.

Evaluating Psychological Studies

This book focuses on implicational philosophy of psychology, investigating the implications of some particular psychological studies. Before getting into our main discussions, we would like to mention three factors that are relevant in the context of evaluating psychological studies and their implications: replication, research participants, and ecological validity.

Replication

Psychological studies, just like other scientific studies, need to be replicated in order to be credible. It is possible that some interesting results fail to be replicated. In fact, psychology, social psychology in particular, is now facing the so-called 'replication crisis' (e.g., Earp & Trafimow 2015): the replicability of social psychological studies, including some famous ones, seems to be remarkably low.

A recent controversy, for example, is about a series of studies of priming effects by John Bargh and colleagues. Priming effects are the unconscious effects that the exposure to a stimulus has on the responses to subsequent stimuli. One famous study (Bargh, Chen, &

Burrows 1996, which has over 5,500 citations on Google Scholar as of October 2020) reports the surprising result that the participants who had completed the simple task of making a sentence out of some given words, including words related to stereotypes of the elderly (e.g., 'grey', 'wise', or 'wrinkle'), walked away more slowly than other participants who had completed the same task without elderly-related words. However, several researchers (e.g., Doyen et al. 2012) reported their failure to replicate the elderly stereotype study and suggested that the popularity of priming studies by Bargh and colleagues is disproportional to their scientific credibility. Daniel Kahneman, who had once mentioned the elderly stereotype study in his best-selling book *Thinking, Fast and Slow* (2011), admitted that he had 'placed too much faith in underpowered studies' in response to a blog post on the controversy (Schimmack, Heene, & Kesavan 2017).

The problem is compounded by the fact that replication failure tends not to be reported in journals (unless, just like in the case of priming studies by Bargh and colleagues, a serious controversy arises). Paul Bloom says that when the project of replicating a study turns out to be unsuccessful, '[u]sually, the project is just abandoned, though sometimes the word gets out in an informal way – in seminars, lab meetings, conferences – that some findings are vaporware ("Oh, nobody can replicate that one")' and '[m]any psychologists now have an attitude that if a finding seems really implausible, just wait a while and it will go away' (Bloom 2017, 224).

We do not necessarily endorse radical pessimism about social psychology; after all, many important studies have been replicated. But, as a general rule, replication should always be kept in mind when evaluating psychological studies, and perhaps some extra care is needed when evaluating studies in social psychology with surprising results.

Replication really matters, but what about the observations of rare conditions about which we cannot expect statistical analysis of data or replication? Despite the lack of statistical analysis or replication, the study of some unusual behaviours can be informative and can help us to understand how the mind works. In the book *Phantoms in the Brain*, V. S. Ramachandran defends the usefulness of observing rare cases as opposed to the statistical study of normal individuals:

> [I]n neurology, most of the major discoveries that have withstood the test of time were, in fact, based initially on single studies and

demonstrations. More was learned about memory from a few days of studying a patient called H.M. than was gleaned from previous decades of research averaging data on many subjects. The same thing can be said about hemispheric specialization (organization of the brain into a left brain and a right brain, which are specialized for different functions) and the experiments carried out on two patients with so-called split brains (in whom the left and right hemispheres were disconnected by cutting the fibers between them). (Ramachandran & Blakeslee 1998, xiii)

We agree with Ramachandran, especially with his idea that we can gain useful insights by observing some rare cases. This is why we will include the split-brain cases (which Ramachandran mentions in this passage) in our discussion of self-knowledge in Chapter 2, and Capgras syndrome (which is a rare condition that Ramachandran discusses in his book) in our exploration of delusion in Chapter 7. Ramachandran's idea is also perfectly compatible with the importance of statistical analysis and replication when it comes to the phase in which we test the insights that we initially gain in observing rare cases. In fact, he only says that major discoveries in neurology were 'initially' based on single studies and demonstrations; his recommendation is 'to begin with experiments on single cases and then to confirm the findings through studies of additional patients' (Ramachandran & Blakeslee 1998, xiii).

Research Participants

Psychological experiments need human participants. Typically, the participants of psychological studies are university students because these are the most easily accessible kind of people for psychology researchers. But this can be a problem. In psychology, we are not just interested in finding out how the mind of a university student works; rather we are interested in finding out how the mind works in general. Can we learn about how the mind works in general from psychological studies involving only university students?

Uncritical optimism on this issue has been questioned in recent years. It has been suggested (Henrich, Heine, & Norenzaya 2010a, 2010b) that most psychological studies published in major journals rely on the participants in Western, educated, industrialized, rich, and democratic (WEIRD) societies, who are in fact highly unusual in many psychological aspects:

[P]eople from Western, educated, industrialized, rich and democratic (WEIRD) societies – and particularly American undergraduates – are some of the most psychologically unusual people on Earth. So the fact that the vast majority of studies use WEIRD participants presents a challenge to the understanding of human psychology and behaviour. [...] Strange, then, that research articles routinely assume that their results are broadly representative, rarely adding even a cautionary footnote on how far their findings can be generalized. (Henrich, Heine, & Norenzaya 2010b, 29)

We will come back to this problem in Chapter 4 when discussing cross-cultural studies of moral judgments (e.g., Haidt, Koller, & Dias 1993; Shweder, Mahapatra, & Miller 1987).

Ecological Validity

Many psychological studies are undertaken in some artificial situations that are not representative of everyday settings, and the tasks proposed in the laboratory may not have the same relevant features as everyday tasks. This raises a methodological problem. In psychology, we are not just interested in understanding how people think and behave in artificial tasks and settings; rather we are interested in understanding how people think and behave in everyday tasks and settings. Can we learn about how people think and behave in everyday tasks and settings from the psychological studies involving only artificial tasks and settings?

Bloom warns us against the tendency to conclude that human agents are irrational on the basis of the experimental findings of irrational biases and errors in artificial tasks and settings. Perhaps biases and errors are exaggerated in artificial settings; they might not be very significant in real-life cases.

Statistically significant doesn't mean *actually significant*. Just because something has an effect in a controlled situation doesn't mean that it's important in real life. Your impression of a résumé might be subtly affected by its being presented to you on a heavy clipboard, and this tells us something about how we draw inferences from physical experience when making social evaluations. Very interesting stuff. But this doesn't imply that your real-world judgments of job candidates have much to do with what you're holding when you make those judgments. What will actually matter much more are such boringly relevant considerations as the candidate's experience and qualification. (Bloom 2017, 224–225)

This is something we should keep in mind, especially when we explore the limitations of human cognition; it is conceivable that the limitation that is found in a controlled experiment does not have much impact in real life.

Further Resources

Articles and Books

Tony Stone and Martin Davies's article on cognitive neuropsychology and philosophy of mind (1993) includes a very interesting discussion of the aim and scope of philosophy and psychology. Alvin Goldman's *Philosophical Applications of Cognitive Science* (2018) includes many examples of how philosophical discussions can be fruitfully informed by psychology and cognitive science.

As we noted, philosophy of psychology contains many topics and issues that we cannot cover in this book. See *Philosophy of Psychology: A Contemporary Introduction* (2004) and *Cognitive Science: An Introduction to the Science of the Mind* (2020) by José Luis Bermúdez; *An Introduction to the Philosophy of Psychology* (2015) by Daniel Weiskopf and Fred Adams; *Mindware: An Introduction to the Philosophy of Cognitive Science* (2000) by Andy Clark; and *The Philosophy of Cognitive Science* (2015) by Mark Cain. We also recommend *The Phenomenological Mind* (2012) by Shaun Gallagher and Dan Zahavi, and *The Disordered Mind: An Introduction to Philosophy of Mind and Mental Illness* (2013) by George Graham.

Online Resources

Paul Thagard's *Stanford Encyclopedia of Philosophy* entry on cognitive science (2019) is helpful as it summarizes some of the key areas of philosophy of psychology.

Tamar Gendler's lecture *Philosophy and the Science of Human Nature* (2011), available at Open Yale Courses, discusses a wide range of issues in philosophy of psychology by combining ancient philosophical wisdom with cutting-edge psychological studies.

Questions

1. How can philosophy and psychology profitably interact in understanding how the human mind works?
2. Can you think of some particular examples in which philosophers and psychologists profitably interact with one another?
3. What can philosophers learn from psychological studies?
4. What can psychologists learn from philosophical arguments and discussions?
5. Is there a clear boundary between philosophical discussion of the mind and psychological discussion of it? Or is the boundary inevitably vague?

1

Rationality

1.1 Introduction

It is a long tradition in Western philosophy to characterize humans as rational animals and to argue that rationality is one of the features that distinguishes them from other animals. It is not just Aristotle who describes the human as the rational animal in his *Metaphysics* (1984). In *Discourse on the Method* (1985), Descartes also characterizes humans in terms of their distinctive reason or understanding; non-human animals do not have reason at all. This trend has continued: Donald Davidson says that rationality distinguishes 'between the infant and the snail on one hand, and the normal adult person on the other' (Davidson 1982, 318).

This view, however, can be (and has been) challenged. One challenge is to deny the sharp contrast between human cognition, which is rational, and non-human cognition, which is not. Humans are rational, but so are non-human animals. For example, Hume writes in his *A Treatise of Human Nature* that 'no truth appears to me more evident than that beasts are endowed with thought and reason as well as man' (Hume 1739/2007, 118).

Another challenge, which is the focus of this chapter, is to deny optimism about human rationality. Non-human animals are not rational, but humans are not rational either. In the memorable beginning of his essay 'An Outline of Intellectual Rubbish', Russell wrote:

Man is a rational animal – so at least we have been told. Throughout a long life I have searched diligently for evidence in favour of this statement. So far, I have not had the good fortune to come across it, though I have searched in many countries spread over three continents. (Russell 1961, 45)

Russellian pessimism about human rationality is echoed in a particularly influential psychological research programme in the 20th century, the heuristics and biases research programme, led by Amos Tversky and Daniel Kahneman. The studies in this programme revealed 'systematic and severe errors' (Tversky & Kahneman 1974, 1124) in human reasoning, which seem to have a 'bleak implication for human rationality' (Nisbett & Borgida 1975, 935). These studies caused heated debates on human rationality, sometimes dubbed 'rationality wars' (Samuels, Stich, & Bishop 2002), both at the theoretical and conceptual level and at the empirical and experimental level. The main aim of this chapter is to examine the relevant psychological studies to see if they really do have bleak or pessimistic implications for human rationality.

We start by presenting a definition of rationality (Section 1.2) before turning to the relevant psychological studies, in particular the ones from the heuristics and biases programme, which reveal a systematic failure to reason according to the rules of logic, probability, and decision-making (Section 1.3). The results of these studies support a pessimistic view of human rationality (Section 1.4). However, objections to the pessimistic interpretation were raised by Gerd Gigerenzer and his ecological rationality research programme (Section 1.5). The objections from this programme are significant because they bring to the fore important ideas that enhance our understanding of human rationality/irrationality. However, we shall argue that these objections do not refute the pessimistic interpretation. Although Gigerenzer's objections do not refute pessimism, they lead us to examine an important issue: whether the difference between optimism and pessimism about rationality hangs on different accounts of the aim of cognition (Section 1.6). In the end, we defend a moderate form of pessimism, according to which humans are not as rational as we might have thought, before appreciating the results of the psychological studies on reasoning.

1.2   Clarifying Rationality

Are humans rational? To answer this question, we need to investigate two sets of issues: (1) 'What does it mean to be rational?', 'What is necessary for a person to be rational?', and 'What is sufficient for a person to be rational?' (the philosophical questions about rationality); and (2) 'Do humans satisfy a sufficient condition for being rational?', 'Do humans fail to satisfy a necessary condition for being rational?', and 'What do empirical studies say about these issues?' (the psychological questions about rationality).

We discuss the philosophical questions in this section and the psychological questions in the next section.

'Rationality' means different things in different contexts (Bortolotti 2014). We will focus on a narrow sense of rationality here: that is, rationality in the context of reasoning. In particular, we (tentatively) accept what Edward Stein (1996) calls 'the standard picture of rationality', according to which rationality consists in reasoning in accordance with the rules of logic, probability, and decision-making (see Box 1A).

But how often should human agents reason in accordance with these rules to be considered rational agents? If the answer is 'Always', then a rational person wouldn't be allowed to make any mistakes; this requirement is far too demanding. It is obvious that human agents are not rational according to such a stringent requirement. A realistic view would take into account the fact that rational agents can make reasoning errors, such as the occasional performance error that is attributed to some interfering factor (e.g., lack of concentration) (see Box 1B), but they do not make systematic reasoning errors. Thus, rationality is compatible with occasional reasoning errors, but it is not compatible with systematic reasoning errors.

The standard picture of rationality is accepted by many, perhaps most, philosophers, and reasonably so. After all, there is a key sense of 'rational' that describes people who follow the rules of logic, probability, and decision-making when they reason and solve problems. There are other senses of 'rational', of course, such as those that describe people who are not overwhelmed by their emotions when they make decisions, or those that describe people who support their arguments with evidence instead of merely stamping their foot in a debate (Bortolotti 2014). But rationality as *logicality*, as we might

BOX 1A: The Standard Picture of Rationality

Definition:
'According to this picture, to be rational is to reason in accordance with principles of reasoning that are based on rules of logic, probability theory, and so forth. If the standard picture of reasoning is right, principles of reasoning that are based on such rules are normative principles of reasoning, namely they are the principles we ought to reason in accordance with.' (Stein 1996, 4)

Example of deductive reasoning:
Jessie believes that either Paula got an A in geometry or Vanessa did, and also that Vanessa did not get an A but got a D instead. From these premises, Jessie concludes that it is Paula who got an A. Jessie is rational: her logical reasoning is in accordance with a rule of logic that one can infer P from (P *or* Q and *not* Q) (*disjunctive syllogism*).

Example of probabilistic reasoning:
Felix assigns the probability 0.8 to the idea that it will rain tomorrow based on the televised weather forecast that there is an 80% chance of rain tomorrow. Felix also assigns the probability 0.9 to the idea that it will rain tomorrow and so he will go to the gym for a workout. Felix is irrational: his probabilistic judgment violates what is known as the 'conjunction rule'; the probability of an event A occurring, $P(A)$, cannot be less than the probability of A and another event B occurring at the same time, $P(A\&B)$.

call it, is widely accepted in philosophy, economics, and psychology. For instance, Phil Gerrans says that 'a rational subject is one whose reasoning conforms to procedures, such as logical rules, or Bayesian decision theory, which produce inferentially consistent sets of propositions' (Gerrans 2001, 161), and Richard Nisbett and Paul Thagard define rational behaviour as 'what people should do given an optimal set of inferential rules' (Thagard & Nisbett 1983, 251).

Having said that, not everybody agrees that the standard picture is the best understanding of human rationality. This controversy lies at the heart of the rationality wars between pessimists about human rationality (often appealing to the heuristics and biases programme) and optimists about human rationality (often associated with the ecological rationality programme). We will come back to this in Section 1.5.

There are some technical issues about the standard picture of rationality that we would like to mention briefly here.

First, the standard picture seems to presuppose that there is just *one* system of logic, *one* theory of probability, and *one* set of principles for decision-making. However, there are different formal systems of logic and different interpretations of probability; even the principles of decision-making can be disputed. Some rules of inference that are valid in standard logic (often called *classical logic*) are not valid in some non-classical logical systems. This raises a question: which system of logic should be adopted in evaluating the reasoning perfor-mance of agents? This is especially tricky if reasoning performance is consistent with one system of logic but not with another. Should we adopt the former and say that an agent's performance is rational? Or should we adopt the latter and say that it is irrational? A similar issue arises when considering interpretations of probability. There are different interpretations of what probabilistic statements (e.g., there is a 80% chance that it will rain tomorrow) actually mean. There are also some probabilistic statements that make sense in some interpre-tations but not in others. This issue is relevant to the debate between pessimists and optimists. Gigerenzer, the most notable optimist, argues that some probabilistic questions in the heuristics and biases experiments are meaningless in light of his favourite interpretation of probability (which is known as the *frequency interpretation*). This issue will be discussed in Section 1.5.

Second, the standard picture assumes that our reasoning should be evaluated against the standards of logic, probability, and decision-making. This implies that, if our intuitive answer to a reasoning task is incompatible with a rule of logic, we should conclude that our intuition is at fault. But why can't we say that it is logic, not intuition, that is at fault? In fact, the development of non-classical logic is sometimes at least partially motivated by some counter-intuitive features of classic logic.

This issue raises a further question: what should we do when facing an apparent discrepancy between logic and intuitive judgment? Should we trust logic and dismiss intuition as irrational? Or should we trust intuition and dismiss logic instead? Jonathan Cohen, another notable optimist, raises a similar issue. If the normative rules, against which our intuitive judgments are evaluated, are themselves evaluated on the basis of our intuitive judgments, then our intuition 'sets its own standards' (Cohen 1981, 317). But then how can our intuitive judgment be irrational? How can our intuitive judgment deviate from the standards *that are set by itself*? Cohen adopts a radical conclusion that human irrationality cannot be proven in principle no matter what psychology shows; 'ordinary human reasoning – by which I mean the reasoning of adults who have not been systematically educated in any branch of logic or probability theory – cannot be held to be faultily programmed' (Cohen 1981, 317). In making this claim, Cohen relies on the distinction between reasoning competence and reasoning performance (see Box 1B).

BOX 1B: Competence vs Performance

When you attempt a task and fail, one of two things may be happening: either you do not have the capacity to accurately perform the task due to some knowledge-gap, or you have the capacity to accurately perform the task but fail to perform it accurately on a particular occasion due to external factors (such as a distraction).

Example: Gina and Tommaso were asked to calculate the square of four by their teacher. Gina did not answer at all because she did not know that the square of a number is the number multiplied by itself. Gina lacked the *competence* to answer the question correctly. Tommaso answered 'twelve'. He knew how to make the square of a number and he was familiar with the four times table, but he was distracted by a sudden noise outside the classroom and gave the wrong answer. Tommaso made a *performance* error.

When Cohen says that 'ordinary human reasoning [...] cannot be held to be faultily programmed', he means that human reasoning *competence* is intact (human agents can apply the rules of good reasoning in ideal conditions), although reasoning *performance* may be imperfect (human agents may make errors in applying the rules of good reasoning due to external factors).

Third, the standard picture presupposes that what matters to rational and successful reasoning is the conformity to the rules of logic, probability, and decision-making. Not everybody agrees. For example, Keith Stanovich (1999) makes a distinction between *rationality* and *intelligence*, where rationality is a broader notion than in the standard picture, and intelligence is what the standard picture captures. In common discourse, intelligence and rationality are often conflated, or it is assumed that intelligence comprises rationality. But IQ tests do not measure the capacity for making good judgments and good choices that we commonly regard as a mark of rationality. If we take intelligence to stand for whatever IQ tests measure, then it does not tell us which behaviours are more likely to be conducive to the agent's well-being *in real life*. Whereas IQ tests measure the capacity to process and manipulate information quickly and efficiently, they are not sensitive to whether the agent forms beliefs that are well supported by the evidence or whether she can critically evaluate the information she receives. To illustrate this distinction, Stanovich describes famous cases of smart people who acted foolishly, by which he means that people who have high intelligence in some domain made bad judgments and bad choices, thereby behaving irrationally. This does not mean that intelligence is not worth studying, just that there are other things that we value. Intelligence and rationality can be seen as having different domains of applications: Stanovich, for instance, suggests that intelligence maps the efficiency of cognitive functioning at an algorithmic level, whereas his more comprehensive notion of rationality tracks thinking dispositions at a higher level, governs decision-making, and takes into account the agent's goals and values. Some notions of rationality like Stanovich's are distinct from the standard picture, where rationality is associated with behaviour that conforms to the rules of logic, probability, and decision-making.

1.3 Systematic Biases and Errors

Here is a tentative answer to the philosophical question (with the qualifications we made at the end of the previous section): 'rationality' consists in reasoning in accordance with the rules of logic, probability, and decision-making.

Now, let us turn to the psychological questions. The crucial question is: 'Do human agents actually reason in accordance with the rules of logic, probability, and decision-making?' We will now review relevant studies, mainly from the heuristics and biases programme, which offer ample evidence that human reasoning systematically deviates from the rules of logic, probability, and decision-making. They include some of the most famous results in 20th-century psychological research.

Wason Selection Task

According to deductive logic, for a conditional statement of the form 'If P then Q' to be falsified, the antecedent (P) must be true and the consequent (Q) must be false. So, the statement 'If you want to go to Brighton, then you need to catch the next train' is false if you do want to go to Brighton but you don't need to catch the next train.

The purpose of the selection task is to establish whether people can recognize when conditional statements are false. In the classic version of the task (Wason 1966), there is a deck of cards and each of them has a number on one side and a letter on the other. Participants can see four cards on the table, the first has a vowel (A) on the visible side, the second an odd number (7), the third a consonant (K), and the last an even number (4) (Figure 1). Participants have to say which cards they need to turn to test the following rule: '*If* a card has a vowel on one side, *then* it has an even number on the other side.' Most participants in the classic version of the task said that the cards to be turned are the card with A on the visible side and the card with 4 on the visible side, or just the card with A on the visible side. However, the correct way to test the rule is to turn the card with A on the visible side and the card with 7 on the visible side, because a conditional statement is falsified when the antecedent ('If a card has a vowel on one side') is true and the consequent ('then it has an even number on the other side') is false. Only 5% of the participants solved the selection task in this version.

Figure 1. Wason selection task with abstract options

Conjunction Fallacy

The next study involves the so-called 'conjunction fallacy' (also known as the *conjunction effect*), which is a mistake people make when they assume that a statement describing the conjunction of two states of affairs (e.g., 'Tomorrow it will be raining and it will be cold') is more probable than a statement describing one of those states of affairs alone (e.g., 'Tomorrow it will be raining').

In one experiment by Tversky and Kahneman (1983), participants first read personality sketches of hypothetical people, and then answered questions about them. Participants were divided into three groups according to their background in probability and statistics: the *naïve* group (those with no background), the *intermediate* group (those with basic knowledge of probability and statistics), and the *sophisticated* group (those with advanced knowledge of probability and statistics). Here is the personality sketch of a hypothetical person, Linda.

> Linda is 31 years old, single, outspoken, and very bright. She majored in philosophy. As a student, she was deeply concerned with issues of discrimination and social justice, and participated in anti-nuclear demonstrations.

> Please rank the following statements by their probability, using 1 for the most probable and 8 for the least probable:

> 1. Linda is a teacher in elementary school.
> 2. Linda works in a bookstore and takes Yoga classes.
> 3. Linda is active in the feminist movement.
> 4. Linda is a psychiatric social worker.
> 5. Linda is a member of the League of Women Voters.
> 6. Linda is a bank teller.
> 7. Linda is an insurance salesperson.
> 8. Linda is a bank teller and is active in the feminist movement.

The result revealed that statements 3 and 7 were regarded, respectively, as the most probable and the least probable, which is explained by the similarity of Linda's personality sketch with the stereotypical image of someone politically active, and the dissimilarity between her personality sketch and the stereotypical image of an insurance salesperson. The crucial statements to consider in this experiment are 6 and 8. The mean rank of the former was lower than the mean rank of the latter, which means that Linda being a bank teller and active in the feminist movement was regarded as *more probable* than her being a bank teller. This, however, is a mistake. Linda being a bank teller *and* active in the feminist movement is the conjunction of her being a bank teller and of her being active in the feminist movement. And the conjunction cannot be more probable than one of the conjuncts. Thus, this mistake is an obvious violation of the conjunction rule. This fallacy was found in all three groups of participants and background knowledge in statistics and probability did not have a significant effect on the participant's performance.

Base-Rate Neglect

In another famous experiment by Kahneman and Tversky (1973), half of the participants read a story, 'cover story', which said that psychologists prepared 100 personality descriptions on the basis of interviewing and testing *30 engineers and 70 lawyers*. The other half of the participants read almost the same cover story, except that the number of engineers and the number of lawyers were switched; *70 engineers and 30 lawyers*. Then participants were presented with personality descriptions – supposedly randomly selected from the 100 personality descriptions – and were asked to judge the probability of that person being an engineer. Here is one such description:

> Jack is a 45-year-old man. He is married and has four children. He is generally conservative, careful, and ambitious. He shows no interest in political and social issues and spends most of his free time on his many hobbies which include home carpentry, sailing, and mathematical puzzles.

One finding was that participants made a judgment on the basis of the stereotypes associated with the two occupations – engineer and lawyer – which is consistent with what we saw in the Linda experiment. Linda was regarded as most likely to be active in the feminist movement, which nicely fits the stereotype provided in her personal description. Similarly, in this study, Jack was most likely judged to be an engineer rather than a lawyer because his personality description nicely fits the stereotype of engineers. The crucial finding was that the base-rate information was largely neglected; the judgment was independent of the base rates provided in the cover stories.

This error constitutes a violation of Bayes' rule, which says that the probability of an hypothesis H given an observation O ('posterior probability', $P(H/O)$) is determined by both how likely O is if H is true ('likelihood', $P(O/H)$), and how probable H is without the observation ('prior probability', $P(H)$). For example, the probability of Jack being an engineer given the personality description is determined by both how likely the personal description (being generally conservative, careful, ambitious, etc.) is if Jack is really an engineer, and how probable it is that Jack is an engineer without the personal description. What happened in the experimental results was that the participants largely ignored the prior probability (i.e., how probable it is that Jack is an engineer without the personal description) which is determined by the base-rate. Thus, Kahneman and Tversky summarize their finding as follows:

> One of the basic principles of statistical prediction is that prior probability, which summarizes what we knew about the problem before receiving independent specific evidence, remains relevant even after such evidence is obtained. Bayes' rule translates this qualitative principle into a multiplicative relation between prior odds and the likelihood ratio. Our subjects, however, fail to integrate prior probability with specific evidence. [...] The failure to appreciate the relevance of prior probability in the presence of specific evidence is perhaps one of the most significant departures of intuition from the normative theory of prediction. (Kahneman & Tversky 1973, 243)

Preference Reversal

Another area of weakness in human reasoning can be found in the psychology and economics literature on *preference reversals*. The principle of procedure invariance tells us that, given two options, if one prefers A to B, then this preference should not change when the method for eliciting the preference changes. Yet participants often state a preference for A over B when they are asked to make a direct choice, but are prepared to pay more to obtain B than they are to obtain A.

Take two lotteries: a relatively safe lottery, where one has a 10% chance of winning nothing and a 90% chance of winning £10; and a relatively risky lottery, where one has a 10% chance of winning £90 and a 90% chance of winning nothing. If asked to choose, people usually prefer to buy a ticket for the safer lottery. In contrast, if asked at what price they would sell their ticket, they set a higher selling price for the ticket of the risky lottery. This phenomenon is observed in different contexts of choice and matching too (Stalmeier, Wakker, & Bezembinder 1997).

The classic example of the violation of procedure invariance in the literature is the Traffic Problem (Tversky & Thaler 1990, 201–202):

(1) The Minister of Transportation is considering which of the following two programs would make the electorate happier:
Program *A* is expected to reduce the yearly number of casualties in traffic accidents to 570 and its annual cost is estimated at $12 million. Program *B* is expected to reduce the yearly number of casualties in traffic accidents to 500 and its annual cost is estimated at $55 million. Which program would you like better?

(2) The Minister of Transportation is considering which of the following two programs would make the electorate happier:
Program *A* is expected to reduce the yearly number of casualties in traffic accidents to 570 and its annual cost is estimated at $12 million. Program *B* is expected to reduce the yearly number of casualties in traffic accidents to 500.
At what cost would program *B* be as attractive as program *A*?

Options 1 and 2 represent two different ways of eliciting people's preferences for one of the two life-saving programmes. In option 1, participants are given all necessary information about the two programmes: how many lives they would save and at what cost. When preferences are elicited in this way (*direct choice*), two-thirds of participants express a preference for programme *B* (which allows more lives to be saved at a higher cost). In option 2, participants are told how many lives would be saved and the cost of programme *A*, but they are not told the cost of programme *B*. Rather, they are asked at what cost programme *B* would become as attractive as programme *A*. When the preference is elicited this way (*price matching*), 90% of participants provide values smaller than $55 million for programme *B*, thereby indicating a preference for programme *A*.

If we take the evidence concerning people's responses to the Traffic Problem as ecologically valid and reliable, it tells us something interesting: people have inconsistent attitudes about what the Minister of Transportation should do concerning the Traffic Problem. They believe that the Minister should implement programme *B* to save the lives of 70 more people a year, even if the programme costs $43 million more than programme *A*. They also believe that the Minister should implement programme *A*, which would save fewer lives, unless programme *B* cost considerably less than $55 million. Depending on the method by which the preference is elicited, participants seem to attribute different monetary value to human lives.

1.4   Pessimism about Rationality

Making Sense of the Results

Overall, these studies reveal 'systematic and severe errors' (Tversky & Kahneman 1974, 1124) in human reasoning that have a 'bleak implication for human rationality' (Nisbett & Borgida 1975, 935). They provide powerful empirical support for the pessimistic conclusion about human rationality that human agents systematically fail to reason in accordance with the rules of deductive reasoning, such as in the Wason selection task, or in accordance with the rules of probability theory, such as the conjunction rule (the Linda experiment) or Bayes' rule (the Jack experiment). Moreover, participants violate basic principles of decision-making (procedure invariance and description invariance), and change their preferences depending on the methods by which their preferences are elicited and the way in which options are presented.

According to Kahneman and Tversky, systematic failures in human reasoning are due to the fact that human agents do not rely on the rules of logic, probability, and decision-making that would guarantee accuracy, but rather rely on *heuristics*. Heuristics are cognitive shortcuts, or cognitive rules of thumb, that 'reduce the complex tasks [...] to simpler judgmental operations' (Tversky & Kahneman 1974, 1124). Heuristics are reliable in many cases, especially in those cases where heuristics and the rules of logic, probability, and decision-making deliver the same answer. However, in other cases, heuristics can lead to systematic errors and deliver different answers from those one would arrive at by applying the rules of logic, probability, and decision-making.

In making a heuristic judgment, you replace a difficult question with an easier one and answer that question instead. For example, the question 'How far is the mountain over there from here?' is a relatively difficult question, which, if you want to answer it in a canonical way, requires you to find a map, identify your place on the map, identify the mountain on the map, measure the distance between them on the map, and then calculate the actual distance while taking into account the scale of the map. Instead of answering the difficult question, you can substitute it with another question, 'How clear does the mountain look to me?', which is a lot easier to answer. When it looks very clear to you, for example, you can conclude that the mountain is very close to you. This substitution strategy works in many cases, but it inevitably leads to systematic errors in other cases: for example, distances are often overestimated when the contours of objects are blurry and are underestimated when the contours of objects are sharp.

Similarly, it is not easy to answer probabilistic judgments such as 'What is the probability of Linda being a bank teller?' or 'What is the probability of Jack being an engineer?' However, instead of answering these questions, one can substitute them with questions of similarity, which are a lot easier: 'How is Linda's description similar to that of a stereotypical bank teller?' or 'How is Jack's description similar to that of a stereotypical engineer?' The substitution in this case is known as an application of the 'representativeness heuristic', in which 'probabilities are evaluated by the degree to which A is representative of B, that is, by the degree to which A resembles B' (Tversky & Kahneman 1974, 1124).

The representativeness heuristic works in many cases, but it inevitably leads to systematic errors in other cases. For instance, it leads to the violation of the conjunction rule when participants are asked to compare the probability of Linda being a bank teller with the probability of Linda being a feminist bank teller. When participants rely on the representativeness heuristic, they compare the similarity between Linda and a stereotypical bank teller and the similarity between Linda and a stereotypical feminist bank teller. Since Linda is not similar to a stereotypical bank teller at all, participants come to the conclusion that Linda is more likely to be a feminist bank teller than a bank teller, which is mathematically fallacious.

Kahneman and Tversky claim that reasoning errors are systematic and severe, but this does not mean that they are unavoidable. A finding is that the conjunction effect is reduced by asking about the *frequency* of an event (how *often* the event occurs) rather than its *probability* (how *probable* it is that the event will occur). A study by

Figure 2.   Wason selection task with concrete options

Klaus Fiedler (1988) compared two versions of the Linda experiment: the original version (probability), which asks the 'probability' of Linda being a bank teller and of her being a feminist bank teller, and a new version (frequency), which instead asks how many people out of 100 who fit Linda's description are bank tellers and how many are feminist bank tellers. Participants are much more likely to give the correct answer to the new (frequency) version of the task (78% correct answer) than to the original (probability) version (9% correct answer).

Similarly, other versions of the Wason selection task were devised based on the hypothesis that performance improves when the rule that is tested is more concrete and refers to situations that partici-pants experience in everyday life. Indeed, there was significant improvement in the results. In one version (Wason & Shapiro 1971), the following statement was tested: 'Every time I go to Manchester, I travel by car.' Participants were presented with four cards that showed on their open sides one of the following: 'Manchester', 'Leeds', 'car', and 'train' (Figure 2). On this occasion, two-thirds of participants were able to choose the right pair of cards to turn to test the rule (the correct pair being the cards with 'Manchester' and 'train' on the visible sides). These performance improvements will be an important issue in our later discussion.

Argument for Pessimism

The psychological experiments on reasoning seem to support the pessimistic conclusion that humans are vulnerable to systematic and widespread irrationality. According to the experimental results, people exhibit poor reasoning performance in a number of tasks, including logical, probabilistic, and decision-making tasks; the conclusion drawn is that people do not reason rationally in those circumstances.

The evidence indicates that people make inferential errors. The errors seem to be due to lack of knowledge of certain inductive rules or an inability to apply them. If so, then people are not fully rational in that their inferences fall short of the best available normative standards. (Thagard & Nisbett 1983, 257)

We argue that the deviations of actual behavior from the normative model are too widespread to be ignored, too systematic to be dismissed as random error and too fundamental to be accommodated by the theory of rational choice and then show that the most basic rules of the theory are commonly violated by decision makers. (Tversky & Kahneman 1986, 252)

The argument for pessimism goes as follows. We provisionally answered the philosophical questions by adopting the standard picture of rationality according to which to be rational is to reason in accordance with the rules of logic, probability, and decision-making (Section 1.3). Then, we moved onto the psychological questions and saw that human reasoning systematically deviates from the rules of logic, probability, and decision-making (Section 1.4). Putting the philosophical and psychological discussions together, we reach a pessimistic conclusion about human rationality.

We now turn to the objections to pessimism, in particular the objections from the ecological rationality programme led by Gigerenzer. As Kahneman and Tversky note, Gigerenzer's objections include two claims: 'a conceptual argument against our use of the term "bias"' and 'an empirical claim about the "disappearance" of the patterns of judgment that we had documented' (Kahneman & Tversky 1996, 582).

Gigerenzer's 'empirical claim' is related to the psychological part of the argument for pessimism. Gigerenzer interprets the psychological studies differently, emphasizing the fact that reasoning performance can be improved when the problems are formulated in a different way. As we saw above, in the frequency version of the experiment run by Fiedler (1988), participants' performances improved significantly. Notice that the proponents of the heuristics and biases programme and the proponents of the ecological rationality programme both recognize the possible performance improvements. Gigerenzer tends to stress the *fragility* of biases; he says that the biases 'disappear' (Gigerenzer 1991). Kahneman and Tversky, in contrast, tend to stress the *robustness* of the biases; they say that biases can be 'reduced by targeted interventions but cannot be made to disappear' (Kahneman & Tversky 1996, 589). But it is far from obvious that this is more than a difference in emphasis or rhetoric. Indeed, Kahneman and Tversky write: 'There is less psychological substance to [Gigerenzer's] disagreement with our position than meets the eye' (Kahneman & Tversky 1996, 589; see also Samuels, Stich, & Bishop 2002).

A more substantial and philosophically interesting disagreement concerns Gigerenzer's 'conceptual argument', which is related to the philosophical part of the argument for pessimism. He rejects the standard picture of rationality, or at least the way in which the standard picture is used in the argument for pessimism. He does not think that reasoning performance should be evaluated in terms of the rules of logic, probability, and decision-making. Among Gigerenzer's conceptual or philosophical objections, we focus on three main objections, which we discuss in turn in the next section.

1.5   Objections to Pessimism

The Feasibility Objection

According to the first objection, which we call the 'feasibility objection', systematic failures to reason in accordance with the rules of logic, probability, and decision-making do not necessarily imply irrationality, because it is unfair and unrealistic to evaluate human reasoning performance in terms of such rules in the first place.

As we noted, the argument for pessimism is based on the standard picture according to which rationality consists in reasoning in accordance with the rules of logic, probability, and decision-making, such as the conjunction rule, Bayes' rule, and the principle of descriptive invariance. But it would be unfairly simplistic and demanding to evaluate human reasoning in terms of the rules of logic, probability, and decision-making. As Gigerenzer notes, such an unfair and unrealistic evaluation 'ignores the constraints imposed on human beings. A constraint refers to a limited mental or environmental resource. Limited memory span is a constraint of the mind, and information cost is a constraint on the environment' (Gigerenzer 2008, 5).

Indeed, not everybody agrees with the claim that standards of good reasoning should be derived from the rules of logic, probability, and decision-making. Some philosophers (e.g., Harman 1999) have argued that human thought should have independent normative standards that reflect human cognitive capacities and limitations. In their accounts, normative standards of rationality are not modelled on formal principles of logic, probability, and decision theory.

Let us consider an example. The standard picture would demand logical consistency among a person's beliefs, which means that a person should not have beliefs that are logically inconsistent with one another. However, the task of maintaining a logically consistent belief system is extremely demanding given realistic computational constraints. The job requires greater computational resources than those available to human cognitive systems. As Stephen Stich puts it, perhaps evaluating human reasoning in terms of the standard picture might be committed to the 'perverse' judgment that 'subjects are doing a bad job of reasoning because they are not using a strategy that requires a brain the size of a blimp' (Stich 1990, 27).

The feasibility objection certainly raises a fair worry about the standard picture in its idealized form: that is, rationality requires reasoning perfectly in accordance with the rules of logic, probability, and decision-making. The standard picture needs to be weakened in light of computational and other relevant constraints (although it is not easy to distinguish relevant constraints from irrelevant ones; see Stich 1990). In this vein, Christopher Cherniak argues against upholding logical consistency as an ideal of rationality for human belief systems and endorses a less demanding version of the standard picture of rationality that includes feasibility considerations. He calls it *minimal rationality* (cf., Cherniak 1990). According to the dictates of minimal rationality, for a belief-like state to be minimally rational it must conform to standards of correct reasoning that are feasible in light of the limitations of human cognitive capacities.

> For our purposes, the normative theory is this: The person must make all (and only) feasible sound inferences from his beliefs that, according to his beliefs, would tend to satisfy his desires. (Cherniak 1990, 23)

However, the pessimistic argument cannot be avoided even when computational constraints are taken into account. It would not be fair to expect that rational agents maintain a perfectly consistent belief system when computational constraints are taken into account. However, even when the constraints are taken into account, it would be fair to expect that rational agents do not make particular errors and mistakes, such as the error of assigning a higher probability to Linda being a feminist bank teller than to Linda being a bank teller. After all, in all of the experiments discussed above, some participants do offer the logically or mathematically correct answer, and they do not have 'a brain the size of a blimp'.

Stanovich (1999) empirically examined this issue by studying the relation between computational capacity (measured by SAT scores) and reasoning performance in reasoning tasks. He found a moderate positive correlation between computational capacity and reasoning performance but concluded that the computational limitation is responsible only for part of the reasoning failures. If correct, this supports the idea that reasoning errors that are found in the heuristics and biases research have little to do with computational constraints; thus, computational constraints cannot be an *excuse* for their reasoning errors.

The Meaninglessness Objection

The Linda experiment and other probabilistic tasks in the heuristics and biases programme ask participants to assess the probability of a single event (e.g., the probability of Linda being a feminist bank teller). However, according to a frequentist interpretation of probability, it is hard to make sense of the probability of a single event.

According to the (simple) frequency interpretation, a claim about the probability of an event (e.g., the probability of winning a coin toss is 0.5) is understood as talking about the frequency of the event relative to the relevant reference class (e.g., the frequency of winning relative to the total number of tosses of that particular coin). The Linda experiment asks the probability of Linda being a feminist bank teller. On a frequentist interpretation, this amounts to asking the frequency of Linda being a feminist bank teller. What does that mean? The frequency of Linda being a feminist bank teller relative to the total cases of her being a feminist bank teller in her life would be 1. Does that mean, then, that the probability of Linda being a feminist bank teller is 1?

Gigerenzer's objection is that asking the probability of a single, non-repetitive event – like Linda being a feminist bank teller – is an ill-formed question. Since the question is ill formed and meaningless, there is no correct answer to it. Thus, it is not a mistake to assign a higher probability to Linda being a feminist bank teller than to Linda being a bank teller.

> The philosophical and statistical distinction between single events and frequencies clarifies that judgments hitherto labeled instances of the 'conjunction fallacy' cannot be properly called reasoning errors in the sense of violations of the laws of probability. (Gigerenzer 1994, 144)

Moreover, as we have already seen (Fiedler 1988), when questions are explicitly framed in the format of frequency with a clearly specified reference class ('Among the 100 people who fit Linda's description, how many are bank tellers and how many are feminist bank tellers?'), participants' performance improves. This reveals that people make apparent 'mistakes' when the question is ill formed (asking the probability of a single event with no specified reference class), but do not make mistakes when the question is well formed (asking the frequency of something being the case among a specified reference class). It would seem, then, that people are far from being irrational.

What we call the 'meaninglessness objection' can be developed in at least two ways. In other words, there are at least two versions of it. The first version, the 'factual version', states that the frequency interpretation of probability is true as a matter of fact and, hence, the probabilistic questions in the heuristics and biases experiments are nonsense as a matter of fact. The second version, the 'psychological version', states that frequentism is psychologically true in the sense that the information about probability is represented in the frequentist format *in the mind of human agents*. Hence, the probabilistic questions in the heuristics and biases experiments are nonsense *psychologically* (i.e., the participants cannot make sense of the questions).

The factual version of the meaninglessness objection is philosophically bold; it presupposes the truth of the frequency interpretation of probability. The interpretation of probability is a highly contested topic in philosophy, which goes beyond the scope of this book. But it is worth pointing out that the factual version involves a controversial argumentative strategy. After all, (the simplistic version of) frequentism has been criticized *exactly because* people think that they can meaningfully talk about the probability of a single event (cf., Hajek 2019). It is true that the probability of a single event does not make sense according to frequentism, but it only shows that frequentism is problematic.

The psychological version of the meaninglessness objection is less bold than the factual version. Unlike the factual version, the psychological version is not committed to a particular claim about the interpretation of probability. The problem with the psychological version, however, is that it is not bold enough; if frequentism is not true as a matter of fact but is merely true psychologically, then the probabilistic questions do make sense as a matter of fact and, thus, reasoning biases are real errors as a matter of fact after all. The psychological version is psychologically problematic as well. It is unlikely that the probabilistic questions in the Linda experiment are psychological nonsense. Apparently, participants do not regard the questions as nonsense; after all, they provided meaningful answers to the questions in the experiments, rather than refusing to answer or demanding clarifications (Samuels, Stich, & Bishop 2002).

The Ecological Rationality Objection

The next objection directly confronts the standard picture of rationality, which defines rationality in terms of the rules of logic, probability, and decision-making. This seems to be where Gigerenzer's fundamental disagreement with pessimists lies. As Gigerenzer notes, his main disagreement with the pessimism in the heuristics and biases programme is that it 'does not question the norms [of logic and probability] themselves' and 'it retains the norms and interprets deviations from these norms as cognitive illusions' (Gigerenzer 2008, 6).

The standard picture is problematic, according to Gigerenzer:

> Humans have evolved in natural environments, both social and physical. To survive, reproduce, and evolve, the task is to adapt to these environments, or else to change them. [...] The structure of natural environments, however, is ecological rather than logical. (Gigerenzer 2008, 7)

The problem identified by Gigerenzer is that the standard picture neglects the role of environment, which is a crucial factor for biological success. As an alternative to the standard picture of rationality, Gigerenzer offers the ecological picture of rationality, which characterizes rationality in terms of cognitive success in the relevant environment. According to the standard picture, rationality requires a fit between the mind and the rules of logic, probability, and decision-making, while ecological rationality requires a 'fit between structures of information-processing mechanisms in the mind and structures of information in the world' (Todd & Gigerenzer 2007, 170).

When we evaluate human reasoning performance in light of the ecological picture rather than the standard picture, the pessimistic interpretation is no longer warranted. For example, the information about probability available in the ancient environment was represented in the frequency format (e.g., '3 rainy days in 10 days' rather than '30% chance of rain'). As we have seen, human reasoning performance is relatively good when the questions are represented in the frequency format. Thus, human probabilistic reasoning seems to be ecologically rational; it worked successfully in the ancient environment in which probability was represented in the frequency format.

A similar argument can be made about the Wason selection task. One might speculate that information about cheaters (those who receive the benefit of cooperation without contributing to it) was particularly salient in ancient societies (Cosmides & Tooby 1992). Indeed, failing to detect cheaters is a serious challenge to the maintenance of altruistic behaviours (e.g., Trivers 1971). It turns out that the Wason selection task becomes less challenging when the content of the statement to be falsified is an example of a social exchange rule. Alternative versions of the selection task were devised to test the hypothesis that a participant's performance improves when the statement tested is a cheater-detection rule (Cosmides 1989). For instance, Richard Griggs and James Cox (1982) asked participants to imagine a police officer checking whether people drinking in a bar respect the following rule: 'If you drink alcohol, then you must be over twenty-one years of age.' The cards had on their visible sides one of the following: 'Beer', 'Coke', '22 years', and '16 years'. In this situation, the majority of participants (correctly) choose the 'Beer' card and the '16 years' card. It could be argued, then, that human deductive reasoning is ecologically rational.

In effect, Gigerenzer introduces an alternative conception of rationality, namely the ecological conception of rationality, and argues that human reasoning meets the requirements of ecological rationality. Thus, we seem to have two conceptions of rationality that yield two different interpretations of the experimental results. Our conclusion is pessimistic ('Humans are irrational') when human reasoning performance is evaluated in light of the standard picture. However, our conclusion is optimistic ('Humans are rational') when human reasoning performance is evaluated in light of the ecological picture.

A problem with this 'ecological rationality objection' is that it seems to conflate biological adaptiveness and rationality. For instance, Stanovich writes:

> Evolutionarily adaptive behavior is not the same as rational behavior. Evolutionary psychologists obscure this by sometimes implying that if a behavior is adaptive it is rational. [...] I think a conflation of these interests is at the heart of the disputes between researchers working in the heuristics and biases tradition and their critics in the evolutionary psychology camp. (Stanovich 2009, 55–56)

Certainly, it could be biologically adaptive to have a cognitive system that is especially good at dealing with frequencies but not very good at dealing with probabilities. But is such a system not only adaptive but also rational? This issue is closely related to the aim or purpose of cognition, which we will discuss in the next section.

Another problem is that the ecological picture seems to imply that humans *used to be rational, but they no longer are.* The concern, expressed again by Stanovich, is that human reasoning styles probably used to be successful in the ancient environment, but are no longer successful in the current environment, where probabilities tend not to be represented in a frequentist format, and information about cheaters no longer has special biological significance:

> Unfortunately, the modern world tends to create situations where some of the default values of evolutionarily adapted cognitive systems are not optimal. [...] [M]odern technological societies continually spawn situations where humans must decontextualize information – where they must deal abstractly and in a depersonalized manner with information. (Stanovich 2004, 122)

It is therefore a challenge to defend optimism even when adopting the ecological picture of human rationality. Our temporary conclusion is that none of the objections reviewed so far constitute a serious threat to the pessimistic interpretation of the experimental results. In the next section, we will explore another issue, which is closely related to the dispute between the standard picture and the ecological picture.

1.6 The Aim of Cognition

Aiming at Truth

Why do we accept the standard picture of rationality rather than, say, the ecological picture? The idea that good reasoning aligns with logical and mathematical rules is often associated with the idea that the aim or purpose of cognition is truth; because the aim of cognition is truth, and because logical and mathematical rules are the best guides to truth, human agents ought to reason in accordance with logical and mathematical rules.

But is the purpose of cognition really truth? Does cognition aim at truth? Perhaps Gigerenzer's fundamental disagreement with the standard picture lies in his dissatisfaction with the idea of truth as the aim of cognition. He does not believe that truth is the aim of cognition, or at least he does not believe that it is the only aim: '[A]daptive behavior has other goals than logical truth or consistency, such as dealing intelligently with other people' (Gigerenzer 2008, 12). From this perspective, human reasoning should not be evaluated in terms of logical and mathematical rules. Rather, it should be evaluated in terms of its contribution to biological and ecological success.

This takes us to the topic of the aim of cognition, which is the last topic in this chapter. We cannot fully address the issue of the aim of cognition here, but we will identify some considerations that need to be taken into account in a full investigation of this issue. As the aim of cognition is too broad a target for our investigation, let us focus on the mental state of believing and explore what its aim might be.

What does the 'aim' of belief mean? There could be more than one correct answer to this question, but our tentative answer is that the 'aim' of belief is the *function* of the belief-forming mechanisms (i.e., the mechanisms that produce beliefs in response to some inputs, including perceptual inputs and other beliefs). To say that the aim of belief is truth is to say that the belief-forming mechanisms have the function of tracking truth (i.e., producing true beliefs, avoiding false ones, etc.) (e.g., Velleman 2000; see also Miyazono 2018).

By 'function' we mean so-called 'aetiological' function; on this understanding, function aligns with evolutionary design (e.g., Millikan 1989; Neander 1991). In other words, X has the aetiological function of doing Y if Xs were selected for doing Y in their evolutionary history. For example, hearts have the aetiological function of pumping blood: hearts were selected for pumping blood in their evolutionary history. Again, kidneys have the aetiological function of filtering metabolic wastes from blood: kidneys were selected for filtering metabolic wastes from blood in their evolutionary history. Similarly, belief-forming mechanisms have the aetiological function of tracking truth if the mechanisms were selected for tracking truth in their evolutionary history.

Thus, our questions are: 'Do belief-forming mechanisms really have the function of tracking truth?' and 'Were they selected for tracking truth in their evolutionary history?'

There are two tempting arguments against the idea that belief-forming mechanisms have the function of tracking truth. Both arguments, in our view, are problematic.

The first argument is that the function of belief-forming mechanisms cannot be tracking truth because 'natural selection does not care about truth; it cares only about reproductive success' (Stich 1990, 62).

This argument might seem compelling at first glance, but it does not stand careful scrutiny. The problem with this argument becomes obvious when we run a parallel argument about hearts. The function of hearts cannot be pumping blood because natural selection does not care about pumping blood; natural selection only cares about reproductive success. The weakness of the parallel argument is clear: the choice between pumping blood and reproductive success as the function of hearts is a false dichotomy. After all, hearts *contributed to reproductive success by pumping blood*, which is why the function of hearts is to pump blood. Similarly, the choice between tracking truth and reproductive success as the function of belief-forming mechanisms is a false dichotomy. Perhaps belief-forming mechanisms *contributed to reproductive success by tracking truth*, in which case the function of the mechanisms is to track truth (Millikan 2009; Wilkins & Griffiths 2012).

The second argument is as follows: the function of belief-forming mechanisms cannot be tracking truth because, as we have seen in the heuristics and biases studies, such mechanisms – and reasoning mechanisms especially – lead to systematic errors and biases. In other words, systematic errors and biases constitute evidence that tracking truth is not the function of belief-forming mechanisms.

This argument is not compelling either. Systematically failing to do X is perfectly consistent with having the function of doing X.

For example, sperm has the function of fertilizing an egg, although most sperm fail to fulfil their function. Although most sperm fail to fertilize an egg, some sperm do fertilize an egg, and that is how sperm has contributed to reproductive success in its evolutionary history. Similarly, it is possible that belief-forming mechanisms have the function of tracking truth, despite them systematically producing false beliefs. Although these mechanisms often produce false beliefs, it is possible that they do produce true beliefs in many other cases, and that is how belief-forming mechanisms have contributed to survival and reproductive success, at least in their evolutionary history. Let us put this a different way. Most sperm do not fertilize an egg, not because sperm do not aim at fertilizing an egg but because some failure can be tolerated as long as some sperm successfully fertilize an egg in biologically crucial contexts. Similarly, human belief-forming mechanisms exhibit systematic errors and biases, not because belief-forming mechanisms do not aim at tracking truth but because some errors and biases (even systematic ones) can be tolerated as long as some beliefs successfully track truth in biologically crucial contexts.

To sum up, the arguments above fail to refute the idea that belief-forming mechanisms have the function of tracking truth. In other words, the idea that truth is the aim of belief has not been ruled out yet. Before closing this chapter, we would like to mention a particularly relevant discussion by Ryan McKay and Daniel Dennett (2009).

Positive Illusions

McKay and Dennett endorse the view that in most cases adaptive beliefs are true beliefs. But there is an exception: positive illusions (i.e., optimistically biased judgments about oneself [see Box 1C for a list of the most common positive illusions]).

According to McKay and Dennett, positive illusions are 'adaptive misbeliefs': in other words, they are false beliefs that are adaptive in themselves. For example, your positive illusion about your health might enhance your actual health and life expectancy. If McKay and Dennett are correct, truth might not be the function of positive illusions (or the mechanisms that produce them).

Please note that positive illusions are importantly different from the errors that are due to the adoption of heuristics. In the case of heuristics, false beliefs are merely tolerated; the errors themselves do not have evolutionary value. However, in the case of positive

BOX 1C: Positive Illusions

Definition:

Positive illusions are patterns of beliefs about oneself, the world, and the future characterized by 'systematic small distortions of reality that make things appear better than they are' (Taylor 1989, 228).

Types of positive illusions:
- Illusion of control – to believe that one can control independent, external events (e.g., Langer & Roth 1975).
- Illusion of superiority – to believe that one is better-than-average in a variety of domains, including attractiveness, intelligence, and moral character (e.g., Brown 2012; Wolpe, Wolpert, & Rowe 2014).
- Optimism bias or unrealistic optimism – to predict that one's future will be largely positive and will yield progress, and that negative events will not be part of one's life (Sharot 2011; Weinstein 1980).

Examples:
- Control: You believe that you have a better chance at winning in a betting situation if you are the one dealing the cards or throwing the dice.
- Superiority: You believe that you are smarter than your colleagues even if the evidence does not support that.
- Optimism bias: You believe that you are immune to a highly infectious disease that other people are catching.

illusions, false beliefs positively contribute to fitness. The function of positive illusions (or, more precisely, the underlying mechanism responsible for positive illusions) is perhaps something other than tracking truth.

Dennett and McKay's argument is certainly compelling. But is it really true that positive illusions do not have the function of tracking truth? As Ruth Millikan (2004) points out, it may be too hasty to draw that conclusion. For example, it is conceivable that the original and basic role of positive illusions is tracking truth, but they later acquired the other derivative roles of contributing to survival and reproduction in a different way, which could interfere with the original function in some cases: '[M]any biological systems ride piggyback on systems developed earlier for other purposes. Systems whose jobs were to distort certain beliefs would have to ride on more general systems whose basic jobs were to produce true beliefs' (Millikan 2004, 86).

Another worry is that some forms of optimism involving a denial of existing threats are maladaptive, and the challenge is how to distinguish them from positive illusions. In 2020, people all around the world experienced the devastating effects of COVID-19. Some people seemed to firmly believe in their relative safety and immunity ('I won't be infected,' 'Even if I were infected, I would just have mild symptoms,' etc.), and due to underestimating their personal risk they also exhibited reckless behaviour. For the purpose of survival, denying health threats does not seem to be a good strategy – especially during a global pandemic. We can imagine that our ancestors were more frequently exposed to life-threatening diseases and viruses. In that ancient environment, the negative impact of simplistic optimism may have easily outweighed its positive impact.

Positive illusions have been conceived as the capacity to respond effectively to threats, not as the denial of those threats, and thus they may be immune from this problem (Bortolotti 2018; Taylor 1989). However, questions remain as to how to distinguish non-adaptive optimism from adaptive positive illusions.

1.7 Summary

- The standard picture of rationality claims that rationality consists in reasoning in accordance with the rules of logic, probability, and decision-making. However, studies of reasoning errors and biases, in particular the ones in the heuristics and biases programme, reveal that we systematically fail to reason in accordance with the rules of logic, probability, and decision-making. Thus, if we adopt the standard picture and take the results of the empirical studies at face value, we draw the pessimistic conclusion that humans are irrational.
- There are three main objections from optimists, most notably Gigerenzer: (1) according to the feasibility objection, the standard picture fails to take relevant constraints into account; (2) according to the meaninglessness objection, the results of the reasoning

studies should be dismissed, in particular the probabilistic ones, because they involve meaningless questions about the probability of single events; and (3) according to the ecological rationality objection, we should replace the standard picture with the ecological picture, which evaluates human cognition not in terms of logical and mathematical rules but rather in terms of biological success in the relevant environment. None of these objections, however, convincingly refutes the pessimistic interpretation of the experimental results.

• The standard picture is related to the idea that the aim of cognition is tracking truth. This idea has some plausibility, but there are some interesting cases, such as the case of positive illusions, in which beliefs seem to have a function that is distinct from tracking truth.

Further Resources

Articles and Books

Among the active participants in the rationality debate, Daniel Kahneman and Gert Gigerenzer are a pleasure to read. We recommend two books where they present their take on the relationship between intuition and rationality in an accessible way: Kahneman's *Thinking, Fast and Slow* (2011) and Gigerenzer's *Gut Feelings: The Intelligence of the Unconscious* (2007).

The *Science* article by Tversky and Kahneman, 'Judgment under uncertainty: Heuristics and biases' (1974), is essential for anyone interested in reasoning and rationality. This and other important papers in the heuristics and biases programme are included in a collection of papers: *Judgment under Uncertainty: Heuristics and Biases* (1982), edited by Kahneman, Slovic, and Tversky. To get a good understanding of the rationality debate, see the articles by Kahneman and Tversky and by Gigerenzer in the journal *Psychological Review* (1996). It would also be helpful to read the following: *Without Good Reason: The Rationality Debate in Philosophy and Cognitive Science* (1996) by Edward Stein, where the notion of the standard picture of rationality is introduced and discussed; the paper by Richard Samuels, Stephen Stich, and Michael Bishop (2002), where the debate is summarized and reinterpreted; and Chapter 1 of Lisa Bortolotti's

Irrationality (2014), where the significance of the debate for our appreciation of human rationality is examined.

Online Resources

Kahneman's research is summarized in his Nobel Prize Lecture in 2002, 'Maps of bounded rationality', which is available online. You can also watch Gigerenzer's TEDx talk 'How do smart people make smart decisions?' (2012).

It may also be useful to read Gregory Wheeler's *Stanford Encyclopedia of Philosophy* entry on bounded rationality (2020), and Andrea Polonioli's interviews with Thomas Sturm on the science of rationality (2017) and with Ralph Hertwig on biases, ignorance, and adaptive rationality (2016), both of which are available on the *Imperfect Cognitions* blog.

Questions

1. What do you mean when you say that a person is rational? How do you judge whether a person is rational or not?
2. What do pessimism and optimism about human rationality have in common? What sets them apart?
3. Is the standard picture of rationality a good measure of how good human reasoning is? Why?
4. To what extent should human agents replace the use of heuristics with the application of the rules of logic, probability, and decision-making? Is it even feasible for human agents to do so?

2

Self-Knowledge

2.1 Introduction

It has been a popular idea in the philosophical tradition – as popular as the idea that humans are rational animals – that humans are self-knowing animals (where self-knowledge is the knowledge humans have about their own mental lives). In fact, both rationality and self-knowledge have been described as *distinctive* of humans: among all animals, human beings are the only ones that can reason rationally and think about their own beliefs, desires, emotions, and so on. The idea of humans as rational animals and the idea of humans as self-knowing animals are not independent of one another. Rationality and self-knowledge are intertwined, and they jointly support human agency. The sophisticated capacity to consider one's own beliefs and reflect on one's own choices (in deliberation and self-examination or in interpersonal settings such as in a discussion with others) seems to rely on good reasoning and self-knowledge.

It turns out that psychological studies in the 20th and 21st century threaten not only the idea that humans are rational animals but also the idea that humans are self-knowing animals. For example, on the basis of a wide range of empirical studies, Timothy Wilson provides a 'not [...] very encouraging' portrait of self-knowledge according to which '[p]eople have limited access to their own personalities, the reasons for their responses, their own feelings, and how they will feel in the future' (Wilson 2002, 158). The main aim of this chapter is to examine relevant psychological studies and see whether their results support such a pessimistic portrait of self-knowledge.

We start by clarifying the idea that humans are self-knowers (Section 2.2) and then examine the implications of relevant psychological studies (Section 2.3). These studies threaten some ideas about how and to what extent humans can attain self-knowledge. In particular, the studies seem to threaten the idea that humans have non-observational access to their own minds (i.e., they can know their minds without observing and interpreting their own outward behaviour). Empirical evidence provides numerous and striking examples of humans actually relying on self-observation or self-interpretation to learn what they are thinking or feeling – figuring out their own minds in the same way that they figure out other minds, by observing and interpreting outward behaviour. The crucial question is whether self-observation and self-interpretation happens *in some cases but not all cases* (in which case humans do have some non-observational access to their minds, as discussed in Section 2.4) or whether it happens *in all cases* (in which case they completely lack non-observational access, as discussed in Section 2.5).

Other interesting questions intersect with issues about the process humans rely on to attain self-knowledge: 'Is self-knowledge fallible?', 'Do we know our minds better than an external observer?', and 'To what extent can human agents know their own mind?' The empirical evidence has something important to contribute to such questions too.

This chapter defends a modest view of human self-knowledge. Although human agents are capable of knowing their own minds non-observationally, they rely on the process of self-observation and self-interpretation more frequently than previously acknowledged, which suggests that their knowledge of themselves is not always peculiar or special.

2.2 Clarifying Self-Knowledge

Self-Knowledge and Its Targets

Claire hears one of her friends saying 'Claire is so mean! I have known her since school and she has never bought me a drink, not even on my birthday!' Claire always thought of herself as a generous person. Her friend must be wrong!

Last night, Jagbir met a handsome man on a roller-coaster ride at the local fair when they were asked to share the same two-seater. Now she can't stop thinking about him. Jagbir thinks she has fallen in love with him. Will she be able to find out who he is?

Claire believes that she is a generous person. Jagbir is convinced that she has fallen in love. But are they right? Are they good self-knowers? More generally, how well do humans know themselves? To answer this question, we need to investigate two issues: the philosophical questions about self-knowledge (e.g., 'What does it mean to have self-knowledge?', 'What is necessary for a person to have self-knowledge?', and 'What is sufficient for a person to have self-knowledge?') and the psychological questions about self-knowledge (e.g., 'Do humans satisfy a sufficient condition for having self-knowledge?', 'Do humans fail to satisfy a necessary condition for having self-knowledge?', and 'What do empirical studies say about these issues?'). We discuss the philosophical questions in this section (Section 2.2) and move on to the psychological questions in the next (Section 2.3).

Self-knowledge is *knowledge* of one's own mind. Here we do not need to commit to a full theory about the nature of knowledge, which is the focus of epistemology; we are only committed to the view that knowledge involves belief (i.e., when X knows that P, X believes that P). This means that self-knowledge involves beliefs about one's mind.

Self-knowledge is knowledge *of one's own mind*. One can know about one's own mental states (such as the desire to eat a cheeseburger or the wish to become an astronaut), one's psychological processes (such as the process of calculating the sum of two numbers), one's psychological capacities (such as the capacity to remember people's names in a list quickly and accurately), one's dispositions (such as the tendency to have paranoid thoughts), one's character traits (such as whether one is generous or mean), one's deep values (such as valuing family more than income), and so on.

We cannot assume that all forms of self-knowledge are similar and equally good. Perhaps humans have relatively good self-knowledge of some of the items above but not others. For example, it is likely that humans have a better grasp of their own beliefs and desires – what Quassim Cassam (2014) calls 'trivial self-knowledge' – than of their own dispositions, character traits, and deep values – what

Cassam calls 'substantive self-knowledge'. Knowing one's own beliefs and desires seems to be relatively simple; people just know what they believe and what they want. In contrast, knowing one's own dispositions, character traits, and deep values requires serious investigation, including observation and analysis of one's past and present behaviour. Claire is angry with her friend for having described her as a mean person, but did her friend have a point? Claire needs to think about her past behaviour. Did she ever buy him a drink? Knowledge of one's own dispositions, character traits, and deep values is typically attained in the same way as knowledge of other people's dispositions, character traits, and deep values – namely by thinking about the past and interpreting the available information. If Claire cannot remember ever buying her friend a drink, then maybe she is not as generous as she thought she was.

Again, knowledge of one's psychological processes is not usually available to conscious awareness and thus cannot be introspected. Jagbir believes that she has fallen in love with the man from the roller-coaster ride, but she may not know what caused her emotional state of arousal during the ride nor what changed in her body when the emotion took hold. Moreover, it is possible that knowing how her emotional state emerged will reveal that it is not love that she is feeling, but rather a sense of excitement caused by the thrill of the ride that she mistakenly categorized as attraction for the handsome man.

As Wilson writes:

> People possess a powerful, sophisticated, adaptive unconscious that is crucial for survival in the world. Because this unconscious operates so efficiently out of view, however, and is largely inaccessible, there is a price to pay in self-knowledge. (Wilson 2002, vii)

We have seen some examples of unconscious reasoning processes in the previous chapter. The heuristics guiding our reasoning processes might not be available to consciousness (although the output of the heuristic processes is usually available). For example, before the studies conducted by Kahneman and Tversky, people may not have been aware of the fact that they relied on the heuristic of representativeness when establishing the probability of events in the Linda experiment (although they were aware of the output of the heuristic process). It is overwhelmingly plausible that human agents do not have introspective access to unconscious cognitive processes of this kind: knowledge about the heuristic processes that guide human reasoning requires agents to interpret the results of sophisticated psychological experiments.

Self-Knowledge: Privileged and Peculiar

Self-knowledge is a form of knowledge. But philosophers tend to assume that self-knowledge is not just an example of knowledge among others; there is something special or distinctive about it. As we will see, the crucial issue in this chapter is whether self-knowledge is really special or distinctive.

In what sense would self-knowledge be special or distinctive? The following example from Alex Byrne is helpful:

> Consider Jim, sitting in his office cubicle. Jim believes that his pen looks black to him; that he wants a cup of tea, that he feels a dull pain in his knee, that he intends to answer all his emails today; that he is thinking about paperclips; that he believes that it is raining. Jim also has various equally humdrum beliefs about his environment: that it is raining, that his pen is black, and so on. Furthermore, he has some opinions about the psychology of his officemate Pam. He believes that her pen looks green to her; that she wants a cup of coffee, that her elbow feels itchy; that she is thinking about him; that she believes that it is raining. (Byrne 2018, 5–6)

Among the three groups of beliefs in this example, one might think that the first group, Jim's beliefs *about his own mind*, is more epistemically privileged than the other two groups, Jim's beliefs *about the environment* and Jim's beliefs *about Pam's mind*.

The notion of 'being epistemically privileged' can be understood in multiple ways: 'epistemically privileged' can mean 'more reliable', 'more likely to be true', 'more likely to be knowledge', and so on. In any case, the basic idea is clear enough: it is relatively easy to imagine that Jim's belief that it is raining is false. Perhaps it was raining one hour ago when Jim looked out of the window. He still believes that it is raining one hour later, but it stopped raining and he did not realize. Again, it is not difficult to imagine that Jim's belief that Pam wants a cup of coffee is false. Perhaps Jim mistakenly assumes that all his co-workers, including Pam, are coffee lovers, but Pam prefers tea to coffee.

In contrast, it is relatively difficult to imagine how Jim's belief that he believes that it is raining is false, or how his belief that he wants a cup of tea is false. When Jim fails to notice that it has stopped raining, his belief that it is raining (his belief about the environment) is false. However, his belief that he believes that it is raining (his belief about his own belief) is true. Again, when Jim fails to notice Pam's preference for coffee, his belief that Pam wants tea (his belief about Pam) is false. However, Jim's belief that he wants a cup of tea (his belief about his own desire) is true. Epistemic privilege is one aspect in which self-knowledge is said to be special and distinctive.

There is another aspect in which self-knowledge is said to be special and distinctive. Self-knowledge is thought to be acquired by a peculiar process that is different in kind from the process of knowing about the environment or about other minds. For example, Jim's belief that he believes that it is raining is acquired by a peculiar process that is different in kind from the process of Jim acquiring the belief that it is raining or the belief that Pam believes that it is raining. The peculiar process is only available to Jim when he tries to know about his own mind, or to Pam when she tries to know about her own mind. The process is not available to Jim when he tries to know Pam's mind, nor to Pam when she tries to know Jim's mind. The peculiarity of the process by which self-knowledge can be acquired has been described in different ways, such as 'introspective', 'direct', 'non-inferential', 'authoritative', or 'a priori' (see Box 2A for some clarification of the meanings of these terms). This peculiarity by which one acquires knowledge of one's own mental states is the second aspect in which self-knowledge is said to be special and distinctive.

What does it mean to say that self-knowledge is peculiar? What is the difference in kind between Jim's access to the contents of his own mind and his access to the contents of other minds or his access to the environment? Fully answering this question requires a discussion of how knowledge of other minds is acquired; this is the topic of Chapter 8, in which we discuss the nature of mindreading (i.e., the process of attributing mental states to others). For now, it can be understood in the following way:

> Our access to others' minds is similar to our access to the non-psychological aspects of our environment. Jim knows that his pen is black by seeing it; Pam could know the same thing by the same method.

BOX 2A: Key Terms in the Philosophical Literature on Self-Knowledge

Introspection (literally, 'looking inward' or 'looking within') is one way of learning about one's own mind, by simply realizing what one's own thoughts and feelings are. For example, Swati knows that she is feeling sad by introspection if all it takes for her to know about her sadness is to turn her attention to how she is feeling.

A priori knowledge is knowledge that can be attained independently of any experience that justifies the knowledge. For example, Swati knows a priori that 2+2=4 or that all bachelors are unmarried without relying on observation or induction.

Direct (non-inferential) self-knowledge is knowledge that can be attained by being aware of one's own mental state without becoming aware of anything else (it is often called 'knowledge by acquaintance'). For example, Swati knows that she feels sad *directly* because her feeling of sadness is something she introspects. Introspecting the feelings requires no inferential process.

First-person authority is the idea that one is more authoritative about the content of one's own mind than about the contents of other people's minds. For example, Swati's friends do not challenge her assertion that she feels sad because they assume that she is the expert when it comes to the contents of her own mind, as they are all experts about the contents of their own minds when they attribute mental states to themselves.

Privileged access is the idea that one's judgment about own mental state is more likely to be true, or more likely to be knowledge, than one's judgment about other issues. For example, when Swati judges that she is sad, that judgment is more likely to be true (i.e., she is in fact sad) or more likely to be knowledge (i.e., she knows that she is sad) than her judgment that one of her friends is sad or that it is raining outside.

Peculiar access is the idea that one can appeal to a peculiar and special method to acquire self-knowledge. For example, Swati appeals to a peculiar and special method when she judges that she is sad. Others cannot appeal to this method when they judge that she is sad.

Likewise, Jim knows that Pam wants a coffee by observing her behavior. Anyone else – including Pam – could know the same thing by the same method. Our peculiar access to our own minds is not like this: one can come to know that one wants a coffee *without observing oneself at all*. (Byrne 2018, 8, our emphasis)

The idea is that peculiarity has something to do with observation, or the lack thereof. Jim's knowledge of his environment and of Pam's mental states is *observational* or *interpretive*: his knowledge of the pen depends on the observation of the pen and its properties, and his knowledge of Pam's mental states depends on him observing and interpreting her behaviour. If Pam answers 'Coffee, please' to the question 'Would you like something to drink?', Jim can observe this exchange and conclude that she wants a cup of coffee. In contrast, Jim does not need any observation of his own behaviour to know that he believes that it is raining or that he wants a cup of tea. The fact that there is no need for observation or interpretation is what makes self-knowledge peculiar. (Note that this does not imply that Jim *cannot* know his mental states by observing his behaviour. It is obvious that Jim, if he wants to, *can* gain knowledge of his mental states by observing his behaviour. The point is that he *does not have to* observe his behaviour to know his own mental states. Observation and interpretation are *not necessary*.)

To sum up, our answer to the philosophical questions about self-knowledge is that self-knowledge is knowledge (a form of belief) of one's own mind and of its constituents, such as one's own mental states, processes, dispositions, character traits, and so on. Self-knowledge seems to be special and distinct in the sense that, first, it is epistemically privileged in comparison to other forms of knowledge and, second, it is acquired through a peculiar and non-observational process.

2.3 Challenges to Peculiarity

Peculiarity and Parity

Let us move on to the psychological questions about self-knowledge. How well do humans know their own minds according to psychological inputs? Do they really have privileged access? How about peculiar access? The psychological studies we will see below could threaten ideas of self-knowledge both as privileged and as peculiar.

We will outline some issues concerning self-knowledge as privileged, but our main focus will be peculiarity.

Several researchers in psychology and philosophy are sceptical about the peculiarity thesis of self-knowledge for empirical reasons (Bem 1972; Carruthers 2009, 2011; Gopnik 1993; Wegner 2002; Wilson 2002). These researchers emphasize the similarity, rather than the difference, between self-knowledge and knowledge of other minds. In other words, their emphasis is not on the *peculiarity* of self-knowledge but rather on the *parity* between self-knowledge and knowledge of other minds.

> Individuals come to 'know' their own attitudes, emotions, and other internal states partially by inferring them from observations of their own overt behavior and/or the circumstances in which this behavior occurs. Thus, to the extent that internal cues are weak, ambiguous, or uninterpretable, the individual is functionally in the same position as an outside observer, an observer who must necessarily rely upon those same external cues to infer the individual's inner states. (Bem 1972, 2)

> [T]he system that is employed when one identifies and attributes mental states to oneself is none other than the mindreading system that underlies one's capacity to attribute mental states to other people. [...] In order to attribute thoughts to oneself, then, the mindreading faculty is forced to interpret the available sensory evidence. This can concern one's physical circumstances and overt behavior, or it can involve one's own visual imagery, affective feelings, and inner speech. The result is that all access to one's own propositional attitudes is sensory-based and interpretive in nature. (Carruthers 2013, 145–146)

But should we deny the idea of peculiar self-knowledge? Is it really true that self-knowledge is observational and interpretive just like knowledge of other minds? We divide this question into two sub-questions. The first sub-question is whether self-knowledge is observational and interpretive in at least some cases. The second sub-question is whether self-knowledge is observational and interpretive in all cases.

If the answer to the first sub-question is 'No' (which implies a 'No' answer to the second sub-question), then the idea of peculiar self-knowledge is unscathed. We call this the 'extreme peculiarity view'. If, in contrast, the answer to the second sub-question is 'Yes' (which implies a 'Yes' answer to the first sub-question), then the idea of peculiar self-knowledge is denied completely. We call this the 'extreme parity view'. Peter Carruthers, for example, defends this extreme position according to which we have no peculiar self-knowledge of our own propositional attitudes and decisions: '[T]here is just a single faculty involved in both forms of activity [knowing one's own mental states and knowing somebody else's], using essentially the same inputs, which are all perceptual or quasi-perceptual in character' (Carruthers 2009, 123).

If the answers are 'Yes' to the first sub-question and 'No' to the second sub-question, the idea of peculiar self-knowledge is partially challenged, but not completely denied. Peculiar self-knowledge can occur; it is just that it is not as widespread as we might assume. We call this the 'moderate view'. Daryl Bem seems to be the defender of the moderate view. In the quote above, he says that we know our mental states 'partially by inferring them from observations of their own overt behavior and/or the circumstances in which this behavior occurs', and this happens not always but rather when 'internal cues are weak, ambiguous, or uninterpretable' (Bem 1972, 2).

Thus, we have three positions: the extreme peculiarity view, the extreme parity view, and the moderate view. Our main task below is to see which view is the one that the empirical evidence recommends.

Dissonance Studies

Let us start by looking at what Bem takes to be the evidence for self-observation: instances of cognitive dissonance.

In a classic study by Leon Festinger and James Carlsmith (1959), participants in one condition (the $1 condition) performed repetitive and boring tasks for one hour. Then they received $1 compensation for playing a role which involved the job of telling the next person who was waiting for her turn that the tasks were fun and enjoyable. Participants in another condition (the $20 condition) performed the same tasks for the same time. They received $20 compensation for playing the role and telling the next person that the tasks were fun and enjoyable. (The remaining participants were in a control group and received no monetary compensation.) Afterwards, all participants indicated how much they enjoyed the tasks. The result was that those in the $1 condition rated the tasks significantly more enjoyable than those in the $20 condition.

Bem argues that this experimental result is explained by the idea of self-observation in a fairly straightforward manner. To see how Bem's idea works, consider the following case. Let us think about a partic-ipant in the $1 condition, Sally, and another in the $20 condition, Christopher. You observe Sally's and Christopher's behaviour and try to figure out how much they enjoyed the tasks. You observe two facts about Sally's behaviour: she told the next person that the tasks were fun (*A1*) and that she received only $1 as compensation (*B1*). On the basis of this pair of observations, you conclude that Sally enjoyed the tasks a lot; you think 'Sally told somebody else that the tasks were fun despite only receiving $1 as compensation, so the tasks must be really fun.' Next, you observe two facts about Christopher's behaviour: he told the next person that the tasks were fun (*A20*) and he received $20 as compensation (*B20*). On the basis of this pair of observations, you conclude that Christopher did not enjoy the tasks very much; you think 'Christopher told somebody else that the tasks were fun, but he obviously did so for the money' (cf., Bem 1967).

Now think about Sally and Christopher themselves. According to Bem's self-perception theory, Sally and Christopher do not have peculiar access to how much they enjoyed the tasks. Thus, they need to figure out how they felt about the tasks by observing their own behaviour, just like you do when you assess how much they enjoyed the tasks. Sally observes two facts about her own behaviour: *A1* and *B1*. Based on this pair of observations, Sally concludes that she enjoyed the tasks a lot. Next, Christopher observes two facts about his own behaviour: *A20* and *B20*. Based on this pair of observations, Christopher concludes that he did not enjoy the tasks. Thus, Bem's self-perception theory nicely predicts and explains Festinger and Carlsmith's result. If Bem is correct, then this experiment supports the idea of self-observation.

But how plausible is Bem's account of Festinger and Carlsmith's experiment? Bem's theory is presented as an alternative to Festinger's own account. According to Festinger's cognitive dissonance theory, the experimental result is explained by the motivation for reducing dissonant ideas rather than the process of self-observation.

In the $1 condition, Sally is aware of three facts: that she told the next person that the tasks were fun (*A1*); that she received only $1 as compensation (*B1*); and that the tasks were boring (*C1*). *A1*, *B1*, and *C1* are dissonant in the sense that they do not fit together well. Sally might be thinking 'If the tasks are boring, why did I tell the next person that the tasks were fun, and I was paid only $1 for it?' So, motivated to dissolve the dissonance creating a feeling of discomfort,

Sally revises her belief about $C1$, which is arguably the easiest observation to revise, thus coming to believe that the tasks were actually fun.

The same thing does not happen in the $20 condition. Christopher is aware of three facts: that he told the next person that the tasks were fun ($A20$); that he received $20 as compensation ($B20$); and that the tasks were boring ($C20$). Christopher's observations are not dissonant. It is coherent to believe that one receives a high compensation for being asked to perform a boring task and to lie to other participants. Christopher does not need to revise his belief about $C20$ to eliminate a feeling of discomfort due to dissonance.

Note that Festinger's account is not committed to the idea of self-observation. In fact, his account seems to presuppose that Sally and Christopher have non-observational access to how much they enjoyed the tasks ($C1$ and $C20$). Otherwise, Sally cannot be aware of $C1$, which is dissonant with $A1$ and $B1$.

Thus we have two accounts of Festinger and Carlsmith's experiment: Bem's self-perception account, which supports the idea of self-observation, and Festinger's cognitive dissonance account, which does not support the idea of self-observation. Which is more plausible? Answering this question is not easy because the two theories predict the same results in many scenarios. In other words, many scenarios (just like the one in Festinger and Carlsmith's study) can be adequately explained by either of the two theories. But only the cognitive dissonance theory predicts that affective or motivational factors (e.g., the feeling of discomfort) are involved in dissonant cases, and this hypothesis seems to be supported by further studies. In any case, we will not pursue the debate between the cognitive dissonance theory and the self-perception theory here (see Cooper 2007 for an overview); it is sufficient to say at this point that it is not obvious that Bem's self-perception account is the best explanation of dissonance cases.

Confabulation Studies

Let us now move on to another body of research relevant to the investigation of self-knowledge: the literature on broad confabulation. In this context, confabulation means 'making up a story' without intending to deceive. It has been defined as an *ill-grounded claim* people make when they do not realize that their claim is ill grounded (Hirstein 2005) or as an *unsubstantiated claim* people make in response to a question that they cannot answer because the relevant information is not known or accessible to them (Turner & Coltheart 2010). For a different understanding of confabulation, where confabulation is a symptom of disorders characterized by severe memory impairments (narrow confabulation), see Chapter 7.

The cases of confabulation that we will consider here are those where agents offer an inaccurate explanation of their own behaviour (see the examples in Box 2B). For example, when asked why one made a decision, one might answer by offering an explanation that does not reflect the actual process behind the decision. Suppose you ask Karl why he chose to watch the film *Casablanca* and he says that he wanted to see a classic film starring Humphrey Bogart when, in fact, his choice was due to the fact that on the way home from work he had seen a poster advertising Morocco as a fun holiday destination and that 'primed' him to select a film that was set in that country. Karl has not lied to you; he is convinced that he is providing an accurate explanation for his choice of film.

Confabulation fits nicely with the idea that humans lack peculiar access to their own minds. If, for example, Karl lacks peculiar access to the real cause of his choice of film, namely the priming effect, then he needs to consider observational inputs to figure out why he made that choice. He eventually reaches the reasonable (but false) conclusion that he wanted to watch a classic film starring Humphrey Bogart. How often do such confabulations happen? Is self-knowledge always confabulatory? Or is it only sometimes confabulatory?

Confabulation studies can be divided into two groups. The first group of studies involves confabulation in unusual circumstances. The most notable example is the study by Michael Gazzaniga (2000), who observed confabulations among so-called 'split-brain patients'. In split-brain cases, the corpus callosum (a bundle of fibres connecting the right hemisphere and the left hemisphere of the brain) is severed as a method of treating severe epilepsy. Gazzaniga's split-brain patient confabulated about the movement of his left hand. The left hand is controlled in the right hemisphere of the brain. The verbal centre of the brain is in the left hemisphere. With the corpus callosum severed, the verbal centre in the left hemisphere loses access to the right hemisphere, which is responsible for the left hand. Thus, the patient (or the patient's left hemisphere) makes up a false story when asked to explain the reason why the left hand does what it

BOX 2B: Some Contexts in Which People Confabulate

Consumer choice:
People offer explanations for their consumer preferences that do not match the most likely causal processes leading to their choices and do not include causally relevant factors. For example, one might choose a product due to an advertisement having made that product salient to them but explain their choice in terms of the product having some qualities that the alternatives do not have. See the stockings experiment (Nisbett & Wilson 1977) reviewed in this section.

Attitude explanation:
People offer explanations for their attitudes (aesthetic or moral judgments, political attitudes, etc.) that are unlikely to reflect the most salient factors contributing to having those attitudes. For example, people in a romantic relationship asked to evaluate their relationship after receiving some negative information about their partner do not realize that their subsequent negative evaluation is largely determined by receiving the negative information (Wilson & Kraft 1993).

Hypnosis:
People under hypnosis tend to explain their actions without acknowledging the role of the hypnotic suggestion on their behaviour. For example, after receiving the hypnotic suggestion that they will see a stranger in the mirror, people under hypnosis claim that the image they see in the mirror is not theirs, and explain this by finding physical differences between themselves and the image (such as different eye colour) (Bortolotti, Cox, & Barnier 2012).

does. The split-brain case provides good evidence that agents attain knowledge of themselves (e.g., of the reasons for their current or past behaviour) based on self-observation and self-interpretation. It is likely that what they do when asked for information they do not have is simply interpret their own behaviour as they would interpret the behaviour of another agent. But there are obvious limitations to these studies. One problem is that the relevant cases can be relatively rare, which makes it difficult to conduct reliable, large-scale empirical studies. Another problem is that it is far from obvious that the finding about these unusual cases can be generalized to more common, everyday cases of self-knowledge. The confabulations in these special cases do not tell us much about how self-knowledge works in general.

The second group of studies investigates confabulation in everyday cases and is more relevant to our discussion about the peculiar nature of self-knowledge. We will now discuss two classic studies of this kind.

The Stockings Experiment. In their landmark paper 'Telling more than we can know: Verbal reports on mental processes', Richard Nisbett and Timothy Wilson (1977) describe an experiment (disguised as a consumer survey) conducted in a bargain store just outside of Ann Arbor, Michigan. Participants were asked to evaluate the quality of four pairs of nylon stockings (*A, B, C*, and *D*, from left to right) and indicate which pair was the best. The result revealed a strong position effect on the choices by the participants: *D* was frequently chosen (*A* = 12%, *B* = 17%, *C* = 31%, and *D* = 40%). Participants' choice was based on the position, not the quality, of the pair of stockings. In fact, all pairs of stockings were exactly the same; there was no difference in quality. However, when asked the reason for their choice, participants did not acknowledge the position effect. Instead, they confabulated and spoke about some qualities of their chosen pair of stockings being the main reason for their choice, such as: 'I chose this pair of stockings because its knit is superior.' When the experimenter explicitly asked participants about the relevance of the position, participants adamantly denied the idea.

Choice Blindness. More recently, Petter Johansson and his colleagues in Lund performed a series of experiments that show a different type of confabulation at play (Johansson et al. 2005; Johansson et al. 2006). The original study by Johansson and colleagues (2005) is inspired by the stockings experiment by Nisbett and Wilson but features two important differences.

First, participants in this experiment chose from a range of non-identical items. The items were photos of the faces of female strangers (Photo *A* and Photo *B*) and participants had to choose which one they found most attractive.

Second, this study involves a deceptive manipulation. After participants made their choice, and before they could be asked about the reason for it, the photos were swapped. Unbeknown to the participants, the experimenter swapped the photo that had been chosen by the participants (say, Photo *A*) with one that had not been chosen (say, Photo *B*). Next, the experimenter asked the participants why they chose Photo *B*, pretending that no swapping had taken place. The surprising result of the experiment was that no more than 26% of the photo swaps were noticed by participants, who we could say were *choice-blind*. Indeed, many participants confabulated by giving articulate and plausible reasons for a choice they apparently never made: 'She looks like an aunt of mine, and she seems nicer than the other one,' 'I thought she had more personality, in a way. She was the most appealing to me,' and so on.

The behaviour observed by Nisbett and Wilson in the stockings experiment and by Johansson and colleagues in the choice blindness studies are striking cases of self-observation and self-interpretation. When explaining why they made their choices, participants do not exhibit any peculiar access to their mental states and processes. Instead, they rely on the same observational and interpretive processes on which they rely when they think about why other people make choices.

For example, think about a hypothetical case in which you observe a participant, Angelina, in the stockings experiment by Nisbett and Wilson. Angelina chooses pair *D* and you are asked why she chose the pair rather than the other pairs. Perhaps you will answer in a way that makes her choice sensible or reasonable; you might say 'She chose it because she thinks that its knit is superior' or 'She chose it because she thinks it is more elastic than the others.' You will not say 'She chose it because of the position effect' unless you are a psychology student. As Nisbett and Wilson point out, '[S]uch factors [e.g., the position effect] should seem particularly implausible as reasons for liking or disliking an object [...] [and] it seems outrageous that such a judgment as one concerning the quality of a nightgown might be affected by its position in a series' (Nisbett & Wilson 1977, 252). The experiment's result can be nicely explained by the self-observation hypothesis: Angelina needs to observe her own behaviour when reporting why she chose pair *D*, just like you need to when you explain why she chose pair *D*.

Again, think about the hypothetical case where you observe a participant, Neville, in the choice blindness study by Johansson and colleagues. Neville chooses Photo A and you are asked why he chose Photo B (since Photo A has been switched with Photo B). Because you do not have any direct or introspective access to Neville's preference for Photo A, you might fail to recognize the swap. Perhaps you will answer the question so that his choice seems sensible or reasonable; you might say 'He chose it because he thinks that the woman in the photo seems nicer than the other one' or 'He chose it because he thinks that the woman had more personality.' The experimental result can be nicely explained by the self-observation hypothesis: Neville needs to observe his own behaviour when reporting why he (allegedly) chose Photo B, just like you do when explaining why he (allegedly) chose it.

Success and Failure of Self-Knowledge

Before moving on, let us consider an issue concerning confabulation studies. It is tempting to think that cases of confabulation involve inaccurate or unsuccessful judgments about one's own mental states. Participants in the studies discussed above *are bad at self-knowledge*. Because of this, confabulation studies might threaten not only the idea of peculiar self-knowledge but also the idea of privileged self-knowledge. But is this really the right interpretation of confabulation studies?

Based on the evidence of pervasive confabulation concerning reasons for attitudes and choices, Krista Lawlor (2003) argues that mental-state self-attributions lack authority as they are not as accurate as third-party attributions and fail to correlate with a person's future behaviour. On the basis that ill-grounded explanations of attitudes and choices are virtually indistinguishable from well-grounded ones and are common, one might argue that we should be genuinely concerned about the reliability of self-knowledge (Scaife 2014, 471). Indeed, some interpret the standard philosophical account of confabulation as an instance of 'failed mind-reading' (Strijbos & de Bruin 2015); confabulation shows that people make mistakes when attributing mental states to themselves:

> [I]f confabulation turns out to be a widespread phenomenon in everyday social practice, this would seriously undermine first-person authority of mental state attribution. (Strijbos & de Bruin 2015, 298)

Consider the stockings experiment once more. Imagine that participants choose the rightmost pair of stockings because of position effects. When asked to explain their choices, they answer that they chose that pair because of its qualities. As they do not mention the role of the position effect in their choice, their explanation is ill grounded. They confabulate. Not only do they offer an ill-grounded explanation, but, as a result of confabulating, they also form the belief that the pair of stockings they chose is the brightest, and that belief is false. Participants who are asked for an explanation of their choice produce an ill-grounded causal claim due to their ignorance of the mental processes underlying their choices.

Whether the form of non-clinical confabulation we are examining here involves a failure of mental-state self-attribution depends on what we take successful mental-state self-attributions to require (Bortolotti 2018a). In their original paper on priming effects, Nisbett and Wilson are clear that participants' verbal reports are inaccurate because participants ignore the mental processes leading to their choices and, as a result, *misidentify* the reasons for their choices. Confabulation is evidence for the view that people are blind *to the processes* responsible for their choices, but this does not imply that they are also blind *to the choices* they made. Independently of whether research participants can identify the reasons for their choices, their choices are *authentic* in the sense that they are sincerely reported and genuinely endorsed. If successful mental-state self-attributions require awareness of one's attitudes and choices, then they are not threatened by confabulation.

Does successful mental-state self-attribution require that people are aware of the mental processes responsible for their choices? This sounds like an implausibly demanding requirement. In the cases where confabulation has been observed and documented (such as consumer choice, moral judgments, and hiring decisions), causal factors leading to the choice are likely to be psychological processes that involve priming effects, socially conditioned emotional reactions, and implicit biases that cannot be directly experienced or easily observed, but rather need to be inferred on the basis of the systematic and scientific study of human behaviour.

Does successful mental-state self-attribution require that people's subsequent behaviour is explained and reliably predicted on the basis of that self-attribution? This also sounds like an implausibly demanding requirement and one that imposes more stability and consistency on people's mental life than is reasonable to expect. We do not know whether people who claim to have chosen a pair of stockings for its texture would choose the softest pair of stockings at their next consumer choice survey, but should they not do so, the fact that mental-state self-attributions fail to shape their future behaviour does not speak so much against self-knowledge as against the crystallization of preference criteria for stockings. This is even more evident in the case of choice blindness.

In the case of the experiment on faces, Johansson and colleagues embrace a *preference misattribution* account of choice blindness, suggesting that participants are (literally) *blind to their choices* and misattribute preferences to themselves. The explanation would be that participants who fail to detect the manipulation chose Photo A because they found that face most attractive; when asked why they chose Photo B (after it was switched for Photo A), they misattribute a preference to themselves and come to think that this face is most attractive. However, some have argued that *preference change* is the best interpretation of the experiment (see Bortolotti & Sullivan-Bissett 2019; Lopes 2014), meaning that participants do not misattribute preferences to themselves when they defend a choice that is different from the one they initially made, but rather change their preference in the course of the study due to the manipulation in the experiment. In this case, participants have an initial preference for Photo A (which explains their choice), but when asked why they chose Photo B, they form a new preference for Photo B (which explains them being able to offer reasons for choosing that photo).

Dominic McIver Lopes (2014) claims that, in the manipulation condition of the experiment, participants give reasons for what has become *their new choice*. For Lopes, it is no surprise that preferences are changeable and amenable to manipulation. The newly ascribed preferences are *real* and are newly formed as a result of the participant's beliefs about the choices they made (Lopes 2014, 29–30). Given that most participants do not detect the manipulation, they come to believe that they chose the face that is presented to them as their choice. Participants do not realize that their preference shifted. In the manipulation condition, reasons are often given in the past tense: 'I *thought* she had more personality in a way,' 'I *chose* her because she smiled,' or 'I *chose* her because she had dark hair' (Johansson et al. 2005, 118). This strongly suggests that people believe that their new preference was there all along, failing to appreciate the preference shift and the role of the manipulation in determining this preference shift. The participant's belief that the choice presented to them was the one that they had made determines the preferences they ascribe to themselves when they give reasons for the choice.

> Perhaps subjects in the manipulation condition changed their preference as a result of their choice. Since they did not notice the manipulation, they believed that they chose the displayed face, and that fact determines their preference. On this hypothesis, [...] subjects' reasons do not accord with their initial preference as revealed by their initial choice, but they do accord with their eventual preference as determined by what they took to be their choice. (Lopes 2014, 29–30)

When asked again about their preferences at a later time (Johansson, Hall, & Sikström. 2008), participants in the manipulated condition chose the face that they provided reasons for choosing in the experiment (i.e., they provided reasons for why they chose the switched photo) and not the face they had originally chosen. According to Lopes, this suggests that *reasons cement preferences*, meaning that when one gives reasons for a choice, the preference expressed in that choice 'sticks' and becomes more stable.

2.4 The Moderate View

So far, we have seen some empirical evidence for self-observation. In some cases, including rather unusual cases (split-brain patients, hypnosis, etc.) and fairly mundane cases (priming effects in consumer choice, choice blindness, etc.), we rely on observation in the same way that we rely on observation to come to know somebody else's mind. This means that the extreme peculiarity view is hopeless. We are then left with two options: the moderate view and the extreme parity view. In the former case, self-observation is at work in some contexts, such as the ones in the experiments above, but not in others. The peculiarity of self-knowledge is limited, but it is not denied. In the latter case, self-observation is always at work; what we have seen in the experiments above is just the tip of the iceberg. There is nothing peculiar about self-knowledge; self-observation is all there is to self-knowledge. Let us examine the two options in more detail.

The moderate view has been supported by many authors in philosophy and psychology. On the psychology side, for example,

Bem defends the idea of self-observation, but adds that self-observation happens 'to the extent that internal cues are weak, ambiguous,
or uninterpretable' (Bem 1972, 2). On the philosophy side, for
example, Byrne defends the idea of peculiar self-knowledge, but adds
that 'there is certainly room for debate about the importance of third
person ("behavioral") access to one's mental states' (Byrne 2018, 2).

According to the moderate view, self-observation is at work in
some contexts, but not in others. The crucial question for this view
is: 'What are the contexts in which self-observation is at work?'

The answer to this question might be found when we look
carefully at the contexts in which people confabulate. Confabulation
experiments seem to put participants in rather peculiar contexts. For
example, the stockings experiment involves a rather peculiar situation
in which the participants are first asked to choose among identical
stockings and then they need to respond to the question 'Why did
you choose this pair?' This situation is unlike our everyday choice
situations where, for example, we choose from different stockings
on display in a supermarket and nobody asks us 'Why?' immediately
after the choice.

Let us consider two hypotheses. The first is that self-observation
happens in the context in which participants are supposed to choose
among identical items. The second hypothesis is that self-observation
happens in the context in which participants are supposed to answer
the 'Why?' question.

Let us begin with the first hypothesis. As Johansson and colleagues
have noted, the stockings experiment 'involved a rather strange and
contrived task' in which experimenters 'have given [the participants]
the artificial choice between identical stockings' (Johansson et al.
2006, 689). Since all items are the same, perhaps participants do
not have a strong preference, or no preference at all, which creates a
context in which 'internal cues are weak'.

However, it is not clear that the choice blindness study can be
explained by this hypothesis. After all, participants choose among
different items (e.g., Photo *A* and Photo *B*) in the experiment. Of
course, it is conceivable that participants do not have a strong
preference despite their choice among different items. After all, the
choice does not have any significant implications for their lives. But
not all cases in which confabulation and choice blindness are observed
involve something inconsequential such as trivial consumer choices
or assessing the attractiveness of strangers' faces. For instance, choice

blindness has been observed in cases where people were asked about their moral principles or political commitments. In this context, the failure to detect the manipulation causes greater concern than in the context of consumer choice or aesthetic judgments. It is perhaps understandable that participants' preferences about the attractiveness of strangers' faces can be easily manipulated, because people may not come to make those choices with existing preferences and may not care much about the attractiveness of faces that they have never seen before. However, preferences about moral and political issues (e.g., 'It is more important for a society to promote the welfare of its citizens than to protect their personal integrity') are expected to be more stable, and they may even count as self-defining for those agents who see themselves as engaged in politics (Bortolotti & Sullivan-Bissett 2019).

Participants in the studies by Hall and colleagues (Hall, Johansson, & Strandberg 2012; Hall et al. 2013) were asked to complete what the authors describe as a 'self-transforming' questionnaire on either foundational moral principles (condition 1) or topical moral issues (condition 2). This happened just before a general election in Sweden at a time when people who were usually not interested in politics were likely to think about these kinds of issues in their daily lives. Participants had to rate their agreement with a statement using a nine-point scale, and then explain their ratings to the experimenter. The transforming part of the experiment was that two of the statements read out by the experimenter were actually the opposite of the statements originally rated. The ratings given were kept the same, but the statement was reversed, so participants were in effect presented with the opposite of the opinion they expressed earlier. The experiment was designed to see whether participants would be led to endorse a view that was in opposition to the one they had just stated.

Once the participant had read the reversed statement, an experimenter would summarize their view back to them with a question such as 'So you don't agree that [statement]?' or 'So you do agree that [statement]?' This mechanism was in place to ensure participants were sure of what they were committing themselves to. The manipulated trials were understood as *corrected* when participants noticed something strange immediately (*spontaneous* detection) or claimed that something was amiss only later at the time of debriefing (*retrospective* correction). Trials were understood as *accepted* when the participant showed no sign of having noticed that the reversal of the opinion they originally expressed was being fed back to them.

In the first condition, in which the questionnaire was on foundational moral principles, around 33% of the trials were spontaneously detected, and a further 8% were retrospectively detected after the experiment. In condition two, nearly 50% of the manipulations were spontaneously detected, but very few participants claimed to detect the manipulations retrospectively. Framed for individuals, 69% of participants *accepted* at least one of the two reversed statements (Hall, Johansson, & Strandberg 2012, 4). The manipulation was performed very subtly, so even participants who noticed something strange did not detect the manipulation as such, although they did declare that they must have previously misread or misunderstood the statement.

There was no correlation between self-evaluation of strength of moral conviction and correction, so those 'participants who believed themselves to hold strong moral opinions in general were no more likely to correct the manipulations' (Hall, Johansson, & Strandberg 2012, 3). Although there was a positive relationship between level of agreement and spontaneous detection, 'a full third (31.3%) of all manipulated trials rated at the endpoints of the scale (1 or 9) remained undetected, which shows that not even extreme levels of agreement or disagreement with statements guarantees detection' (Hall, Johansson, & Strandberg 2012, 3). However, those participants who claimed to be politically active were more likely to spontaneously detect the manipulation in condition two when compared to politically active participants in condition one. From this we learn that those who identified as politically active were less likely to be manipulated into misidentifying their attitudes or were less likely to have their attitudes changed. It would be interesting to examine whether there are any other individual differences that can explain the correction/acceptance rates among participants.

Let us now consider the second hypothesis that self-observation happens in the context in which participants are supposed to answer the 'Why?' question. Nisbett and Wilson (1977) said the following in the opening of their classic article:

> 'Why do you like him?' 'How did you solve this problem?' 'Why did you take that job?' In our daily life we answer many such questions about the cognitive processes underlying our choices, evaluations, judgments and behavior. (Nisbett & Wilson 1977, 231)

Nisbett and Wilson are certainly right: we face many 'Why?' questions in daily life. But there are some reasons to think that 'Why?' questions (unlike 'What?' questions such as 'What do you think?' or 'What do you want?') create the context in which self-observation is likely. Perhaps 'Why?' questions create the context in which 'internal cues are weak, ambiguous, or uninterpretable' (Bem 1972, 2). For example, a 'Why?' question might be taken as asking the cause of the decision rather than the decision itself. Participants do not have strong internal cues about the cause of their decision and, thus, they have no choice but to appeal to self-interpretation.

Nisbett and Wilson propose a distinction between 'content' (i.e., what occupies one's consciousness at that time) and 'process' (i.e., the causal origin of content) (but see also Wilson 2002). We confabulate about the latter, but not about former. In fact, Nisbett and Wilson accept that 'we do indeed have direct access to a great storehouse of private knowledge' of the content of consciousness and the content belongs to 'private facts that can be known with near certainty' (Nisbett & Wilson 1977, 255).

Alternatively, the 'Why?' question might be taken as asking participants to justify their decision. The 'Why?' question creates the context in which participants are supposed to justify their decision rather than simply report their psychological states and processes. Under the psychological pressure to justify their decision, participants appeal to self-observation which enables them to explain their own behaviour in terms of beliefs and desires that make their behaviour reasonable or justifiable (Sandis 2015). For example, a participant, Jeremiah, chooses pair *D* because of the position effect. He interprets the experimenter's question about his choice as a request for a justification. This is a difficult request; there is no good reason for Jeremiah's choice as the stockings to choose from were identical (unless we believe that we are in a situation in which the position of an item is a good reason to choose it). Under the psychological pressure to justify his choice, Jeremiah says that pair *D* has the best texture, which latches onto generally plausible reasons for choosing stockings and other similar items.

Note that this is not to say that Jeremiah's answer is plausible or unproblematic. Even as a justification for his particular choice of the rightmost pair of stockings within a set of four identical pairs of stockings, his answer is still problematic. A justification is not supposed to disclose the causal processes that led to his choice, but rather to highlight what good reasons there are for that choice, regardless of whether those reasons did motivate him to make the choice (Sandis 2015). The problem is that the reason he provided to justify his choice does not match the features of the situation because all pairs of stockings are the same.

2.5 The Extreme Parity View

Extreme Parity and Parsimony

Now let us turn to the extreme parity view. According to this view, self-observation is always at work. Self-observation is all there is to self-knowledge. Shaun Nichols and Stephen Stich summarize the view:

> [The extreme parity view] proposes to maintain the parallel between detecting one's own mental states and detecting another person's mental states quite strictly. The *only* information used as evidence for the inference involved in detecting one's own mental state is the information provided by perception (in this case, perception of oneself) and by one's background beliefs (in this case, background beliefs about one's own environment and previously acquired beliefs about one's own mental states). (Nichols & Stich 2003, 156)

Note that we do not have direct evidence for the extreme parity view. We only have the evidence for self-interpretation in some limited contexts such as abnormal cases (e.g., split-brain cases) and experimental contexts (e.g., the stockings experiment).

The extreme parity view is counterintuitive. For example, it does not explain those occasions in which we deliberate. The extreme parity view gets something right: people 'read their own minds', self-observe, and self-interpret much more frequently than they realize. But by being extreme, the view misses some important nuances. People sometimes deliberate (rarely and not very rationally) and it is overwhelmingly implausible to think otherwise. When making a decision that will have wide-ranging and long-term implications (e.g., which subject to study at university or whether to move to a foreign country), people consider the advantages and disadvantages of each outcome, ask for advice, and generally 'make up' their own mind without the need to self-observe.

Despite the lack of direct evidence for it, and despite its being counterintuitive, the extreme parity view can be defended by an indirect argument; we call this the 'parsimony argument' for the extreme parity. The extreme parity view gives a parsimonious explanation of the available data. The extreme parity view explains all cases of self-knowledge in a simple and unified manner in terms of self-observation. We do not need to posit additional peculiar methods for gaining self-knowledge. As Carruthers has noted, 'In order to warrant the extra complexity, it needs to be shown that [the extreme parity view] on its own is inadequate, or else some positive evidence of an additional method should be provided' (Carruthers 2011, 366).

Parsimony arguments are often used in philosophy (and in science). If we have two theories, theory *A* and theory *B*, which are equally good at explaining the available data, and if *A* is more complicated than *B*, then we ought to choose *B* since it is more parsimonious. So, if we have two hypotheses about self-knowledge, the moderate view and the extreme parity view, which are equally good at explaining the available data, and if the moderate view is more complicated than the extreme parity view, then we ought to choose the extreme parity view since it is more parsimonious.

The Parsimony Argument

Premise 1: The moderate view and the extreme parity view are equally good at explaining the available data.

Premise 2: The moderate view is more complicated than the extreme parity view.

Premise 3: If the moderate view and the extreme parity view are equally good at explaining the available data, and if the former is more complicated than the latter, then we ought to choose the extreme parity view.

Conclusion: We ought to choose the extreme parity view.

Should we accept the parsimony argument in this case? Is the extreme parity view really defendable?

Our focus will be on premise 1, namely that the moderate view and the extreme parity view are equally good at explaining the available data. Can this premise be challenged? Challenging premise 1 involves providing some cases that the extreme parity view cannot explain but that the moderate view can. Are there such cases?

The Interpretive Sensory-Access Theory

Nichols and Stich point out that '[i]t seems obvious that people can sit quietly without exhibiting any relevant behavior and report on their current thoughts' (Nichols & Stich 2003, 157). For example, it is possible that a person, Joan, knows that she believes that there is an apple on the table, or that she wants to eat an apple, while sitting still in the living room. This case seems to pose a serious problem for the extreme parity view (but not for the moderate view, which allows for the possibility of peculiar and non-observational access). Being unable to explain such an obvious fact, Nichols and Stich say that the extreme parity view is 'crazy' and 'is hard to take seriously' (Nichols & Stich 2003, 156).

Carruthers notes that the case can be explained by a sophisticated version of the extreme parity view where materials for self-interpretation go beyond the observation of bodily behaviour. According to Carruthers' (2009) interpretive sensory-access (ISA) theory, the materials for self-interpretation include both external cues (including own behaviour and environment) and inner sensory cues (including inner speech and mental imagery). The ISA theory can deal with the case of immobile Joan: although there is no informative external cue in the case, Joan can access her internal sensory cues (including inner speech and mental imagery) that help her to learn about her beliefs, desires, and so on. Joan can attribute to herself the belief that there is an apple on the table on the basis of her inner speech sentence 'An apple is on the table' or mental imagery of an apple on the table.

There is a sense in which the ISA theory is not that extreme; after all, the theory permits peculiar and non-interpretive access to internal cues (such as inner speech and mental imagery). That said, the ISA theory is extreme in that it denies any peculiar access to propositional attitudes (such as beliefs or desires). According to the ISA theory, metacognitive access to propositional attitudes is always self-interpretive, where self-interpretation is based not only on external cues but also on internal sensory cues.

Note that although the ISA theory recognizes the peculiar access to internal sensory cues, it is still more parsimonious than the moderate view. Any sensible account of metacognition, including the moderate view, would recognize the peculiar access to inner speech, mental imagery, and so on. Thus, the ISA theory, which recognizes the peculiar access to internal sensory cues but does not recognize the peculiar access to propositional attitudes, is more parsimonious than the moderate view, which recognizes peculiar access to propositional attitudes in addition to peculiar access to internal sensory cues. This means that the parsimony argument is still applicable.

There are, however, some worries about the ISA theory. It requires at least two theoretical assumptions: a psychological assumption and a metaphysical assumption. The psychological assumption is that internal sensory cues regularly accompany propositional attitudes. For example, the inner speech sentence 'An apple is on the table' regularly accompanies the belief that an apple is on the table. Otherwise (i.e., if there is no such a regularity), the theory fails to explain the case of immobile Joan. If Joan's belief that an apple is on the table is not regularly accompanied by the inner speech sentence 'An apple is on the table' (or other internal sensory cues), then she is not able to identify her belief. The metaphysical assumption is that internal sensory cues do not constitute propositional attitudes. For example, the inner speech sentence 'An apple is on the table' does not constitute the belief that an apple is on the table, although the former reliably accompanies the latter. Otherwise (i.e., the inner speech sentence does constitute the belief), admitting peculiar access to the inner speech sentence amounts to admitting peculiar access to the belief, which contradicts the ISA theory's denial of peculiar access to propositional attitudes.

One might worry about the compatibility of the psychological and metaphysical assumptions. If internal sensory cues regularly accompany propositional attitudes, then one might think that there must be an explanation of the regular co-occurrence of sensory cues and propositional attitudes. A simple explanation of the regular co-occurrence is that internal sensory cues are constitutive of propositional attitudes.

Setting this worry aside, another problem is that the ISA theory might fail to explain the case of immobile Joan after all because her internal cues are not informative enough for her to identify her propositional attitudes. Even though Joan has access to her internal sensory cues (such as the inner speech sentence 'An apple is on the table' or the mental image of an apple on the table), these sensory cues are not sufficient for her to identify her belief that there is an apple on the table.

For example, having the mental image of an X in your mind does not specify whether you are thinking about X or Y when you cannot discriminate X from Y in your visual imagination. Suppose that Joan recognizes a mental image of a geometrical shape with lots of angles. Suppose that she also has two hypotheses: that she is believing something about a chiliagon (i.e., a polygon with 1,000 sides) and that she is believing something about a myriagon (i.e., a polygon with 10,000 sides). Can she tell which one is correct? This is really difficult because distinguishing chiliagons from myriagons in one's visual imagination is extremely difficult. As Descartes notes, the thing that I visually imagine when thinking about a chiliagon 'differs in no way from the representation I should form if I were thinking of a myriagon, or any figure with very many sides' (Descartes 1984, 50).

One might think, however, that this problem can be solved by inner speech. For example, Joan can conclude that she is believing something about a chiliagon when she recognizes the inner speech word 'chiliagon' or that she is believing something about a myriagon when she recognizes the inner speech word 'myriagon'. But inner speech has its own problems too.

Having an inner speech sentence P in your mind does not specify whether you are believing that P, desiring that P, imagining that P, supposing that P, and so on. For example, what is Joan supposed to know about her propositional attitudes when she recognizes the inner speech sentence 'Caesar died in his bed'? Does she believe that Caesar died in his bed, or does she imagine that Caesar died in his bed? As Hume points out, sensory cues (or 'ideas') are the same between somebody imagining that Caesar died in his bed and somebody believing that Caesar died in his bed. The believer 'form[s] all the same ideas as [the imaginer] does' and the believer 'can't conceive any idea that [the imaginer] can't conceive, or conjoin any ideas that [the imaginer] can't conjoin' (Hume 1739/2007, 66).

To sum up, it is not clear that the ISA theory can successfully explain the case of immobile Joan; internal sensory cues might not be informative enough for knowing about one's own propositional attitudes.

2.6 Summary

- Empirical data, especially those concerning confabulation, suggest that agents rely on self-observation to identify their own mental states – at least in some cases. This is consistent with what we called the moderate view, according to which humans know their own minds by self-observation in some cases but not always.

- The view that our self-knowledge always relies on self-observation and self-interpretation (what we called the extreme parity view) is certainly attractive because of its simplicity, but it faces the difficult challenge of explaining the case of immobile Joan. It is also not clear that the ISA theory can meet this challenge.
- According to the moderate view, our self-knowledge relies on self-observation and self-interpretation in some cases. This suggests that there are parts or domains of the mind to which people do have peculiar and direct access and parts or domains to which people do not have peculiar and direct access. The best thing to do if one wants to know about the parts or domains of the latter kind is to observe and interpret one's own behaviour or learn from third-person testimony. This picture is compatible with the idea that the mind is fragmented, which will be discussed in Chapter 3.

Further Resources

Articles and Books

The stockings experiment discussed in this chapter is included in Richard Nisbett and Tim Wilson's article 'Telling more than we can know: Verbal reports on mental processes' (1977), which is considered to be one of the most influential psychology papers of the 20th century. Wilson's book *Strangers to Ourselves: Discovering the Adaptive Unconscious* (2002) is an excellent overview of salient psychological studies on the limitations of introspection, and it offers some interesting philosophical reflections on the implications of those studies.

For a thorough investigation of the phenomenon of confabulation, we recommend a book by William Hirstein, *Brain Fiction: Self-Deception and the Riddle of Confabulation* (2005), where clinical and non-clinical instances of confabulation are examined. For more information about cognitive dissonance and the self, see Elliott Aronson's useful article (2019) that discusses the notion of hypocrisy.

For an empirically informed and philosophical discussion of self-knowledge, we recommend Peter Carruthers' work, especially the target article (2009) in *Behavioral and Brain Sciences* and the book *The Opacity of Mind: An Integrative Theory of Self-Knowledge*

(2011). Some papers that discuss the role of the empirical evidence on confabulation in the self-knowledge literature include work by Robin Scaife (2014) and Derek Strijbos and Leon de Bruin (2015). Other important contributions by philosophers include: Shaun Nichols and Stephen Stich's *Mindreading: An Integrated Account of Pretence, Self-Awareness and Understanding Other Minds* (2003), Quassim Cassam's *Self-Knowledge for Humans* (2014), and Annalisa Coliva's *The Varieties of Self-Knowledge* (2016).

Online Resources

Brie Gertler's *Stanford Encyclopedia of Philosophy* entry on self-knowledge (2020) has some useful discussion of the implications of the empirical evidence on theories of self-knowledge. Eric Schwitzgebel's *Stanford Encyclopedia of Philosophy* entry on introspection (2019) is good background reading on the idea of self-knowledge as privileged and peculiar.

Keith Frankish's article on the limitations of self-knowledge (2016) in *Aeon* and Joelle Proust's article on metacognition (2016) in the *Brains* blog are both accessible and engaging. Lisa Bortolotti also wrote an accessible article for *Aeon* on everyday instances of confabulation (2018b), where the stockings experiment is mentioned.

Mitchell Green's introductory lectures on the value and limits of self-knowledge (2019) are available at University of Edinburgh online courses. Petter Johansson's TED talk (2018) is an excellent introduction to the phenomenon of choice blindness.

Questions

1. Do you know yourself better than your family members or friends do?
2. If you have any special access to information about yourself, does this apply only to the content of your feelings and thoughts or does it extend to your character traits too?
3. In what way, if any, does the literature on confabulation undermine self-knowledge claims?
4. In what context does it make more sense to hypothesize a type of self-knowledge that is not limited to self-observation and interpretation?

3

Duality

3.1 Introduction

Our discussion so far seems to suggest that the mind is fragmented or divided rather than united. For instance, the fact that many people are vulnerable to reasoning biases, which we discussed in Chapter 1, suggests that their minds are fragmented. Recall the Linda experiment, where most research participants considered the conjunction 'Linda is a bank teller and is active in the feminist movement' more probable than 'Linda is a bank teller' because the description of Linda matched that of a feminist. Participants committed the conjunction fallacy because they chose the option that they felt was more 'representative' of Linda. Stephen Jay Gould describes his own experience with the Linda experiment as follows:

> I know that [the feminist bank teller hypothesis] is least probable, yet a little homunculus in my head continues to jump up and down, shouting at me – 'but she can't just be a bank teller; read the description'. (Gould 1991, 469)

Gould says that he knows that the feminist bank teller hypothesis is *mathematically* less probable than the bank teller hypothesis because a conjunction of two events can never be more probable than one of the conjuncts, but while part of him is convinced that the bank teller hypothesis is more probable, another part of him still leans towards the feminist bank teller hypothesis. It is as if Gould's mind is, by his own admission, fragmented.

The phenomenon of self-observation, discussed in Chapter 2, lends support to the idea of the fragmented mind as well. To self-observe is to treat one's own mind as if it is somebody else's. You learn about your own mind by observing and interpreting your own behaviour just like you do when you learn about somebody else's mind by observing and interpreting her behaviour. This means that, in a sense, we are *strangers to ourselves*. This is also the title of Timothy Wilson's (2002) book, which provides an overview of the significance of the studies on the limitations of introspection.

The very idea of self-observation suggests that the part of a person's mind that is observing and interpreting is distinct from, and maybe even alienated from, the part of the mind that is being observed and interpreted. As we mentioned in Chapter 2, the most extreme example of this fragmentation or alienation is in the context of confabulation by split-brain patients (Gazzaniga 2000), where the brain is literally divided into two (i.e., the right hemisphere and the left hemisphere become physiologically alienated from one another). But the idea of a fragmented mind can be generalized to other, less extreme forms of self-observation too. According to Wilson, human agents are alienated from an important part of themselves – their 'adaptive unconscious'.

> Many human judgments, emotions, thoughts, and behaviors are produced by the adaptive unconscious. Because people do not have conscious access to the adaptive unconscious, their conscious selves confabulate reasons for why they responded the way they did. (Wilson 2002, 105)

We believe that the idea of a fragmented mind is plausible as it makes sense of some phenomena we have already described and other phenomena we will describe in the following chapters. This chapter will clarify the idea of a fragmented mind in light of the empirical evidence and various theoretical considerations. In particular, this chapter will address the literature on the dual-process theory (Section 3.2), which is an informative account of mental fragmentation. The dual process theory states that human cognition is the result of the interaction between two kinds of processes: Type-1 processes and Type-2 processes. This theory provides us with a plausible solution for the so-called 'rationality paradox', which concerns how to reconcile human apparent rationality with human apparent irrationality. There are, however, some issues with the dual process theory. The following questions arise: 'What are Type-1/Type-2 processes?', 'What distinguishes Type-1 processes from Type-2 processes?', and 'How do Type-1 and Type-2 processes interact? Do they compete with each other all the time? Or are Type-1/Type-2 processes dominant most of the time?' (Section 3.3).

This chapter also addresses whether the dual-process theory implies the dual-system theory (i.e., Type-1/Type-2 processes correspond to two distinct cognitive systems) (Section 3.4) and the dual-state theory (i.e., Type-1/Type-2 processes correspond to two distinct mental states or attitudes) (Section 3.5).

3.2   The Dual-Process Theory

Basic Ideas

What does it mean to say that the mind is fragmented or divided rather than united? By 'fragmented' we do not just mean that the mind has many parts, constituents, or systems. The crucial part of what we call 'fragmentation' is the idea that different parts of the mind can pull us in different directions, or more specifically that there can be some kind of conflict between different parts of the mind. Plato's doctrine of the tripartite structure of the soul is a classic expression of a fragmented mind. According to Plato, the soul is composed of three parts: appetite, spirit, and reason. Crucially, Plato does not only say that the soul is divided into parts, he also says that different parts can be in conflict with one another, pulling the soul in different directions. Plato explains this idea in the famous Chariot Allegory:

> Remember how we divided each soul in three at the beginning of our story – two parts in the form of horses and the third in that of a charioteer? [...] The horse that is on the right, or nobler, side is upright in frame and well jointed, with a high neck and a regal nose; his coat is white, his eyes are black, and he is a lover of honor with modesty and self-control; companion to true glory, he needs no whip, and is guided by verbal commands alone. The other horse is a crooked great jumble of limbs with a short bull-neck, a pug nose, black skin, and bloodshot

white eyes; companion to wild boasts and indecency, he is shaggy around the ears – deaf as a post – and just barely yields to horsewhip and goad combined. (Plato 1995, 43–44)

The idea of a fragmented mind has been expressed in many ways by different authors in philosophy and psychology (see Frankish & Evans 2009), and several accounts describe a sort of duality in the human mind (see Box 3A for three versions of duality).

Currently, the best expression of the idea of mental fragmentation can be found in the dual-process theory (Evans 2003, 2010; Evans & Over 1996; Kahneman 2011; Sloman 1996; Stanovich 1999, 2011; Stanovich & West 2000). The dual-process theory has been applied to different domains, including reasoning, learning, and social cognition (for an overview, see Evans 2008). There are also dual-process theories of other psychological phenomena, such as moral judgments (Chapter 4) or mindreading (Chapter 6).

The focus of this chapter is the dual-process theory of reasoning according to which reasoning performance is determined by the interaction between two reasoning processes of different kinds: Type-1 processes and Type-2 processes. Typically, Type-1 processes

---

BOX 3A: Theories of Duality in Human Cognition

Dual process:
'Dual-process theories hold that there are two distinct processing modes available for many cognitive tasks: one (type 1) that is fast, automatic and non-conscious, and another (type 2) that is slow, controlled and conscious.' (Frankish 2010, 914)

Dual system:
'Human cognition is composed of two multipurpose reasoning systems, widely known as System 1 and System 2, the former supporting type 1 processes, the latter supporting type 2 ones.' (Frankish 2010, 914)

Dual attitude (or dual state):
'Dual attitudes are defined as different evaluations of the same attitude object: an automatic, implicit attitude and an explicit attitude.' (Wilson, Lindsey, & Schooler 2000, 101)

are evolutionarily older, unconscious, automatic, low effort, and associative, whereas Type-2 processes are evolutionary more recent, conscious, controlled, high effort, and rule-based. Just like the two horses in Plato's Chariot Allegory, Type-1 processes and Type-2 processes can pull us in different directions. In the Linda experiment, for example, Type-2 processes should follow the mathematically canonical procedure and reach the conclusion that the bank teller hypothesis is more probable than the feminist bank teller hypothesis: 'I know that [the feminist bank teller hypothesis] is least probable.' In contrast, Type-1 processes follow a heuristic procedure driven by judgments of representativeness and reach the conclusion that the feminist bank teller hypothesis is more probable than the bank teller hypothesis: '[A] little homunculus in my head continues to jump up and down, shouting at me – "but she can't just be a bank teller; read the description"' (Gould 1991, 469).

We will now discuss two issues concerning the dual-process theory. In the rest of this section, we focus on the reasons for accepting the dual-process theory. Next (in Section 3.3), we focus on the details of the theory.

Empirical Reasons: Reasoning Biases

There are both empirical and philosophical reasons for favouring the dual-process theory (or at least supporting the basic idea of it). We will start with the empirical reasons and then turn to the philosophical reasons.

A clarification is needed with regard to the empirical reasons for favouring the dual-process theory. It would not be accurate to assume that the dual-process theory is an empirical theory in psychology that is directly testable via experiments. Instead, it is one of general hypotheses in psychology that can make sense of a series of relevant studies as interconnected, just like the massive modularity hypothesis, the language of thought hypothesis, and the adaptive unconsciousness hypothesis. In fact, Jonathan Evans and Keith Stanovich argue that the dual-process theory is a 'broad framework' or 'metatheory'; it 'cannot be falsified by the failure of any specific instantiation or experimental finding' and its central role is to 'stimulate new research and accumulate enough supportive evidence' (Evans & Stanovich 2013b, 263). The dual-process theory has been successful in making sense of relevant empirical studies as interconnected. In *Thinking*,

Fast and Slow, for example, Daniel Kahneman (2011) interprets the entire heuristics and biases programme in light of the dual-process theory.

Wason Selection Task

Having said that, the dual-process theory has been associated with some particular empirical findings. For example, the dual-process theory *of reasoning* was originally introduced in an interpretation of the Wason selection task experiments, which we saw in Chapter 1. In one experiment (Wason & Evans 1974), participants were asked to select cards that need to be turned over to verify the given hypothesis and to explain the reason for selecting the cards. Participants' actual choices were strongly influenced by a primitive matching bias (selecting cards depicting the items that are explicitly mentioned in the hypothesis), but the reasons offered by participants have little to do with their matching bias. Rather, their reasons were apparently logical, *post hoc* rationalizations. (This reminds us of the stockings experiment by Nisbett and Wilson [1977] discussed in Chapter 2, where participants' choices were strongly influenced by the position effect, of which they were not aware. When asked to justify their choice, they offered a *post hoc* rationalization that had nothing to do with the position effect.)

To explain the result of the Wason selection task experiments, Wason and Evans propose a dual-process account, which posits two distinct processes:

1. The processes underlying reasoning performance (e.g., matching bias) are not generally available for introspection.
2. Introspective accounts of reasoning performance reflect one's tendency to construct a justification for one's own behaviour consistent with one's knowledge of the situation.

Belief Bias

The dual-process theory of reasoning has been associated with the belief bias, which is the tendency of one's beliefs to influence one's judgment of logical validity such that inferences with believable (i.e., plausible given one's background beliefs) conclusions are more likely to be regarded as valid than ones with unbelievable conclusions.

An inference is logically valid if its conclusion is guaranteed to be true when all of its premises are true. In an experiment (Evans,

Barston, & Pollard 1983) on logical validity, participants were asked to evaluate four types of inferences.

- *Valid-Believable*: A valid inference with a believable conclusion. For example, 'No cigarettes are inexpensive. Some addictive things are inexpensive. Therefore, some addictive things are not cigarettes.'
- *Valid-Unbelievable*: A valid inference with an unbelievable conclusion. For example, 'No addictive things are inexpensive. Some cigarettes are inexpensive. Therefore, some cigarettes are not addictive.'
- *Invalid-Believable*: An invalid inference with a believable conclusion. For example, 'No addictive things are inexpensive. Some cigarettes are inexpensive. Therefore, some addictive things are not cigarettes.'
- *Invalid-Unbelievable*: An invalid inference with an unbelievable conclusion. For example, 'No cigarettes are inexpensive. Some addictive things are inexpensive. Therefore, some cigarettes are not addictive.'

The result showed a significant belief bias: inferences with believable conclusions are more likely to be regarded as valid than those with unbelievable conclusions (92% of participants took Valid-Believable inferences to be valid, while only 46% took Valid-Unbelievable inferences to be valid). But there is also another tendency: valid inferences are more likely to be regarded as valid than invalid ones (46% of participants took Valid-Unbelievable inferences to be valid, while only 8% took Invalid-Unbelievable inferences to be valid). Evans and colleagues interpret these results in terms of the dual-process theoretical idea that these two tendencies reflect an interplay between two kinds of processes: a non-logical process responsible for the belief bias and a logical process responsible for sensitivity to logical structure.

Philosophical Reasons: The Rationality Paradox

We will now move on to philosophical reasons for favouring the dual-process theory. The main theoretical consideration concerns what is known as 'the rationality paradox', which can be summarized as a simple question: 'We can put a man on the moon, so why can't we solve those logical reasoning problems?' (O'Brien 1998, 23).

As we have seen, human agents deviate from the rational norms of reasoning: for example, people systematically judged that it was more probable that Linda was a feminist bank teller than a bank teller. But this is paradoxical. If people are so irrational that they make frequent mistakes in basic reasoning problems, like in the Linda experiment, then how did humans achieve remarkable things in science, technology, culture, and other areas? How can creatures who systematically fail to solve the Linda experiment and other basic problems of reasoning solve the much more difficult and complicated logical and mathematical problems that are required, for example, in the project of sending humans to the Moon and bringing them back to Earth safely? Note that the answer to this problem cannot (just) be about individual differences. For example, the answer cannot just be that NASA's employees are super smart or especially immune to biases and errors. The real paradox is that one and the same person can be rational in some contexts and irrational in other contexts. For example, a science professor who can easily solve complicated maths problems might fail in the Linda experiment.

A special case of the rationality paradox concerns the fact that the remarkable achievements by humans include scientific achievements, which, in turn, include psychological achievements such as the findings of human reasoning errors in the heuristics and biases programme. But how can creatures who systematically fail in the Linda experiment and other basic problems of reasoning successfully solve logical and mathematical tasks that are required for designing and conducting successful psychological studies on reasoning and reveal reasoning errors such as the conjunction fallacy?

This version of the rationality paradox can be put in the form of a self-defeating paradox, which we call the 'self-defeating rationality paradox'. Suppose that the empirical evidence supports the sceptical view that humans systematically make errors in some basic reasoning problems, such as the Linda problem. However, an implication of this is that humans are not really capable of doing psychology; after all, doing psychology requires the cognitive capacity for solving logical and mathematical tasks that are much more difficult than those required in the Linda experiment. But if humans are not capable of doing psychology, then we should not trust the findings of psychology, including those about reasoning biases. This means that we lose the empirical evidence for the sceptical view of reasoning. The sceptical view defeats itself!

The Self-Defeating Rationality Paradox

Premise 1: The experimental psychology of reasoning reveals that human reasoning capacity is not sufficiently reliable (see Chapter 1).

Premise 2: If human reasoning capacity is not sufficiently reliable, then we should not trust the product of human reasoning capacity, including scientific findings and theories, and in turn the experimental psychology of reasoning.

Conclusion: Thus, the experimental psychology of reasoning is self-defeating.

The rationality paradox (and its special case: the self-defeating rationality paradox) seems to suggest that, on the one hand, humans systematically fail to solve even basic reasoning tasks in some contexts (such as in the heuristics and biases experiments), and, on the other hand, they systematically succeed in solving difficult ones in other contexts (such as when calculating the orbit of a space rocket or analysing experimental data in a psychological study).

The dual-process theory helps us to make sense of this rather puzzling situation. According to the dual-process theory, human cognitive performance is determined by the complex interplay between Type-1 and Type-2 processes. Type-1 processes are dominant in some contexts, while Type-2 processes are dominant in other contexts. Systematic reasoning failures are typically seen in Type-1-dominant contexts, while systematic reasoning successes are typically seen in Type-2-dominant contexts.

(However, we should be sceptical about the simplistic idea that people always make mistakes in Type-1-dominant contexts, or people do not make any mistakes in Type-2-dominant contexts. For instance, people might appeal to heuristic processes in Type-1-dominant contexts, but heuristics work perfectly fine in many cases: 'In general, these heuristics are quite useful' [Tversky & Kahneman 1974, 1124].)

With the dual-process theory, we can also respond to the self-defeating rationality paradox. Premise 1 can be true only when it is understood as a claim about Type-1-dominant contexts. Thus, the argument should look like this:

Premise 1: The experimental psychology of reasoning reveals that human reasoning capacity *in Type-1-dominant contexts* is not sufficiently reliable.

Premise 2: If human reasoning capacity *in Type-1-dominant contexts* is not sufficiently reliable, then we should not trust the product of human reasoning capacity, including scientific findings and theories, and in turn the experimental psychology of reasoning.

Conclusion: Thus, the experimental psychology of reasoning is self-defeating.

But now we see what's wrong with this argument. In particular, Premise 2 is false because even if human reasoning capacity in Type-1-dominant contexts is not sufficiently reliable, human reasoning capacity in Type-2-dominant contexts might be sufficiently reliable, in which case we might trust the product of human reasoning capacity, including scientific findings and theories, in a Type-2-dominant context.

3.3   Processes and Interactions

Type-1 and Type-2 Processes

Let us now move on to consider the details of the dual-process theory. So far, we have not offered a detailed characterization of it; we have only said that reasoning performance is determined by the interaction between Type-1 and Type-2 processes. There are at least two crucial questions to be asked:

- *Process*: What are 'Type-1 processes' and 'Type-2 processes'?
- *Interaction*: How do Type-1 processes and Type-2 processes interact?

Let us begin with the process question. Type-1 processes and Type-2 processes are distinguished by their properties. It is assumed that there are two clusters of properties: the cluster of Type-1 properties and the cluster of Type-2 properties. Type-1 processes instantiate Type-1 properties and Type-2 processes instantiate Type-2 properties.

We should not expect that Type-1/Type-2 properties in Table 1 are always co-instantiated and that Type-1/Type-2 processes are the ones with all of the Type-1/Type-2 properties. In fact, dual-process theorists are not usually committed to such a strong claim: 'The main

Table 1. Type-1 and Type-2 properties (Evans 2008)

Type-1 cluster properties	Type-2 cluster properties
Unconscious or preconscious	Conscious
Implicit	Explicit
Low effort	High effort
Automatic	Controlled
Rapid	Slow
High capacity	Low capacity
Default process	Inhibitory
Holistic and perceptual	Analytic and reflective
Evolutionarily old	Evolutionarily recent
About evolutionary rationality	About individual rationality
Shared with animals	Uniquely human
Non-verbal	Verbal
About modular cognition	About fluid intelligence
Associative	Rule-based
Domain-specific	Domain-general
Contextualized	Abstract
Pragmatic	Logical
Parallel	Sequential
Stereotypical	Egalitarian
Universal	Heritable
Independent of general intelligence	Linked to general intelligence
Independent of working memory	Limited by working memory capacity

misuse of such tables is to treat them as strong statements about necessarily co-occurring features – in short to aid in the creation of a straw man' (Stanovich & Toplak 2012, 5).

Some propose to distinguish essential and accidental items in the list. *Essential* properties are what define Type-1/Type-2 processes and *accidental* properties are statistically but not necessarily correlated with essential properties. Evans and Stanovich argue that essential Type-1 properties are the property of not requiring working memory and the property of being autonomous; essential Type-2 properties are the property of requiring working memory and the property of involving 'cognitive decoupling', which is the 'ability to distinguish supposition from belief and to aid rational choices by running thought experiments' (Evans & Stanovich 2013a, 236).

Type-1 properties and Type-2 properties form statistically (but not necessarily) correlated property clusters: Type-1 clusters and Type-2 clusters. An intriguing suggestion by Richard Samuels (2009) is that Type-1/Type-2 clusters constitute natural kinds, or 'homeo-static property clusters' (Boyd 1991). In other words, Type-1/Type-2 properties are statistically (but not necessarily) co-instantiated, and this tendency to co-instantiate is not an accident; it is due to under-lying mechanisms.

Samuels proposes the following analogy. Influenza is associated with its characteristic symptoms, such as coughing and fever, that tend to be (but are not always) co-instantiated, and any co-instantiation can be explained by an underlying causal mechanism, namely the presence of the flu virus. Similarly, Type-1/Type-2 properties tend to be (but are not always) co-instantiated, and any co-instantiation can be explained by an underlying causal mechanism. The causal mechanism is 'System 1/System 2', which will be discussed in Section 3.4.

Interaction between Type-1 and Type-2 Processes

Let us move to the interaction between Type-1 and Type-2 processes. One might think that Type-1 and Type-2 processes operate in a parallel manner and that they compete with one another for the final output. In the Linda experiment, for example, Type-1 processes are operating and eventually generate the answer that the feminist bank teller hypothesis is more probable than the bank teller hypothesis. Type-2 processes are also operating and eventually generate the answer that the bank teller hypothesis is more probable than the feminist bank teller hypothesis. And the final output (the person's answer to the question) is determined as the result of the competition between these two kinds of processes. This model of interaction between Type-1 and Type-2 processes is known as 'the parallel-competitive model' (e.g., Sloman 1996). This model implies that the reasoning mistake in the Linda experiment is due to the 'weakness' of Type-2 processes; they were defeated in the competition by Type-1 processes.

The parallel-competitive model states that Type-1 and Type-2 processes operate in parallel. Alternatively, we might think that Type-1 and Type-2 processes operate in a sequential manner (i.e., Type-2 processes come after Type-1 processes). More precisely, we might think that Type-1 processes are the default processes and Type-2 processes intervene in Type-1 processes only when necessary. This model of interaction is known as 'the default-intervention model' (e.g., Evans & Stanovich 2013a). This model implies that participants' reasoning mistakes in the Linda experiment were due to the 'laziness' (Kahneman 2011, 32), rather than the 'weakness', of Type-2 processes; Type-2 processes simply fail to intervene in Type-1 processes.

The default-intervention model states that Type-2 processes are 'lazy'; Type-1 processes are the default position and Type-2 processes come into play only when necessary. That said, Type-2 processes at least have the capacity to intervene in Type-1 processes. But we can think of another model that denies that Type-2 processes have this capacity. Type-2 processes are not 'lazy', they are 'incompetent'. Type-2 processes are not able to intervene in Type-1 processes; at best they can rationalize the output from Type-1 processes in a *post hoc* manner. Type-2 processes are similar to lawyers rather than police officers. Unlike police officers, lawyers are not able to intervene in a defendant's behaviour. Their job is rather to rationalize and justify the defendant's behaviour in a *post hoc* manner. Let us call this 'the lawyer–client model' (Haidt 2001). This model implies that participants' reasoning mistakes in the Linda experiment are due to the 'incompetence', rather than the 'laziness' (in the case of the default-intervention model) or 'weakness' (in the case of the parallel-competitive model), of Type-2 processes; they are not able to intervene in Type-1 processes in the first place.

Despite sounding radical, the lawyer–client model is plausible to some extent. For example, it is consistent with the selection task experiment discussed in Chapters 1 and 3 (Wason & Evans 1974). Participants' performance is largely determined by unconscious Type-1 processes, which exhibit the primitive matching bias. In contrast, Type-2 processes are not vulnerable to such a bias, but they are not capable of intervening in Type-1 processes in the first place. Type-2 processes just rationalize the performance of Type-1 processes in a *post hoc* manner. A similar analysis is applicable to the stockings experiment discussed in Chapter 2 (Nisbett & Wilson 1977). In this experiment, choice is largely determined by unconscious Type-1 processes, which are strongly influenced by the position effect. In contrast, Type-2 processes are not vulnerable to such an effect, but they are not capable of intervening in Type-1 processes in the first place. Type-2 processes just rationalize the Type-1 choice in a *post hoc* manner.

Which model is correct? This is not an easy question to answer, but a conciliatory answer is available: each model captures some of the interactions between Type-1 and Type-2 processes. In fact, it is far from obvious that we need to choose only one model and reject the alternatives. The idea is that in many cases, Type-2 processes just 'wait and see' (which is consistent with the default-intervention model). Even when they are operating, their main job is to rationalize what Type-1 processes do (which is consistent with the lawyer–client model). But sometimes Type-2 processes do intervene, which creates a real competition between Type-1 and Type-2 processes (which is consistent with the parallel-competitive model).

We will come back to this issue in the discussion of moral judgment in Chapter 4.

3.4   The Dual-System Theory

Exactly Two Systems?

We now turn to more controversial ideas that are often associated with the dual-process theory (see Box 3A). The first idea, known as 'the dual-system theory', extends the dual-process theory 'by making specific proposals about the underlying cognitive mechanisms responsible for type-1 and 2 processing' (Evans 2012, 125). Type-1 and Type-2 processes are attributed to 'two distinct cognitive systems, with different structures, functions and evolutionary histories' and thus 'we have, in effect, two minds' (Frankish 2010, 919).

Gould talks about the internal disagreement within him, between a part of him, a 'little homunculus', who says that Linda 'can't just be a bank teller; read the description', and another part of him, 'I', who 'knows that [the feminist bank teller hypothesis] is least probable'. The dual-system theory takes this description rather seriously and interprets it as a disagreement between two distinct systems: System 1 and System 2.

Is the dual-*system* theory plausible? Should we really attribute Type-1 processes and Type-2 processes to two distinct systems? It depends on what we mean by 'systems'. Different authors use the term 'system' in different ways. In the early stage of the development of dual-process theory, authors did not draw a sharp theoretical distinction between the 'process' talk and the 'system' talk, often going back and forth between them relatively freely (e.g., Stanovich 1999). This suggests that, for these authors, the distinction between the 'process' talk and the 'system' talk is more or less a kind of terminological choice, or perhaps the two are different ways of expressing the same thing. The dual-system theory, in this deflationary terminology, is not very interesting; it simply collapses into the dual-process theory.

Recently, however, authors have tended to be more careful about the distinction between the 'process' talk and the 'system' talk, and are often in favour of the former. For example, Keith Stanovich and Maggie Toplak avoid the 'system' talk because it tends to be associated with some unwarranted assumptions: 'the two processes in dual-process theory map explicitly to two distinct brain systems' and 'what is being referred to [by the term "System 1" or "System 2"] is a singular system' (Stanovich & Toplak 2012, 4). For Stanovich and Toplak, if the dual-system theory comes with these assumptions, then it is not defensible. Evans joins Stanovich and Toplak and avoids the 'system' talk because '[a] cognitive or neural system, in a well-defined sense, should be described with some fairly specific assumptions about its inputs, outputs and functions', and '[i]t has been evident for some time that what people have been calling System 1 is in fact a multitude of automatic systems' (Evans 2011, 90).

These authors avoid the 'system' talk because it implies the implausible idea that there are exactly two cognitive systems in the human brain. This is what Samuels calls the 'token thesis' according to which 'each mind contains two particular cognitive mechanisms or systems [...] each human mind exhibits a fundamental, bipartite division into particular systems' (Samuels 2009, 133).

The token thesis is implausible and the dual-process/system theorists explicitly deny such an idea. For example, according to Stanovich (2004, 2011), what is called 'System 1' is a collection of autonomous systems or mechanisms ('the autonomous set of systems' or 'TASS'). Many of these systems are modular: that is, they are informationally encapsulated and are dedicated to specific tasks (see Box 3B).

Again, 'System 2' is divided into at least two parts: the algorithmic part and the reflective part. The distinction between the algorithmic part and the reflective part corresponds to the distinction between cognitive ability and thinking disposition. Cognitive abilities are the 'measures of the ability of the algorithmic mind to sustain decoupled representations (for purposes of inhibition or simulation)', while thinking dispositions are the 'measures of the higher-level regulatory states of the reflective mind' (Evans & Stanovich 2013a, 230).

BOX 3B: Modularity

Definition of modularity:
'[M]odular systems can be defined as systems made up of struc-
turally and/or functionally distinct parts. While non-modular
systems are internally homogeneous, modular systems are
segmented into modules, i.e., portions of a system having
a structure and/or function different from the structure or
function of other portions of the system.' (Calabretta & Parisi
2005, 309)

What is a mental module?
It is a system within the human mind that is responsible for
specific cognitive tasks. Some of the module's characteristics
include fast processing and informational encapsulation, which
means that the module is not affected by information from
other systems (Fodor 1983).

Massive modularity hypothesis:
'[It] maintains that our cognitive architecture – including the
part that subserves "central processing" – is largely or perhaps
even entirely composed of innate, domain-specific computational mechanisms or modules.' (Samuels 1998, 575)

The dual-system theory is not that plausible if it is understood as
the token thesis. Can there be another interpretation of it?

Samuels suggests another, more promising, interpretation of the
dual-system theory which he calls the 'type thesis'. The dual-system
theory is not about *the number of cognitive mechanisms* found in the
human mind but rather about *the number of kinds of mechanisms*
found in the human mind. That is, the claim is not that there are two
cognitive mechanisms; rather there are two kinds of mechanisms. In
Samuels' words: '[E]ach mind is comprised of two types or kinds of
cognitive system [...] each exhibits a fundamental, bipartite division
into kinds or types of cognitive system' (Samuels 2009, 133).

A similar proposal is to interpret the dual-system theory as what
Evans calls the 'two-minds hypothesis', according to which there
are two minds, both of which include multiple systems: 'there are
forms of cognition which are ancient and shared with other animals,

and those that are recently evolved and distinctively human' (Evans 2012, 125) and 'each mind can have access to multiple systems in a meaningful sense of that term' (Evans 2012, 125–126).

Two Agents?

In his book *Thinking, Fast and Slow*, Kahneman talks about the dual-system theory in the following way: 'systems' in the dual-system theory are 'agents within the mind, with their individual personalities, abilities, and limitations' (Kahneman 2011, 28). It turns out, however, that his descriptions are only useful metaphors. For him, 'System 2 calculates products' is shorthand for '[m]ental arithmetic is a voluntary activity that requires effort, should not be performed while making a left turn, and is associated with dilated pupils and accelerated heart rate' (Kahneman 2011, 29). This suggests that Kahneman's version of the dual-system theory collapses to the dual-process theory.

But why can't we take the agential talk literally rather than metaphorically? Kahneman argues that the literal interpretation 'is considered a sin in the professional circles in which I travel, because it seems to explain the thoughts and actions of a person by the thoughts and actions of little people inside the person's head' (Kahneman 2011, 28–29). Against Kahneman, however, one might argue that the dual-agent theory is helpful since, for example, it helps us to make sense of why two conflicting beliefs can coexist. In the Linda experiment, for example, Gould believes that '[the feminist bank teller hypothesis] is least probable' but, at the same time, he also believes that Linda 'can't just be a bank teller' (Gould 1991, 469). In other words, he has two conflicting beliefs: the belief that (1) the feminist bank teller hypothesis is less probable than the bank teller hypothesis; and the belief that (2) the former is more probable than the latter.

But this creates a puzzle. Can a person simultaneously adopt two beliefs that obviously conflict with one another? Alfred Mele describes the puzzle as follows: believing two contradictory beliefs simultaneously 'is not a possible state of mind: the very nature of beliefs precludes one's simultaneously believing that p is true and believing that p is false' (Mele 2001, 7). The idea of two sub-agents explains how conflicting beliefs can coexist. It is certainly puzzling that one agent believes two obviously conflicting beliefs simultaneously. But the puzzle is resolved if it turns out that each of the two beliefs is attributed to one of two sub-agents. Attributing belief 1 to sub-agent 1 and belief 2 to sub-agent 2 is no more puzzling than attributing two distinct beliefs to two distinct agents. Let us call this 'the conflicting belief argument' for the dual-agent theory. The conflicting belief argument, or something similar to it, has been expressed in psychology and philosophy. Here are two examples.

Sloman on Criterion S

Steven Sloman (1996) proposes something similar to the conflicting belief argument (although his commitment to the dual-agent theory is not very clear). Attributing two reasoning systems to a single human is warranted if what he calls 'Criterion S' is satisfied, and a reasoning task satisfies Criterion S 'if it causes people to simultaneously believe two contradictory responses' (Sloman 1996, 11). According to Sloman, Criterion S is satisfied in the Linda experiment. Gould believes that (1) the feminist bank teller hypothesis is less probable than the bank teller hypothesis, and that (2) the former is more probable than the latter.

Davidson on Mental Partitioning

In defending what he calls 'the partitioning of the mind', which is somewhat similar to the idea of a dual cognitive agent, Donald Davidson (2004) argues that two conflicting beliefs cannot be attributed to a single agent because doing so makes the mind of the agent unintelligible – it compromises the very practice of explaining and predicting the behaviour of the agent by attributing beliefs and desires to the agent. Thus, two conflicting beliefs need to be attributed to two independent parts of the agent: '[I]f parts of the mind are to some degree independent, we can understand how they are able to harbor inconsistencies'; '[T]he point of partitioning [in the mind] was to allow inconsistent or conflicting beliefs and desires and feelings to exist in the same mind, while the basic methodology of all interpretation tells us that inconsistency breeds unintelligibility' (Davidson 2004, 184).

However, the conflicting belief argument is not very compelling. The first problem is that it is not clear why two conflicting beliefs cannot be attributed to a single agent. An agent believing two conflicting beliefs simultaneously would make the agent irrational, but we have already seen several times in this book that humans can be irrational (to at least some extent in some cases). The attribution of two conflicting beliefs to the same agent is problematic only for someone who embraces a rather idealized conception of agents where agents need to be rational (in the sense of having mutually consistent beliefs).

The second problem of the conflicting belief argument concerns the crucial assumption in this argument, namely the assumption that there are two conflicting *beliefs*. Note that this assumption is crucial for the conflicting belief argument, which relies on one agent having two conflicting *beliefs* (e.g., Gould believing that the feminist bank teller hypothesis is less probable and that it is more probable than the bank teller hypothesis). There is no puzzle if the assumption is false (e.g., Gould *believes* that the feminist bank teller hypothesis is less probable than the bank teller hypothesis and *imagines* that the former is more probable than the latter).

Does Gould really simultaneously believe that the feminist bank teller hypothesis is less probable and that it is more probable than the bank teller hypothesis? Isn't it more plausible that, after learning the correct answer, Gould no longer believes that the feminist bank teller hypothesis is more probable? He *believes* that the feminist bank teller hypothesis is less probable than the bank teller hypothesis. In contrast, it is not clear that Gould also believes that the feminist bank teller hypothesis is more probable than the bank teller hypothesis. It is certainly true, from his description, that he cannot rid himself of the thought that the feminist bank teller hypothesis is very likely to be true. But this thought does not have to be understood as a belief. This possibility is discussed in the next section.

3.5   The Dual-State Theory

Two States

Another idea that tends to be associated with the dual-process theory is that Type-1 processes and Type-2 processes involve two kinds of mental states (or attitudes). Let us call this 'the dual-state theory'.

Psychologists working on people's attitudes have observed that attitudes are typically unstable and that they are likely to change when people are asked to reflect on the object of their evaluation, suggesting that people have some Type-1 attitudes that are largely unconscious and implicit and some Type-2 attitudes that emerge only after reflection is prompted and are conscious and explicit. What is particularly interesting is that the content of Type-1 attitudes about an object of evaluation contrasts with the content of Type-2 attitudes. For instance, experiments indicate that research participants are likely to shift their commitments when they are asked to give reasons for previously held attitudes (Hodges & Wilson 1993) and are more vulnerable to the effects of evidence manipulation when they are asked to give reasons for their attitudes (Wilson, Hodges, & LaFleur 1995).

Here is one example from the dual-attitude literature. Couples who have been dating for a few months are asked to provide reasons why they are attracted to their partner and are then asked to rate their commitment to the relationship and the likelihood that they will live together or get married in the future (Seligman, Fazio, & Zanna 1980). Participants' responses are elicited via questioning. Guided by the formulation of the questions, some couples are invited to offer intrinsic reasons for being together ('I date X because ...'), whereas others are invited to offer extrinsic and more instrumental reasons ('I date X in order to ...'). Research participants invited to give extrinsic reasons ended up rating their attitudes towards their partners more negatively and tended not to predict living together or getting married in the future. They did not seem to realize that their reports were biased by the way in which the questioning was conducted: the fact that they provided reasons for their attitudes does not guarantee that they reported an attitude that accurately represented how they felt and what they thought about the relationship.

Timothy Wilson and Dolores Kraft (1993) designed a similar study on attitudes towards one's partner (but without evidence manipulation). Participants were asked to report their attitude towards their relationship. They were then divided in two groups and were asked, first, to report their attitude towards their relationship again and, second, to predict the future of their relationship. In one group, they were also asked to list reasons for the success or failure of their relationship before making the prediction. Results show that participants who were asked for reasons for the state of their relationship experienced a shift between their initial attitude towards the relationship and their prediction.

Psychological models attempt to explain the instability of attitudes when people are asked to provide reasons for them. One model appeals to retrieval mechanisms and the idea that attitudes towards an object or person are constructed mainly on the basis of those aspects of the object or person to be evaluated that are easily accessible when the relevant information is retrieved (Wilson et al. 1984). By looking for reasons for a previously reported attitude, people justify their attitude based on the most accessible reasons for having that attitude. These reasons might be different from what caused the initial attitude and may give rise to a different attitude. Jaideep Sengupta and Gavan Fitzsimons give up the idea that people have persistent attitudes independent of context and say that 'attitudes are freshly computed based on available contextual cues' (Sengupta & Fitzsimons 2004, 711). That means that attitudes are fleeting, being formed from scratch every time they are elicited.

A new search for reasons may cause participants to form an entirely new attitude towards their relationship. Initially, participants may report an attitude that reflects how they feel about their relationship at that time (maybe an attitude formed via a Type-1 process). The attitude reported after a search for reasons may be affected by the weighing of benefits and costs (maybe an attitude formed via a Type-2 process). It is not surprising that different processes give rise to different attitudes. This explains the effects of evidence manipulation that participants experience in the dating couples study.

Non-Doxastic Dual-State Theory

It is tempting to think that the dual-process theory implies the dual-state theory. Type-1 processes and Type-2 processes give rise to two kinds of mental states. Uriah Kriegel nicely expresses this idea: '[w]herever there is a duality of processes, there is likely also a duality of products' and '[t]he associationist system likely produces one mental state, the rationalist system another' (Kriegel 2012, 474). Again, it is tempting to think that the dual-state theory is implied by the dual-system theory. Keith Frankish writes that '[d]ual-system theorists typically assume that the two reasoning systems have separate databases, and it is attractive to link the two types of belief we have distinguished with the two systems' (Frankish 2009, 274).

Let us consider this proposal in relation to Gould's response to the Linda experiment. Gould has a mental state, *M1*, about the feminist bank teller hypothesis being less probable than the bank teller hypothesis; he also has a mental state of a distinct kind, *M2*, about the feminist bank teller hypothesis being more probable than the bank teller hypothesis.

There are various versions of the dual-state theory, with different accounts of what *M1* and *M2* actually are. We can roughly distinguish doxastic dual-state theory from non-doxastic dual-state theory. According to the former, both *M1* and *M2* are broadly doxastic states ('doxastic' means 'related to beliefs') (e.g., *M1* and *M2* are different kinds of beliefs). According to the latter, at least one of them is not doxastic (e.g., *M1* is a belief and *M2* is a non-doxastic state).

Gendler on Aliefs and Beliefs

Let us start with Tamar Gendler's non-doxastic dual-state proposal. Gendler (2008a) explicitly justifies her proposal, the alief/belief distinction, based on the heuristics and biases programme and the dual-process theory. On her view, *M1* is belief and *M2* is what she calls an 'alief'. Gould *believes* that the feminist bank teller hypothesis is less probable than the bank teller hypothesis, while he *alieves* that the feminist bank teller hypothesis is more probable than the bank teller hypothesis.

Gendler introduces the concept of aliefs with some examples. One example involves an experience of the Grand Canyon Skywalk. A man, let us call him Wilhelm, is convinced that the solid clear glass floor of the Grand Canyon Skywalk is safe, but when he is actually on it he suddenly feels extreme fear and becomes unable to move. In this case, Wilhelm believes that the Skywalk is perfectly safe (otherwise he would not have stepped on it in the first place). Nonetheless, according to Gendler, Wilhelm alieves that the Skywalk is dangerous, which explains his affective and behavioural responses.

Gendler's general characterization of an alief is as follows:

> A paradigmatic alief is a mental state with associatively linked content that is representational, affective and behavioral, and that is activated – consciously or nonconsciously – by features of the subject's internal or ambient environment. Aliefs may be either occurrent or dispositional. (Gendler 2008a, 642)

This characterization suggests that an alief is a composite mental state that is constituted by the following components:

1. a representational component (e.g., 'Really high up and a long way down.');
2. an affective component (e.g., 'Not a safe place to be!'); and
3. a behavioural component (e.g., 'Get off!').

However, understanding aliefs in this way makes Gendler's proposal problematic (e.g., Currie & Ichino 2012; Dogett 2012). Aliefs are presented as composite entities that are constituted by representational, affective, and behavioural components. But why is it that the representational, affective, and behavioural components constitute a composite state? Why can't we simply explain cases like the Skywalk case in terms of representational, affective, and behavioural processes without positing a composite state that is constituted by them? Introducing a composite state seems to be explanatorily redundant.

In some places, Gendler hints at a different, less problematic characterization of aliefs: '[T]o have an alief is to have an innate or habitual propensity to respond to an apparent stimulus in a particular way' (Gendler 2011, 41). These remarks suggest another understanding of aliefs: an alief is understood not as a composite mental state that is constituted by representational, affective, and behavioural components, but rather as a propensity or disposition to go through a series of cognitive, affective, and behavioural processes that are statistically (but not always) correlated. To say that Wilhelm in the Skywalk case alieves that the Skywalk is dangerous is to say that he is disposed to go through some particular cognitive (e.g., thinking about the idea of falling down), affective (e.g., fear), and behavioural (e.g., unable to move) processes (see Schwitzgebel 2013 for a dispositional account of beliefs).

Doxastic Dual-State Theory

Frankish on Type-1 and Type-2 Beliefs
Keith Frankish (2009) proposes a doxastic dual-state theory according to which what we commonly call 'belief' may actually be two or more different types of mental states with distinct features: Type-1 beliefs and Type-2 beliefs. On his view, *M1* is a Type-2 belief and *M2* is a Type-1 belief. Gould Type-2 believes that the feminist bank teller hypothesis is less probable than the bank teller hypothesis, while he Type-1 believes that the feminist bank teller hypothesis is more probable than the bank teller hypothesis.

A key feature of beliefs is consciousness: we might think of beliefs as conscious states, but some beliefs are actually never actively thought about and they remain in the background. Frankish's example is that we have many beliefs about how a tap works, but we rarely think about these beliefs or express them out loud.

Another key feature is control: we tend to think of beliefs as mental states that we decide to adopt, but many beliefs are formed automatically as a result of sub-personal mechanisms. Consider the following example: people may glance out of the window and pick up an umbrella on their way out of the house; the best explanation for their action is that they believe that it is raining or that it will be raining soon. However, they have never decided to believe that it is raining or that it will be raining soon; they have not weighed up the reasons for and against the claim that it is raining.

There are some other relevant features of belief that Frankish considers, but simply by reflecting on consciousness and control it is easy to see that beliefs come in two types: those that are conscious and are typically the outcome of deliberation, and those that are unconscious and automatic. Frankish calls the former Type-1 beliefs and the latter Type-2 beliefs, aligning them with the dual-system theory, where Type-1 beliefs are understood as outputs of System 1 and Type-2 beliefs as the outputs of System 2. Type-1 beliefs work like behavioural dispositions, which are reflected in non-verbal behaviour but are not explicitly stated or challenged. Type-2 beliefs work like opinions, which are reflected in verbal behaviour but do not necessarily impact on people's actions – when they do, it happens via the causal relationship between Type-1 and Type-2 beliefs. Frankish argues that the notion of Type-2 belief captures what in the philosophical literature has been known as an 'acceptance', almost like a policy to which agents explicitly commit. A useful example here is that of implicit racial bias. Many people have a Type-2-belief that all humans are equal, independent of their skin colour (their explicit policy). However, those people might also behave in ways that suggest that they have racist Type-1-beliefs (e.g., non-conscious and non-controlled associations between black people and violence).

Schwitzgebel on In-Between Beliefs

We would also like to mention Eric Schwitzgebel's proposal. Although it is not strictly speaking a dual-state theory, it is relevant to our discussion – it could be described as a multiple-state theory since it recognizes beliefs, non-beliefs, and attitudes in-between belief and non-belief. Schwitzgebel suggests that it would be helpful to consider some mental states as neither beliefs nor non-beliefs: he calls them *in-between cases* (Schwitzgebel 2001).

Schwitzgebel discusses the example of Antonio, who is sometimes disposed to believe that there is a benevolent deity and is sometimes disposed to believe that God is just a beautiful metaphor. How Antonio feels about God and what he thinks about God changes depending on the context: on a beautiful spring day Antonio may be disposed to believe in God but at a dull church social event he may not. According to Schwitzgebel, there are numerous cases of in-between believing and a dispositional account of belief can handle those cases.

In-between cases of believing are cases where a mental state has some, but not all, of the dispositional properties of a belief. One dispositional property of a belief is that if you have a belief, then you are disposed to behave in a way that manifests your commitment to the truth of the content of your belief. Here is an example from Schwitzgebel where a person asserts something that sounds like a belief but does not have the right dispositional properties:

> Daiyu's belief that most pearls are white has entirely atypical effects. It does not cause her to say anything like 'most pearls are white' (which she would deny; she'd say instead that most pearls are black) or to think to herself in inner speech that most pearls are white. She would not feel surprise were she to see a translucent purple pearl. If a friend were to say to Daiyu that she was looking for white jewelry to accompany a dress, Daiyu would not at all be inclined to recommend a pearl necklace. Nor is she disposed to infer from her belief that most pearls are white that there is a type of precious object used in jewelry that is white. (Schwitzgebel 2012, 14)

For Daiyu's mental state to be a belief it needs to have the dispositional properties of a belief. When a mental state fails to have the dispositional properties of a belief, such as when Daiyu does not infer from her mental state with the content 'Most pearls are white' that a precious object used in jewellery is white, then we cannot call that mental state a belief. Depending on how many of the dispositional properties of a belief Daiyu's mental state has, it could be an in-between case or something else altogether. It is therefore conceivable that mental states resulting from System 1 fail to have the dispositional profile of well-behaved beliefs because they are not used in inference or are not explicitly endorsed. It is also conceivable that mental states resulting from System 2 fail to have the dispositional profile of well-behaved beliefs because they do not drive behaviour.

The three proposals above (Gendler's belief/alief distinction, Frankish's Type-1/Type-2 distinction, and Schwitzgebel's in-between cases of believing) contribute to a better understanding of the complexity of human mental lives and help us acknowledge how heterogeneous human mental states can be. It is worth noticing, though, that each of these views seems to rely quite heavily on the over-idealized concept of agency that we challenged earlier.

Gendler's proposal is supposed to answer puzzle cases such as the Skywalk case. 'Why is it that Wilhelm in the Skywalk case feels extreme fear and becomes unable to move despite his belief that the Skywalk is perfectly safe?' This is puzzling given the assumption that Wilhelm's feelings and behaviour are always coherent with what he believes. But why should we accept this assumption? Isn't this an over-idealized assumption about human agency?

Again, the idea that Antonio cannot really believe that God exists given his often-conflicting thoughts and emotions concerning God is grounded in the idea that, for Antonio to have that belief, his behaviour would have to be more coherent. Similarly, consider Sylvia, who systematically prefers to sit next to a white person rather than a black person on the bus (see Chapter 6 for a more thorough discussion of such cases). The idea that she cannot Type-1 believe that black people are equal to white people, but maybe only Type-2 believe it, is grounded in the idea that for Sylvia to Type-1 believe that black people are equal to white people her behaviour would always have to match her Type-1 belief. Antonio and Sylvia are unlikely to be as consistent in their thoughts and actions as we would like them to be – which does not necessarily tell us anything deep about the metaphysics of belief, but may simply be a by-product of their (and our) inescapable irrationality.

3.6   Summary

- The basic idea of the dual-process theory of reasoning is plausible. The theory's empirical plausibility comes from its consistency with a variety of empirical studies, including the study of reasoning biases. The theory's theoretical plausibility relies on the fact that it enables us to solve the rationality paradox as well as the self-defeating rationality paradox.
- However, there are a number of issues with the theory. In particular, there is no agreement on how Type-1 processes and

Type-2 processes should be characterized, nor is there agreement on how Type-1 processes and Type-2 processes interact.

- The dual-process theory is often associated with the dual-system theory. But it is not a trivial task to find the interpretation of 'system' according to which the dual-system theory is plausible. It should not be interpreted as the token thesis (the idea that there are exactly two systems in the brain). Perhaps it should rather be interpreted as the type thesis (the idea that there are two kinds of systems in the brain).

- The dual-process theory is also associated with the dual-state theory. Frankish proposes a doxastic dual-state theory that distinguishes Type-1 beliefs from Type-2 beliefs. Gendler, in contrast, proposes a non-doxastic dual-state theory that distinguishes aliefs from beliefs. These attempts to distinguish between different types of states are promising and insightful but tend to assume that agents' behaviour is rational.

Further Resources

Articles and Books

We highly recommend Jonathan Evans' article (2003) in *Trends in Cognitive Science* and his review article (2008) in *Annual Review of Psychology*. Keith Frankish's review article (2010) in *Philosophy Compass* and Frankish and Evans' historical overview of the dual-process theory (2009) are accessible and informative.

Daniel Kahneman's best-selling book *Thinking, Fast and Slow* (2011) integrates the heuristics and biases programme into the dual-process (or the dual-system) framework. Keith Stanovich's *Who is Rational?: Studies of Individual Differences in Reasoning* (1999) provides an interesting take on the strengths and limitations of the dual-system theory and poses a question concerning how to think about individual differences in reasoning performance. *Rationality and Reasoning* (1996) by Jonathan Evans and David Over offers a dual-process account of deductive reasoning and its biases.

The dual-process theory and the dual-system theory have also been the target of challenges and have generated controversy. For an overview of the debate, see the journal *Perspectives on Psychological Science*, Volume 8, Issue 3 (2013), which includes a target article by

Evans and Stanovich, followed by critical discussions. For psychological and philosophical discussions on the dual-process theory and
the dual-system theory, we recommend the collection *In Two Minds:
Dual Processes and Beyond* (2009), edited by Evans and Frankish.

Online Resources

For an accessible introduction to some of the themes discussed in this
chapter, see Eric Mandelbaum's *Stanford Encyclopedia of Philosophy*
entry on associationist theories of thought (2017). On YouTube you
will find Keith Frankish's talk on the dual-system distinction (2013).
There is an interesting post on dual-system theory and the relative
benefits of the two systems in *Scientific American*, authored by Scott
Barry Kaufman and Jerome L. Singer in 2012.

Questions

1. Which cognitive tasks in your everyday life are most likely to be
   due to Type-1 processing? Which are most likely to be handled by
   Type-2 processing?
2. What are the implications of the fragmentation of the mind,
   and in particular of the distinction between Type-1 and Type-2
   processes or systems, for the prospects of improving the quality
   of human reasoning via education and training?
3. If you have a Type-1 attitude and a Type-2 attitude (this can be
   about racial differences, religious affiliation, or your romantic
   partner), which one is your *real* attitude?

4

Moral Judgment

4.1 Introduction

This chapter continues the discussion of the fragmentation of the mind but with a change of focus. In the previous chapter we discussed a fragmentation that concerns reasoning, in particular the fragmentation between Type-1 reasoning processes that are (typically) unconscious, automatic, low effort, associative, and so on, and Type-2 reasoning processes that are (typically) conscious, controlled, high effort, rule-based, and so on. In this chapter we discuss a different but related form of fragmentation, namely the fragmentation of the processes by which we arrive at moral judgments.

As we saw in the previous chapter, the dual-process theory is a useful theoretical framework for making sense of reasoning processes. The dual-process framework has also been applied in other fields of psychological study, such as research on learning and on social cognition (see Evans 2008 for an overview). We will argue in this chapter that the dual-process framework is also useful for making sense of the processes by which people make moral judgments, such as the judgment that it is wrong to harm an innocent child or that it is right to help an elderly stranger who is suffering.

Emerging views in the psychological and neuroscientific studies of moral judgments suggest a dual-process structure according to which moral judgments are determined by the interaction between two kinds of processes: *emotion-based* processes and *reasoning-based* processes. This chapter will investigate details of the dual-process structure of moral judgments. Of particular importance are the empirical studies of moral judgments by Jonathan Haidt and Joshua Greene. Both Haidt and Greene propose influential dual-process-theoretical accounts of moral judgments, but their accounts are importantly different in a number of ways. One of the objectives of this chapter is to clarify and discuss the difference between their two accounts.

We will begin by discussing a series of influential studies of moral judgments by Eliot Turiel and his colleagues and critiques of these studies by Richard Shweder and Jonathan Haidt (Section 4.2). This debate will lead us to discuss the dual-process theory of moral judgment according to which moral judgments are the product of the interaction between emotion-based processes and reasoning-based processes. There are, however, several important details that need to be specified. One issue is what we call 'the interaction question' (discussed in Section 4.3), which asks: 'How do emotion-based processes and reasoning-based processes interact?' In Haidt's model, reasoning processes have a relatively weak role (of rationalizing affective judgments in a *post hoc* manner), but they have a stronger role (of competing with affective processes or intervening in them) in Greene's model. Another issue is what we call 'the process question' (discussed in Section 4.4), which asks: 'What are emotion-based processes and reasoning-based processes?' Greene suggests the intriguing idea that the distinction between emotion-based processes and reasoning-based processes corresponds to the philosophical distinction between utilitarianism and deontology. This chapter will examine whether this view is defensible.

4.2 Harm and Emotion

Moral and Conventional

Let us start with the influential developmental psychological studies of moral judgments by Turiel and followers.

Moral–Conventional Tasks

One of Turiel's main hypotheses is that the distinction between moral rules and conventional rules is psychologically real, and this distinction is made by both adults and children (even at an early stage of cognitive development). See, for example, the two stories below. Children are aware of the difference between a violation of a moral rule ('a moral violation') and a violation of a conventional rule ('a conventional violation'). Below is an example of each:

> A number of nursery school children are playing outdoors. There are some swings in the yard, all of which are being used. One of the children decides that he now wants to use a swing. Seeing that they are all occupied, he goes to one of the swings, where he pushes the other child off, at the same time hitting him. The child who has been pushed is hurt and begins to cry. (Turiel 1983, 41)

> Children are greeting a teacher who has just come into the nursery school. A number of children go up to her and say 'Good Morning, Mrs. Jones.' One of the children says 'Good Morning, Mary.' (Turiel 1983, 41)

Turiel's hypothesis is consistent with the empirical findings, in particular those involving what are known as 'moral–conventional tasks' in which adults and children reliably distinguish moral violations from conventional violations in multiple ways (Nucci 2001; Nucci & Turiel 1978; Smetana 1981; Turiel, Killen, & Helwig 1987). First, moral violations are typically regarded as more serious than conventional transgressions: for example, pushing the other child off the swing is worse than calling the teacher by her first name. Second, the wrongness of moral violations is more authority-independent than the wrongness of conventional violations: for example, pushing the other child off the swing is still wrong even if an authority figure (say, a teacher) says that it is OK, while calling the teacher by her first name is OK if an authority figure (say, the teacher herself) says that it is OK. Third, the wrongness of moral violations is more universal than the wrongness of conventional violations: for example, pushing the other child off the swing is wrong even in a country with a very different culture and values, while calling the teacher by her first name might be OK in a country with a very different culture and values.

Another important finding is that moral judgments and conventional judgments are justified differently. The wrongness of moral violations, but not the wrongness of conventional violations, tends to be explained or justified in terms of 'harm' in a broad sense (i.e., negative impacts on welfare, justice, or the rights of individuals involved). For example, the wrongness of pushing the other child off the swing tends to be explained or justified in terms of the harm that the act causes to the child, while the wrongness of calling the teacher by her first name is not usually justified by reference to the harm to the teacher.

These findings suggest that moral judgments are clearly distinguished from conventional judgments. Moral judgments, unlike conventional judgments, are the responses to perceived harms, and moral violations are judged to be seriously wrong, authority-independently wrong, universally wrong, and so on. Let us call this view 'the harm account' of moral judgments.

The studies by Turiel and colleagues are remarkable and they strongly support the harm account. However, several researchers, most notably Richard Shweder and Jonathan Haidt, are sceptical. Their main worry is that the findings by Turiel and colleagues might only be true about some particular group of people; they might not be generally applicable to other cultural or socio-economic groups. For example, an interview study (Shweder, Mahapatra, & Miller 1987) found that people in Bhubaneswar, India, tended to moralize harmless violations. For instance, people in Bhubaneswar treated a wide range of harmless violations related to food, clothing, sex roles, and other practices as moral violations, exhibiting the moral-type response to them (i.e., regarding the relevant violation as seriously wrong, authority-independently wrong, universally wrong, etc.). For example, 'A widow in your community eats fish two or three times a day', which does not seem to harm anyone, was treated as a moral violation rather than a conventional one.

However, this is not a conclusive objection to the harm account. As Turiel, Killen, and Helwig (1987) point out, on closer scrutiny the scenarios in the study by Shweder, Mahpatra, and Miller (1987) might involve some kind of harm *given Indian people's background assumptions about how the world works*. For example, 'A widow in your community eats fish two or three times a day' is harmful according to an Indian worldview because the act will offend their deceased husband's spirit and will cause the widow to suffer greatly. Again, 'The day after his father's death, the eldest son had a haircut and ate chicken' (another item in the study by Shweder and colleagues) is harmful because the deceased father's soul will not receive salvation if the proscription of eating chicken is violated.

Thus, despite the challenge by Shweder and colleagues, one can still maintain that the harm account is universally true: moral judgment is a response to perceived harm both in the United States and in India. The difference between Indian people and American people lies in the fact that people in the two cultures have different worldviews; this has wide-ranging implications for what does and does not constitute a harmful action in each culture or worldview (e.g., a widow's eating fish is harmful for Indian people, but it is not harmful for American people).

Morality and Harm

Jonathan Haidt sets out to resolve the dispute between Shweder and Turiel. Haidt's aim is to overcome the limitation of the study by Shweder and colleagues, and find more convincing evidence against the harm account.

The Dog Eating Study
This study (Haidt, Koller, & Dias 1993) examines how participants from the United States and Brazil respond to harmful and harmless stories.

> *Dog*: A family's dog was killed by a car in front of their house. They had heard that dog meat was delicious, so they cut up the dog's body, cooked it, and ate it for dinner.

> *Chicken*: A man goes to the supermarket once a week and buys a dead chicken. Before cooking the chicken, he has sexual intercourse with it. He then cooks the chicken and eats it.

> *Flag*: A woman is cleaning out her closet and finds her old national flag. She doesn't want the flag anymore, so she cuts it up into pieces and uses the rags to clean her bathroom.

> *Promise*: A woman was dying and on her deathbed she asked her son to promise that he would visit her grave every week. The son loved his mother very much, so he promised to visit her grave every week. However, after his mother died, the son was too busy to keep his promise.

These stories are prepared to be affect-laden. Some of the stories involve disrespect or disobedience (e.g., *Flag* and *Promise*), while others involve the emotion of disgust (e.g., *Dog* and *Chicken*). At the same time, these stories are prepared to be harmless. *Dog*, for example, involves a dead dog, which cannot be harmed. The dog eating is a private and secret act and, thus, nobody will be psychologically disturbed by watching the act or knowing about it.

Just like in the studies by Turiel and colleagues, participants were asked to answer some questions about each story, such as:

> *Interference*: 'Should [the actor] be stopped or punished in any way?'
> *Universality*: 'Suppose you learn about two different foreign countries. In country A, people [do that act] very often, and in country B, they never [do that act]. Are both of these customs OK, or is one of them bad or wrong?' (Haidt, Koller, & Dias 1993, 617)

Participants in this study were from three cities in two countries: Philadelphia (United States), Porto Alegre (which is a relatively Westernized city in Brazil), and Recife (a less Westernized city in Brazil). They were also assigned to either a high socio-economic status (SES) group or a low SES group in the city they were in.

The study found that both the city and the SES group influenced the moralizing tendency of the participants (where moralizing tendency is the tendency to treat a violation as a moral violation, measured by their response to the Interference question and the Universality question). The more Westernized participants were, the less moralizing they were. The higher SES group was less moralizing than the lower SES group. The majority of high SES people in Philadelphia did not moralize offensive harmless acts, while the majority of low SES people in Recife did moralize them. For example, most of the high SES people in Philadelphia said that the act in *Chicken* should not be stopped or punished, and that the custom concerning the act in *Chicken* is not universal. In contrast, most of the low SES people in Recife said that the act in *Chicken* should be stopped or punished, and that the custom concerning the act in *Chicken* is universal.

In addition to the questions about Interference and Universality, participants answered a question about the harm involved in the story (e.g., 'Do you think anyone was harmed by what the man did to the dead dog?'). It turned out that, against the harm account, an answer of 'Yes' to this question about harm was not a very good predictor of participants' moralizing tendency: many participants moralized *Dog* and other stories even though participants regarded them as harmless. Thus, stories like *Dog* are harmless for those participants *whatever background assumptions they might have about how the world operates*. This means that the study by Haidt and colleagues poses a more serious problem for the harm account than the study by Shweder and colleagues.

During their interview, some participants actually tried to come up with potential harmful aspects of the act in question (e.g., eating dog meat is harmful because it would make a person sick). But it is likely that this type of reaction is a *post hoc* rationalization of their intuitive response. Indeed, participants did not revise their judgment when the interviewer explicitly denied any alleged harm in the act (e.g., the dog meat was thoroughly cooked and was thus perfectly safe to consume). In light of this, participants tried to find some other harmful aspect of the act. This suggests that it is not the case that participants first recognize a harmful aspect of dog eating and then make a moral judgment about it. Rather they first intuitively make a moral judgment that dog eating is wrong and then give a *post hoc* reason for that judgment by appealing to whatever harmful consequence they can think of. Their reaction is thus analogous to the participants of the stockings experiment by Nisbett and Wilson (1977) who first chose a pair of stockings unconsciously influenced by its location and then gave a *post hoc* justification for their decision by appealing to some superior quality of that particular pair of stockings.

The upshot of this is that the harm account is no longer true outside some limited cultural or socio-economic groups. Shweder's and Haidt's criticism of the harm account is intimately related to the criticism of the psychological studies that heavily rely on WEIRD participants (Henrich, Heine, & Norenzayan 2010a, 2010b), which we mentioned in the Introduction.

Shweder distinguishes the culture in which the ethics of autonomy (in which a moral agent is regarded as an autonomous and individual being) is dominant, the culture in which the ethics of community (in which a moral agent is essentially tied to the community to which they belong) is dominant, and the culture in which the ethics of divinity (in which morality is essentially tied to spirituality and the essence of moralizing for attaining spiritual purity and sanctity) is dominant. The harm account is closely related to the first kind of culture where the ethics of autonomy is dominant; it is not applicable to other cultures.

Haidt stresses the importance of what he calls 'moral founda-tions' (Graham, Haidt, & Nosek 2009; Graham et al. 2013; Haidt

& Joseph 2004). Moral foundations are 'cognitive modules upon which cultures construct moral matrices' (Haidt 2012, 124). The five moral foundations are: the care/harm foundation, the fairness/cheating foundation, the loyalty/betrayal foundation, the authority/subversion foundation, and the sanctity/degradation foundation. Different foundations are dominant in different groups. The harm account is closely related to the care/harm foundation; it is not applicable to the cultural socio-economic groups in which the care/harm foundation is not dominant.

Morality and Affect

We have seen that the studies by Shweder and Haidt cast doubt on the harm account of moral judgment. They suggest that moral judgments are not necessarily a response to perceived harm. These studies, in particular Haidt's study, suggest an alternative view that moral judgments are a response to affectively charged transgressions rather than to harmful transgressions. In fact, the main strategy in the dog eating study was to elicit moral judgments by presenting the 'stories that are affectively loaded – disrespectful or disgusting actions that "feel" wrong – yet that are harmless' (Haidt, Koller, & Dias 1993, 615).

A classic question about moral judgment is: 'Are moral judgments based on reasoning or on emotion?' A view would be that, when I judge, for example, that killing an innocent person is wrong, I am making the judgment on the basis of my reasoning about the consequences of killing or about relevant rules and duties. Another view would be that, when making a moral judgment about killing, I am making a judgment on the basis of my *affective* disapproval of the killing.

The dog eating study seems to support the latter view. It turns out, however, that the latter view is ambiguous. For example, the phrase 'I am making this judgment on the basis of my affective disapproval of killing' is open to at least two interpretations. It can mean that my judgment is *causally influenced by* affective disapproval. It can also mean that my judgment is (partly) *constituted by* affective disapproval. The former view takes affective inputs to be a cause of moral judgments (in which case affective inputs and moral judgments are separate or distinct events). For example, my judgment about killing an innocent person is caused by my affective disapproval of killing an innocent person. The latter view, in contrast, takes affective inputs to be a part of moral judgments (in which case affective inputs and moral judgments are not separate). For example, my judgment about killing an innocent person is (partly) constituted by my affective disapproval of killing an innocent person. Or, simply put, the judgment *just is* affective disapproval.

We therefore have two slightly but importantly different views about moral judgments and emotions: the view that moral judgments are causally influenced by affective inputs (we call this 'causal moral sentimentalism') and the view that moral judgments are partly constituted by affective inputs (we call this 'constitutive moral sentimentalism').

Causal moral sentimentalism and constitutive moral sentimentalism are distinct claims, but they are not completely independent. Suppose that it turns out that changes in affective inputs co-vary with changes in moral judgments. For example, one makes different moral judgments depending on whether or not one feels affective disapproval of an act. This is typically taken to be evidence for causal moral sentimentalism. But it could be taken to be evidence for constitutive moral sentimentalism as well: the best explanation of the co-variation would be that moral judgments are (partly) constituted by affective inputs. Thus, causal moral sentimentalism and constitutive moral sentimentalism can be supported by the same (or at least a similar) body of empirical evidence.

The studies by Haidt and colleagues mentioned above are coherent with causal/constitutive moral sentimentalism. Moral judgment (or the moral-type response) can be activated by offensive stories that do not involve harm, such as *Flag* or *Chicken*, which can be explained by the fact that: (1) even without the presence of harm, those stories evoke affective reactions of the relevant kind; and (2) moral judgment is caused/constituted by the affective reactions.

Causal/constitutive moral sentimentalism has been supported by other empirical studies too (Greene & Haidt 2002; Haidt 2007). In one remarkable study (Wheatley & Haidt 2005), for example, highly hypnotizable participants participated in group hypnosis sessions in which they were given the post-hypnotic suggestion to feel a flash of disgust either when they read the word 'often' or when they read the word 'take'. Participants were then brought out of their hypnotic state and were asked to evaluate some moral transgressions presented as vignettes, such as the one below. There were two versions of each vignette, one with the word 'often' and one with the word 'take':

Congressman Arnold Paxton frequently gives speeches condemning corruption and arguing for campaign finance reform. But he is just trying to cover up the fact that he himself [will take bribes from/ is often bribed by] the tobacco lobby, and other special interests, to promote their legislation. (Wheatley & Haidt 2005, 781)

The result was that participants rated the transgression in the vignette as being morally worse when a hypnotic trigger word was present in the vignette than when the word was absent. For example, in response to the 'take' version of the Paxton vignette, participants who received the post-hypnotic suggestion that they should be disgusted with the word 'take' rated Congressman Paxton's act as morally worse than the 'often' version of it. This result can be nicely explained by the causal/constitutive moral sentimentalist idea that disgust with a word causes/constitutes their harsh moral judgment of a vignette containing the word.

These results strongly support the idea that affective inputs causally/constitutively influence moral judgments. However, it is important to note that these results do not necessarily show that affective processes dominate moral judgment, nor do they imply that reasoning processes do not play any role in moral judgment. Think back to the discussions of reasoning in earlier chapters. In Chapter 1 we saw that our reasoning is often based on heuristic processes, but in Chapter 3 we also argued that heuristic Type-1 processes interact with Type-2 processes. A similar thing can be said about emotion and reasoning in moral judgment: moral judgment is often affective, but affective processes might interact with reasoning processes. In other words, there can be an analogy between the dual structure concerning reasoning where Type-1 processes and Type-2 processes interact with each other and the dual structure concerning moral judgment where affective processes and reasoning processes interact with each other.

Indeed, the analogy between heuristic Type-1 processes in reasoning and affective processes in moral judgment seems apt (e.g., Sunstein 2005). An affective moral judgment can be understood as a form of heuristic Type-1 judgment. As Kahneman noted, a heuristic judgment replaces a difficult question with an easy one, for example replacing a difficult probabilistic judgment (e.g., 'What is the probability of Linda being a bank teller?') with an easy stereotypical judgment ('Is Linda like a stereotypical bank teller?'). We can make sense of affective influence on moral judgment in the same way. Perhaps what we do is replace a difficult question of morality ('Is this the right thing to do?') with an easy question of emotion ('How do you feel about this action?').

We will examine the dual-process theory of moral judgment in the next section.

4.3   Interaction between Affective Processes and Reasoning Processes

Models of Interaction

We have discussed some basic ideas of the dual-process theory of moral judgment according to which affective processes and reasoning processes interact with each other. We will now clarify this theory by investigating two crucial questions (which correspond to the process question and the interaction question discussed *in Chapter 3*):

- *Process*: What are 'affective processes' and 'reasoning processes'?
- *Interaction*: How do affective processes and reasoning processes 'interact'?

Let us start with the interaction question. In *Chapter 3* we discussed three models of interaction or relation between Type-1 and Type-2 processes of reasoning: the parallel-competitive model, the default-intervention model, and the lawyer–client mode. Analogously, we can think of three models of interaction between affective processes and reasoning processes (see Box 4A).

Haidt (2001) proposes the social intuitionist model of moral judgment, which is a good example of the lawyer–client model. (Or, more precisely, the lawyer–client analogy is something we borrow from Haidt himself.) Reasoning processes are more like 'a lawyer trying to build a case than a judge searching for truth' (Haidt 2001, 814). Haidt also proposes the analogy of the press secretary for a secret administration: 'Moral reasoning is often like the press secretary for a secretive administration – constantly generating the most persuasive arguments it can muster for policies whose true origins and goals are unknown' (Haidt 2007, 1000).

BOX 4A: Models of Interaction between Type-1 and Type-2 Processes

The parallel-competitive model of moral judgments
Affective processes and reasoning processes compete with each other as equally strong competitors. Affective processes are dominant in some cases, and reasoning processes are dominant in others.

The default-intervention model of moral judgments
Affective processes are the default processes and reasoning processes play a relatively weaker role. Affective processes are active by default, but in some cases reasoning processes can intervene and dominate.

The lawyer–client model of moral judgments
Affective processes are dominant (almost) all of the time and the role of reasoning processes is even weaker. The primary role of reasoning processes is not to intervene but rather to rationalize the output of emotion-driven moral judgments in a *post hoc* manner, just like a lawyer rationalizes the claims of her client in a *post hoc* manner.

The social intuitionist model has two major claims: first, that 'moral intuitions (including moral emotions) come first and directly cause moral judgments'; and, second, that '[m]oral reasoning is usually an *ex post facto* process used to influence the intuitions (and hence judgments) of other people' (Haidt 2001, 814). The social intuitionist model is nicely illustrated by what Haidt calls 'moral dumbfounding' (Haidt, Bjorklund, & Murphy 2000).

Julie and Mark are brother and sister. They are traveling together in France on summer vacation from college. One night they are staying alone in a cabin near the beach. They decide that it would be interesting and fun if they tried making love. At the very least it would be a new experience for each of them. Julie was already taking birth control pills, but Mark uses a condom too, just to be safe. They both enjoy making love, but they decide not to do it again. They keep that night as a special secret between them, which makes them feel even closer to each other. What do you think about that? Was it wrong for them to make love? (Haidt 2001, 814)

In response to this story, people first intuitively think that it is wrong for Julie and Mark to have sexual intercourse. When asked 'Why is it wrong?', they search for a *post hoc* justification of the intuitive answer. It turns out that the Julie and Mark story is cleverly constructed in such a way that it is very difficult to come up with a truly satisfactory justification of the intuitive answer. Some might appeal to the dangers of inbreeding, which is not a good justification: it is said that Julie and Mark carefully use two forms of birth control. Others might appeal to the bad effect on the relationship between Julie and Mark, which, again, is not a good justification: it is said that Julie and Mark feel even closer to each other. Eventually, many people end up saying something like 'I know it's wrong, but I just can't come up with a reason why.'

Note that the social intuitionist model is not committed to the radical claim that reasoning processes only provide *post hoc* rationalizations of intuitive responses. Haidt carefully distances himself from Hume's radical claim that 'reason is, and ought only to be the slave of the passions, and can never pretend to any other office than to serve and obey them' (Hume 1739/2007, 266). Hume's model seems to be that the relationship between affective processes and reasoning processes is just like the one between slaves and their master, where the slaves can only obey the order of their master. In contrast, Haidt's model is that the relationship between them is more like the one between a lawyer and their client: 'Good lawyers do what they can to help their clients, but they sometimes refuse to go along with requests' (Haidt 2012, 68). Reasoning processes might overweigh affective processes when a person has enough time to consider the question, when the person has a strong motivation to be accurate, when affective input is relatively weak, and so on. (Thus, the social intuitionist model contains an element of the default-interventionist model.)

Still, the social intuitionist model insists that it is atypical that reasoning processes refuse to go along with intuitive responses; *post hoc* rationalization is the typical activity and is the main job of reasoning processes. When it comes to determining one's moral judgment and its content, the role of affective processes is overwhelmingly more important than that of reasoning processes.

In response, several philosophers have challenged Haidt's social intuitionist model and the more general argument for the dominating role of raw emotional reactions in the formation of moral attitudes. For instance, Jeanette Kennett and Cordelia Fine (2009) have pointed out that Haidt attacks the causal role of reason in moral judgment by emphasizing: (1) the importance of automatic evaluations and intuitive processes in explaining human behaviour (which we reviewed in Chapter 3); (2) the fact that biases affect reasoning (which we reviewed in Chapter 1); and (3) the pervasiveness of *post hoc* justifications offered by human agents for their behaviour (which we reviewed in Chapter 2).

According to Kennett and Fine, based on (1) to (3), Haidt effectively argues that human agents are not *reason responders*. Agents can be characterized as reason trackers and reason responders. They are reason trackers when they recognize something as a reason for a judgment or an action, and can judge or act according to such a reason. They are reason responders when, in addition to tracking reasons, they respond to those reasons as reasons for a judgment or an action. Whereas non-human animals can track reasons, they most likely can't respond to reasons. Reason tracking seems to be something automatic and often unconscious that maps onto System 1. Reason responding seems to be something deliberate and conscious that maps onto System 2.

Traditionally, moral philosophers have attributed to human agents the capacity to respond to reasons and the capacity to be guided by reasoning in their moral judgment. However, Haidt seems to suggest that the capacity for responding to reasons in human agents is an illusion. When it appears that human agents are responding to reasons, in reality they are typically playing the lawyer or the press secretary role, offering reasons as a *post hoc* justification for a moral judgment they have already arrived at by socially constructed intuitions. According to Kennett and Fine, this picture of moral judgment does not do justice to the fact that human agents have the capacity for moral agency and minimizes the role of reasoning in the formation of moral judgments. How are competent adult human agents different from non-human animals, young children, and incompetent adults when making moral judgments if we cannot describe them as reason responders? Haidt underestimates the fact that human agents can 'effortfully override judgments based on moral intuitions' (Kennett & Fine 2009, 93) because they have values and are responsive to reasons.

Despite their challenge to Haidt (namely that he exaggerates the illusory nature of reason responsiveness in human agents), Kennett and Fine recognize the importance of his work and appreciate the fact that the empirical evidence on moral judgment has forced philosophers to think more carefully about the role of intuitions.

> It is certainly very plausible that much of the processing underpinning our everyday moral judgment and behaviour is done automatically and with little effortful cognition. Nonetheless, a close examination of the social cognitive psychology literature suggests that Haidt's (2001) claim that 'moral reasoning is rarely the direct cause of moral judgment' (p. 815) is to overstate the primacy of automatic processes in social judgment, and to underplay the contribution of controlled processes. (Kennett & Fine 2009, 88)

More Than a *Post Hoc* Rationalization

The lawyer-client model of interaction (such as the social intuitionist theory) can be challenged for empirical reasons as well. In particular, Greene and colleagues conducted a series of fMRI experiments whose results better fit the parallel-competitive model or the default-intervention model than the lawyer–client model.

The Trolley/Footbridge Study

In this influential study, Greene and colleagues (2001) compare two different kinds of sacrificial dilemmas: personal and impersonal dilemmas involving the option of sacrificing someone's life to save others. Personal sacrificial dilemmas involve the option of sacrificing someone's life in an 'up close and personal' manner (e.g., the footbridge dilemma), while impersonal sacrificial dilemmas involve the option of sacrificing someone's life in an impersonal manner (e.g., the trolley dilemma).

> *The Trolley Dilemma*: A runaway trolley is headed for five people, who will be killed if it proceeds on its present course. The only way to save them is to pull a lever that will divert the trolley onto an alternate set of tracks where it will kill only one person instead of five. Should you divert the trolley?

> *The Footbridge Dilemma*: A trolley threatens to kill five people. You are standing next to a large stranger on a raised footbridge that spans the tracks and stands in between the oncoming trolley and the five

people. In this scenario, the only way to save the five people is to push this stranger off the bridge and onto the tracks below. He will die if you do this, but his body will stop the trolley from reaching the others. Should you push the stranger onto the tracks?

Although these two dilemmas share the same structure of saving five people by sacrificing one, the philosophical community are aware that they tend to elicit different responses: people tend to favour the sacrificing option in the case of the trolley dilemma (i.e., the response in favour of pulling the lever), while they tend to favour the anti-sacrificing option in the case of the footbridge dilemma (i.e., the response against pushing the stranger off the bridge). In this experiment, Greene and colleagues used fMRI to monitor the brain activities of participants while they responded to personal dilemmas (e.g., the footbridge dilemma), impersonal dilemmas (e.g., the trolley dilemma), and non-moral dilemmas. It was found that personal moral dilemmas, when compared to impersonal and non-moral dilemmas, evoke increased activities in brain areas associated with social/ affective processing (medial frontal gyrus, posterior cingulate gyrus, and bilateral superior temporal sulcus). In contrast, impersonal and non-moral dilemmas, when compared to personal dilemmas, evoke increased activity in brain areas associated with working memory and abstract reasoning (dorsolateral prefrontal and parietal areas).

This result does not sit well with the lawyer–client model, in which reasoning processes typically play a minor role of *post hoc* rationalization. The experiment seems to suggest that, at least in the case of impersonal dilemmas, reasoning processes (which are manifested as a pro-sacrificing response to impersonal dilemmas) can either compete with affective processes (the parallel-competitive model) or intervene in them (the default-intervention model).

Greene and colleagues also analysed participants' response times. It turns out that participants were slow to approve of the personal sacrificial option (e.g., pushing the stranger off the bridge) but relatively quick to disapprove of it. In contrast, approving of the impersonal sacrificial option (e.g., pulling the lever) and disapproving of it took an equally long time. This result is especially coherent with the default-intervention model. Since personal dilemmas elicit a strong affective reaction against the sacrificial option, approving of it can be a simple and quick matter (i.e., just letting the affective reaction manifest itself in the judgment), while disapproving of it requires reasoning processes to intervene in the affective processes and override the affective reaction, which can be slow.

The trolley/footbridge dilemmas (Greene et al. 2001) examine relatively 'easy' dilemmas in the sense that one form of response tends to be dominant in them: the sacrificial response (e.g., the response in favour of the pulling the lever) is dominant in impersonal dilemmas such as the trolley case, while the anti-sacrificial response (e.g., the response against pushing the stranger off the bridge) is dominant in personal dilemmas such as the footbridge case. Another contrasting experiment (Greene et al. 2004) examines a rather 'difficult' dilemma, known as the crying baby dilemma, in which people's reactions tend to split.

> *The Crying Baby Dilemma*: Enemy soldiers have taken over your village. They have orders to kill all remaining civilians. You and some of your townspeople have sought refuge in the cellar of a large house. Outside, you hear the voices of soldiers who have come to search the house for valuables. Your baby begins to cry loudly. You cover his mouth to block the sound. If you remove your hand from his mouth, his crying will summon the attention of the soldiers, who will kill you, your child, and the others hiding in the cellar. To save yourself and the others, you must smother your child to death. Should you smother your child?

It turns out that engaging in difficult dilemmas such as the crying baby dilemma causes increased activity in the anterior cingulate cortex, which is associated with dealing with two or more incompatible behavioural responses. Researchers also found that the sacrificial response to a difficult dilemma (e.g., the response in favour of smothering the child to save oneself and others) is correlated with increased activity in the dorsolateral prefrontal cortex, which is the seat of cognitive control and is necessary for overriding impulsive responses. These results provide further evidence of the view that reasoning processes can do something more than *post hoc* rationalization: reasoning processes can compete with affective processes or intervene in them.

Putting the evidence together, a reasonable view is that, as the phenomenon of moral dumbfounding suggests, reasoning processes rationalize the output of affective processes in a *post hoc* manner in some cases (i.e., the lawyer–client model). However, as the studies by Greene and colleagues suggest, reasoning processes can do something more than that in other cases: they either compete with affective processes (i.e., the parallel-competitive model) or intervene in them (i.e., the default-intervention model). This conclusion is consistent with what we suggested in the previous chapter concerning the interaction between Type-1 processes and Type-2 processes of reasoning: the conciliatory view according to which the parallel-competitive model, the default-intervention model, and the lawyer–client model are all correct to some extent, but wrong to some extent.

4.4   Affective Processes and Reasoning Processes

The Mapping Thesis

We will now move on to the process question about the dual-process theory of moral judgment. The dual-process theory says that moral judgments are produced by the interaction between affective processes and reasoning processes. But what are 'affective' processes and 'reasoning' processes?

Different theorists have slightly different terminology. Haidt distinguishes 'moral intuition' from 'moral reasoning'. Moral reasoning is defined as 'conscious mental activity that consists of transforming given information about people in order to reach a moral judgment'. It is also said to be 'intentional, effortful, and controllable' (Haidt 2001, 818). Moral intuition, in contrast, is defined as 'the sudden appearance in consciousness of a moral judgment, including an affective valence (good–bad, like–dislike), without any conscious awareness of having gone through steps of searching, weighing evidence, or inferring a conclusion' (Haidt 2001, 818). It is called moral *intuition*, rather than moral *emotion*, because the intuitive input can be unconscious and too fast to be regarded as an emotion.

Greene draws a distinction between 'cognitive' and 'emotional' processes. He defines 'cognitive' processes as the processes that deal with 'cognitive' representations: that is, representations that are 'inherently neutral representations, ones that do not automatically trigger particular behavioral responses or dispositions' (Greene 2008, 40). Emotional processes, in contrast, are the processes that deal with 'emotional' representations: that is, representations that 'do have such automatic [behavioural] effects, and are therefore behaviorally valenced' (Greene 2008, 40).

Let us recall our discussion of the process question about the dual process of reasoning. Type-1 and Type-2 processes of reasoning are distinguished by clusters of properties: the cluster of Type-1 properties and the cluster of Type-2 properties. Type-1 processes instantiate Type-1 properties and Type-2 processes instantiate Type-2 properties. We can think of a similar approach to the dual process of moral judgment. Affective processes and reasoning processes of moral judgment are distinguished by clusters of properties: the cluster of 'affective' properties (fast, effortless, automatic, unconscious, behaviourally valenced, etc.) and the cluster of 'reasoning' properties (slow, effortful, controllable, conscious, behaviourally neutral, etc.).

In the context of the process question, the most philosophically interesting issue is about Greene's claim that the distinction between affective processes and reasoning (or cognitive) processes (which is a distinction concerning the type of processes in the brain) nicely maps onto the distinction between utilitarianism and deontology (which is a distinction concerning fundamental moral principles). Utilitarianism, which was developed by Jeremy Bentham and John Stuart Mill, states that the moral worth of an action (e.g., whether it is good or bad) is determined by the amount of utility or happiness the act brings about. Deontology, which was developed by Immanuel Kant, states that the moral worth of an action is determined by rules concerning duties and rights.

The result of the trolley/footbridge study (Greene et al. 2001) suggests that the distinction between affective processes and reasoning processes maps onto the distinction between personal moral dilemmas (e.g., in the footbridge dilemma) and impersonal moral dilemmas (e.g., in the trolley dilemma). The latter distinction, in turn, maps onto the distinction between the anti-sacrificial response (e.g., not pushing the stranger off the bridge in the footbridge dilemma) and the sacrificial response (e.g., pulling the lever in the trolley dilemma). The distinction between the anti-sacrificial response and the sacrificial response also maps onto the distinction between utilitarian moral judgment and deontological moral judgment. For example, the option of not pushing the stranger off the bridge, an anti-sacrificial response, is a typical deontological option that respects the right of the stranger or the duty of not using a stranger merely as a means to an end. The option of pulling the lever, a sacrificial response, is a typical utilitarian option that maximizes utility or happiness: the total utility is larger when one person is killed to save five people than when five people are killed. Putting all of these distinctions together, we can conclude that the distinction between affective processes and reasoning processes maps onto the distinction between deontological and utilitarian judgments. In Greene's words, 'there is a natural mapping' (Greene 2008, 63) between the two types of brain processes and the two types of moral principles (see Table 2).

Let us call Greene's idea 'the mapping thesis' (Greene calls it 'the central tension principle') and formulate it as follows:

> *The Mapping Thesis*: Deontological judgments are typically produced in affective processes, and utilitarian judgments are typically produced in reasoning processes.

With the mapping thesis at hand, Greene goes on to make some provocative claims: that 'the psychological essence' of deontology lies in emotional processes and 'the psychological essence' of utilitarianism lies in reasoning processes; that utilitarianism and deontology 'are not so much philosophical inventions as they are philosophical manifestations of two dissociable psychological patterns, two different ways of moral thinking, that have been part of the human repertoire for thousands of years'; and that 'the moral philosophies of Kant, Mill, and others are just the explicit tips of large, mostly implicit, psychological icebergs' (Greene 2008, 38).

The mapping thesis bridges the gap between brain processes and principles of moral philosophy. By bridging the two, the thesis might enable us to draw some interesting consequences on the latter from the research of the former. In fact, Greene argues that his findings have a devastating consequence for philosophical deontology, which is perhaps the most controversial part of his project. Deontology, according to Greene, is discredited because it is the product of the affective, automatic, and heuristic processes 'that are rather inflexible, and therefore likely to be unreliable, at least in some contexts' (Greene

Table 2.   The mapping thesis

Ethical theories	Type of processes	Properties
Deontology	emotional, intuitive, affective	fast, effortless, automatic, unconscious, behaviourally valenced
Utilitarianism	reasoning, cognitive	slow, effortful, controllable, conscious, behaviourally neutral

2008, 60). The psychological essence of deontology lies with the affective processes that are tracking something irrelevant to morality, namely how 'up close and personal' a transgression is. For example, the affective/deontological process is activated in the footbridge dilemma but not in the trolley dilemma because pushing the stranger off the bridge is something very 'up close and personal' while pulling the lever to save five people is not. Upon reflection, however, being 'up close and personal' does not seem to be a morally relevant property. Sacrificing someone's life in an up-close and personal way and sacrificing someone's life in a distant and impersonal manner do not seem to be morally different. Thus, we should be sceptical about the deontological judgment that pushing the stranger off the bridge is wrong.

Greene's argument runs parallel to the following argument against the trustworthiness of heuristic Type-1 processes. Heuristics such as representational heuristics are inflexible and are thus likely to be unreliable in some contexts. Representational heuristics track something irrelevant to the probability of a given hypotheses, namely similarity to stereotypes (e.g., how Linda's description is similar to that of a stereotypical bank teller). Thus, we should be sceptical of heuristic judgments (e.g., the judgment that Linda is more likely to be a feminist bank teller than a bank teller).

But, of course, these philosophical consequences follow *only* *if* the mapping thesis is true. (Note that we are not saying that these consequences follow *if* the mapping thesis is true: see Berker 2009; Kahane 2011; and relevant chapters in Sinnott-Armstrong 2008b.) The crucial question, then, is whether the mapping thesis really is true or not. We will examine this question in the rest of this chapter.

Content Interpretation

Evaluating the mapping thesis depends on what the thesis actually means. How should we interpret it? In particular, what is meant by 'deontological' judgments and 'utilitarian' judgments in the thesis?

An appropriate interpretation of the mapping thesis needs to satisfy two conditions. First, an appropriate interpretation makes it the case that the mapping thesis is empirically plausible in light of relevant empirical studies, such as the one by Greene and colleagues. Let us call this 'the psychological adequacy condition'. Second, an appropriate interpretation makes it the case that the mapping thesis is philosophically adequate in the sense that 'utilitarian judgments' and 'deontological judgments' in the thesis are genuinely relevant to utilitarianism and deontology in moral philosophy. Let us call this 'the philosophical adequacy condition'.

Two conditions need to be satisfied simultaneously. Suppose that an interpretation of the mapping thesis satisfies the psychological adequacy condition but not the philosophical adequacy condition. The mapping thesis is empirically supported, but it has nothing to do with utilitarianism or deontology in moral philosophy and, thus, it does not really bridge the gap between brain processes and principles of moral philosophy. Suppose, in contrast, that an interpretation of the mapping thesis satisfies the philosophical adequacy condition but not the psychological adequacy condition. The mapping thesis is relevant to moral philosophy, but it is not supported by empirical evidence and, thus, we do not have reason to take it seriously.

Let us now see if there is an interpretation of the mapping thesis that is both psychologically and philosophically adequate. One possibility, which we call 'the content interpretation', would be to define 'deontological' judgments and 'utilitarian' judgments in the mapping thesis in terms of the content of the judgments. According to the content interpretation, a 'deontological/utilitarian' judgment is the judgment with 'deontological/utilitarian' content. For example, the judgment that it is wrong to push the stranger off the bridge is deontological because its content 'it is wrong to push the stranger off the bridge' is deontological. In contrast, the judgment that it is right to pull the lever to save five people is utilitarian because its content 'it is right to pull the lever to save five people' is utilitarian.

According to the content interpretation, 'deontological/utilitarian' judgments are the judgments with 'deontological/utilitarian' content. But what is 'utilitarian content' or 'deontological content', exactly? What makes it the case that content is utilitarian or deontological? Let us accept the following answer, which is suggested by Greene (2008):

> The content P is utilitarian if P is justifiable more easily in terms of deontological principles than in terms of utilitarian principles; and it is deontological if P is justifiable more easily in terms of utilitarian principles than in terms of deontological principles.

For example, the judgment that pushing the stranger off the bridge is wrong is deontological: the judgment has deontological content, namely 'it is wrong to push the stranger off the bridge', which is easily justifiable in terms of deontological principles by reference to rights and duties (but not very easily justifiable in terms of utilitarian principles).

Note that it is not easy to justify the content 'it is wrong to push the stranger off the bridge' in terms of utilitarian principles, but it is possible. Somebody who is committed to rule utilitarianism (a form of utilitarianism that evaluates rules, rather than acts, in terms of their utilitarian consequences) might agree with a deontologist that we should not push the stranger off the bridge because the absolute rule prohibiting any kind of sacrificing for the sake of saving more people maximizes utility in the long run. (For example, the rule allowing sacrificing in some cases can easily be abused.) Still, the content 'it is wrong to push the stranger off the bridge' is deontological because justifying it from a utilitarian point of view is relatively difficult and requires 'a lot of fancy philosophizing' (Greene 2008, 39), such as introducing the distinction between act utilitarianism and rule utilitarianism.

Now, with the content interpretation, the mapping thesis is understood as follows:

> Deontological judgments in the content sense (i.e., judgments with deontological content) are typically produced in affective processes, and utilitarian judgments in the content sense (i.e., judgments with utilitarian content) are typically produced in reasoning processes.

This version of the mapping thesis is certainly plausible in light of the findings by Greene and colleagues (2001): the anti-sacrificial response (e.g., not pushing the stranger off the bridge), which has deontological content (i.e., the content that is more easily justifiable in terms of deontological principles than utilitarian principles), was found to be associated with affective processes, while the sacrificial response (e.g., pulling the lever to save five people), which has utilitarian content (i.e., the content that is more easily justifiable in terms of utilitarian principles than deontological principles), was found to be associated with reasoning processes. Thus, the content interpretation is psychologically adequate.

The content interpretation, however, faces problems concerning philosophical adequacy. There are multiple ways of making a judgment with utilitarian/deontological content. For example, someone might judge that pushing the large stranger off the bridge is wrong not because she cares about deontological principles but because she likes large people, or because she dislikes the idea of pushing someone with her own hands. Or perhaps her judgment is made by flipping a coin, reading tealeaves, or some other random process. All of these count as deontological judgments according to the content interpretation, but they have nothing to do with utilitarianism/deontology in moral philosophy. This suggests that the content interpretation is too weak to be philosophically adequate.

A version of this problem is that, when a rule utilitarian chooses to not push the stranger off the bridge by explicitly invoking rule-utilitarian considerations, we need to classify her judgment as deontological because its content is deontological. But it does not sound right to say that her judgment is deontological; she is clearly a (rule) utilitarian. Thus, again, the content interpretation is not philosophically adequate.

Commitment Interpretation

Thus, we need a better interpretation of 'utilitarian' and 'deontological' judgments in the mapping thesis. Another proposal would be to define them not in terms of their content but rather in terms of the moral commitment of the person who makes the judgment. One proposal, which we call 'the commitment interpretation', is that 'deontological/utilitarian' judgments of person X are the ones that reflect X's (implicit or explicit) commitment to deontological/utilitarian principles (or at least something close enough). For example, the judgment that it is wrong to push the stranger off the bridge is deontological, not because its content 'it is wrong to push the stranger off the bridge' is deontological, but because the person who makes the judgment is (implicitly or explicitly) committed to deontological principles (or at least something close enough), and this commitment is reflected in the judgment. Again, the judgment that it is right to pull the lever to save five people is utilitarian, not because its content 'it is right to pull the lever to save five people' is utilitarian, but because the person who makes the judgment is (implicitly or explicitly) committed to utilitarian principles (or at least something near enough), and this commitment is reflected in the judgment.

Note that we allow for the possibility that person X is *implicitly*, but not *explicitly*, committed to deontological/utilitarian principles, otherwise almost nobody outside of the philosophical community could make deontological/utilitarian judgments. This would be too strong, ruling out the very possibility of studying the psychology of deontological/utilitarian judgments by non-philosophical subjects. For the same reason we allow for the possibility that person X is committed to something *similar to* deontological/utilitarian principles, but not deontological/utilitarian principles *themselves*. Again, almost nobody outside of the philosophical community is committed to deontological/utilitarian principles themselves.

Now, on the commitment interpretation, the mapping thesis would look like this:

> Deontological judgments in the commitment sense (i.e., judgments that reflect a person's commitment to deontological principles) are typically produced in affective processes, and utilitarian judgments in the commitment sense (i.e., judgments that reflect a person's commitment to utilitarian principles) are typically produced in reasoning processes.

The commitment interpretation is certainly philosophically adequate. When a person is committed to utilitarian principles and she makes a judgment out of the commitment, the judgment is certainly relevant to the moral theory of utilitarianism.

The difference between the content interpretation and the commitment interpretation is clear. For example, judging in favour of pulling the lever on the basis of flipping a coin is 'utilitarian' in the content sense (because its content is utilitarian), but not 'utilitarian' in the commitment sense (because it does not reflect the person's commitment to utilitarian principles). Again, judging against pushing the stranger off the bridge on the basis of reading tealeaves is 'deontological' in the content sense (because its content is deontological), but not 'deontological' in the commitment sense (because it does not reflect the person's commitment to deontological principles).

The commitment interpretation certainly satisfies the philosophical adequacy condition, but it faces problems concerning the psychological adequacy condition. The studies by Greene and colleagues do not support this version of the mapping thesis.

Here is an immediate problem. The studies by Greene and colleagues seem to show that anti-sacrificial judgments are based on affective reactions. However, the affective rejection of pushing the stranger off the bridge does not look like a deontological judgment in the commitment sense. A mere affective aversion is nothing like a genuine deontological judgment that reflects one's deontological commitments concerning duties, rights, and so on. There is a huge gap between a person's affective aversion to pushing the stranger off the bridge and her rejecting the idea of pushing him because of her genuine deontological commitment with regard to the stranger's rights.

In response, Greene (2008) argues that deontological notions such as rights or duties are the product of *post hoc* rationalization. In the stockings experiment by Nisbett and Wilson (1977), for example, participants first choose a pair of stockings because of their location and then rationalize their decision in a *post hoc* manner (referring to the colour, texture, etc., of the chosen stockings). Similarly, according to Greene, deontologists first make an affective judgment against pushing the stranger off the bridge, and then rationalize that judgment in a *post hoc* manner, referring to rights, duties, etc. In Greene's words:

> Deontology, then, is a kind of moral confabulation. We have strong feelings that tell us in clear and uncertain terms that some things simply *cannot be done* and that other things simply *must be done*. But it is not obvious how to make sense of these feelings, and so we, with the help of some especially creative philosophers, make up a rationally appealing story: There are these things called 'rights' which people have, and when someone has a right you can't do anything that would take it away. It doesn't matter if the guy on the footbridge is toward the end of his natural life, or if there are seven people on the tracks below instead of five. (Greene 2008, 63)

Greene, in effect, rejects the claim above that a mere affective aversion to pushing the stranger off the bridge is nothing like a genuine deontological judgment that pushing him off the bridge is wrong because of one's own duty (to not harm the innocent man) or the stranger's right (to not be harmed). The latter is nothing but the former rationalized in a *post hoc* manner.

How about utilitarianism? Are sacrificial responses in the dilemmas (e.g., the judgment in favour of pulling the lever in the trolley dilemma) utilitarian in the commitment sense? Do sacrificial responses in the dilemmas reflect the person's (implicit or explicit) commitment to utilitarian principles? Guy Kahane (Kahane 2012; Kahane et al. 2015) argues that they are not utilitarian in the commitment sense. Kahane and colleagues characterize utilitarianism as the 'radical and demanding view' that 'the right act is the one that maximizes aggregate well-being, considered from a maximally impartial perspective that gives equal weight to the interests of all persons, or even all sentient beings' (Kahane et al. 2015, 206). The sacrificial responses in the dilemmas have nothing to do with a commitment to utilitarian principles characterized above. For example, endorsing the option of pulling the lever to save five people seems to be utilitarian on the face of it, but one can endorse this option without being committed to the radical and demanding doctrine of impartially maximizing aggregate well-being. In fact, it is unlikely that the participants of the studies by Greene and colleagues are (implicitly or explicitly) committed to such a radical and demanding doctrine (or something close enough). It is not likely, for example, that they give equal weight to the interests of all people and all sentient beings.

A related problem is that it is possible for one to endorse a sacrificial option such as pushing the stranger off the bridge to save five people not because she wants to maximize aggregate well-being but rather because she does not hesitate to sacrifice the stranger's life in order to fulfil some purposes. In other words, the endorsement of a sacrificial option could be the expression of a reduced aversion to sacrificing someone else's life rather than of genuine care for the greater good. This hypothesis is consistent with findings that the tendency to make sacrificial responses in moral dilemmas is correlated with psychopathic and anti-social traits (e.g., Bartels & Pizarro 2011; Kahane et al. 2015; Koenigs et al. 2012; see also Chapter 8).

The commitment interpretation therefore seems problematic too. This puts us in a dilemma. The content interpretation is psychologically adequate, but it is not philosophically adequate. The notion of 'utilitarianism/deontology' in the mapping thesis is too weak or too liberal to be genuinely relevant to the principles of moral philosophy. The commitment interpretation, in contrast, is philosophically adequate, but it is not psychologically adequate. The studies by Greene and colleagues do suggest that sacrificial judgments are produced by reasoning processes, but sacrificial judgments might not count as utilitarian judgments in the commitment sense (see Conway et al. 2018 for more discussions).

4.5 Summary

- According to the dual-process theory of moral judgment, moral judgments are the product of the interaction between affective processes and reasoning processes. Several issues emerge when we consider the details of how moral attitudes are formed.
- One issue is about how affective processes and reasoning processes interact with each other (the *interaction* question). There are three models: the parallel-competitive model, the default-intervention model, and the lawyer–client model. The main job of reasoning processes is to rationalize the output of affective processes in a *post hoc* manner according to the lawyer–client model, while reasoning processes have a more substantial role (they constantly compete with, or occasionally intervene in, affective processes) according to the parallel-competitive model and the default-intervention model.
- Another issue arises in relation to understanding what affective processes and reasoning processes are (the *process* question). The mapping thesis aims to bridge the distinction in the brain between affective processes and reasoning processes and the distinction in moral philosophy between deontology and utilitarianism. But it is not easy to find an interpretation of the mapping thesis that is both psychologically adequate (i.e., supported by evidence) and philosophically adequate (i.e., relevant to philosophical theories of morality).

Further Resources

Articles and Books

A good place to start to learn about Jonathan Haidt's social intuitionism about morality is 'The emotional dog and its rational tail: A social intuitionist approach to moral judgment' (2001), which he considers his most important article. There, he defends the primacy of affect over reason in moral judgment. Also see his *The Righteous Mind: Why Good People Are Divided by Politics and Religion* (2012). Commentaries on social intuitionism can be found in articles by Steve Clarke (2008), Neil Levy (2014), and S. Matthew Liao (2011). The book *Regard for Reason in the Moral Mind* (2018) by Joshua May is a challenge to social intuitionism and a defence of moderate rationalism in moral reasoning.

The trolley/footbridge study by Joshua Greene and colleagues is in their *Science* article (2001). See Greene (2003) for a discussion of how to bridge the gap between the empirical study of brain activities and the philosophical discussion of moral principles. Greene's *Moral Tribes: Emotion, Reason, and the Gap between Us and Them* (2013) includes a remarkable combination of philosophical defence of and empirical support for utilitarianism.

Our focus in this chapter was on Haidt's theory and Greene's theory of moral judgment, but there are other important theories that cannot be ignored. For example, the universal moral grammar theory explains moral judgment by using concepts and models that are analogous to those used in linguistics. We recommend John Mikhail's review article (2007) and Mark Hauser's *Moral Minds: How Nature Designed Our Universal Sense of Right and Wrong* (2006).

The *Moral Psychology* series from MIT Press (edited by Walter Sinnott-Armstrong) contains important contributions by philosophers, psychologists, and neuroscientists. Volume 2 (*The Cognitive Science of Morality: Intuition and Diversity*, 2008a) and Volume 3 (*The Neuroscience of Morality: Emotion, Brain Disorders, and Development*, 2008b) are particularly relevant to the topic of this chapter.

Online Resources

On YouTube you will find a 2017 interview by *Philosophy Overdose* with Jesse Prinz on moral judgment, a 2013 lecture by Jonathan Haidt on whether there is a rationalist delusion in moral psychology, and a 2014 lecture by Joshua Greene on the roles of emotion and reason in moral judgment. We also recommend a 2012 *Philosophy Bites* podcast in which Liane Young is interviewed about mind and morality, and social intuitionism. Henry Richardson's *Stanford Encyclopedia of Philosophy* entry on moral reasoning (2018) is useful too.

Questions

1. Think about everyday cases in which the moral judgment by you, or someone you know, is largely driven by emotion. Again, think about everyday cases in which the moral judgment by you, or someone you know, is largely driven by reasoning.

2. Which do you think are more trustworthy or reliable: emotion-driven moral judgments or reasoning-driven moral judgments? Does that vary depending on context?
3. Can we learn something about morality by studying the brain? For example, what does Greene's fMRI study imply about the philosophical debate between utilitarianism and deontology?
4. Compare the dual-process theory of reasoning (Chapter 3) and the dual-process theory of moral judgment. What are the similarities? What are the differences?

5

Moral Motivation and Behaviour

5.1 Introduction

Chapter 4 discussed the roles of affective processes and reasoning processes in moral judgments. The dual-process theory states that moral judgments are determined by the interplay between affective processes and reasoning processes. However, when it comes to moral *behaviour* and *motivation* rather than moral *judgments*, one might think that affective processes are much more important than reasoning processes.

Suppose that by reading a newspaper Anna comes to know that thousands of children in Africa have been suffering from a life-threatening disease. Anna reasons, on the basis of a utilitarian calculation, that it is morally better to spend the £50 she has in her wallet on helping the children by donating the money to a charity than spend it on a ticket to the next football game. However, this moral reasoning might fail to motivate her behaviour; she might find herself at the next football match despite her moral reasoning. In contrast, when Anna emotionally empathizes with the suffering children, rather than running a utilitarian calculation about them, it is more likely that she would visit a charity's website and make an online donation.

In this chapter, we will discuss the role of moral emotions, and affective empathy in particular, in moral motivation and behaviour. Our focus will be on empathy-induced moral behaviour, such as the act of donating money to prevent children from suffering out of empathy for them. Empathy seems to play an important role in moral behaviour at least in many cases (although there are cases in which moral behaviour has little to do with empathy, such as the case in which a promise with a friend is kept out of duty rather than empathy with the friend).

In general, when we evaluate the moral worth of an action, some theories, such as Kantian deontology, focus on the *motivation* for the act. According to these theories, whether an action is morally worthy is determined by whether a person acts based on the right kind of motivation (e.g., the motivation to fulfil one's own moral duty). Other theories, such as utilitarianism, focus on the *consequences* of the act. According to these theories, whether an action is morally worthy is determined by whether the action brings about the right kind of consequences (e.g., the consequence of making African children happier).

This chapter will investigate both the motivations and the consequences of empathy-induced moral behaviour. In particular, it will examine two hypotheses about such behaviour. The first hypothesis concerns the motivation of empathy-induced behaviour. This hypothesis – what we call 'the empathy–altruism hypothesis' (Batson 1991, 2011, 2018) – is that empathy-induced behaviour is genuinely motivated by altruism (Sections 5.2 and 5.3). When Anna empathizes with suffering children in Africa, her empathy motivates her to help the children out of genuine concern for their well-being. The second hypothesis concerns the consequence of empathy-induced behaviour. The hypothesis – what we call 'the empathy–benefit hypothesis' – is that empathy-induced behaviour has morally beneficial consequences (Sections 5.4, 5.5, and 5.6). When Anna empathizes with suffering children in Africa, she donates some of her money to a charity, which has morally beneficial consequences.

Central to this chapter is the discussion of influential experimental studies by Daniel Batson (1991, 2011, 2018). As we will see, his studies are crucially relevant both to the empathy–altruism hypothesis and to the empathy–benefit hypothesis. We will suggest that the experimental results support the former but do not support the latter.

5.2   The Empathy–Altruism Hypothesis

Empathy

Our central topic in this chapter is the relationship between empathy and (moral) behaviour. One hypothesis, the empathy–altruism hypothesis, says that empathy-induced behaviour is genuinely altruistic. The other hypothesis, the empathy–benefit hypothesis, says that empathy-induced behaviour has morally beneficial consequences. We will begin by discussing the empathy–altruism hypothesis.

Evaluating the empathy–altruism hypothesis requires both philosophical and psychological investigations. Philosophical investigation involves clarifying the key concepts in the empathy–altruism hypothesis. Psychological investigation, in contrast, involves evaluating empirical evidence for the empathy–altruism hypothesis. This section focuses on the former and the next section (Section 5.3) focuses on the latter.

There are two key concepts in the empathy–altruism hypothesis: 'empathy' and 'altruism'. We will now clarify them in turn.

It is widely agreed that empathy is an affective state (and thus it is sometimes called 'affective empathy') and that it can be distinguished from 'cognitive empathy'. 'Cognitive empathy' refers to mindreading, which is the capacity to predict and explain the behaviour of others by attributing to them relevant mental states such as beliefs or desires. (Or, perhaps, 'cognitive empathy' refers to a particular form of mindreading that is based on simulation rather than theorizing. See Chapter 8 for further discussion.) We can coherently imagine a person who has a good mindreading capacity or cognitive empathy but is not affectively empathic. Such a person might predict the behaviour of a suffering child in Africa by attributing beliefs and desires to that child, but would have difficulty affectively empathizing with the child's suffering. Perhaps people with psychopathy exemplify this: their mindreading capacity seems to be intact, which enables them to deceive and manipulate other people successfully, while their affective empathy seems to be compromised, which explains their sometimes cruel behaviour (see Chapter 8 for further discussion).

Apart from the distinction between (affective) empathy and cognitive empathy, there is virtually no consensus among researchers about what (affective) empathy is and there is little consensus about how to use the term 'empathy'.

The term 'empathy' has been used in many different ways by different authors (**Box 5A**; also see Maibom 2012). In presenting the empathy–altruism hypothesis, Batson defines 'empathy', which he equates with 'empathic concern', as an 'other-oriented emotion elicited by and congruent with the perceived welfare of someone in need' (Batson 2018, 29). When, for example, Anna empathizes with a suffering child in Africa, she feels something negative about the child (other-oriented), which is elicited by the suffering of the child, and the feeling is congruent with the child's suffering in the sense that the valence of the feeling (negative) mirrors the valence of the perceived welfare of the child (negative).

Other authors understand 'empathy' as involving not only the congruence of valence (positive or negative) but also qualitative congruence or similarity. It is not just that Anna feels something negative, and that this negativity is congruent with the negativity of what a child in Africa feels (congruence of valence); she feels something that is qualitatively the same as, or at least qualitatively similar to, what the child feels (qualitative congruence). For example, Paul Bloom defines empathy as 'the act of feeling what you believe other people feel – experiencing what they experience' (Bloom 2016, 3). Jesse Prinz characterizes empathy as 'a matter of feeling an emotion that we take another person to have' (Prinz 2011, 215). This sense of 'empathy' is what Batson calls 'feeling as another feels'

BOX 5A: Varieties of 'empathy' (Batson 2018)

- 'Empathy' as empathic concern, which is other-oriented emotion elicited by and congruent with the perceived welfare of someone in need.
- 'Empathy' as knowing another person's thoughts and feelings.
- 'Empathy' as feeling the same emotion that another person feels.
- 'Empathy' as imagining how another person feels.
- 'Empathy' as imagining how you would feel in another person's place.
- 'Empathy' as feeling distress at witnessing another person's suffering.
- 'Empathy' as a general disposition, or trait, to feel for others.

(Box 5A), which is distinguished from what he calls 'empathy' or 'empathic concern'.

Batson clearly distinguishes his conception of 'empathy' or 'empathic concern' from 'empathy' on Bloom's and Prinz's conception. Bloom's and Prinz's conception of empathy is not necessary for Batson's conception of empathy: for example, Anna can feel empathic concern for hungry children in Africa without being hungry or feeling something like hunger herself. Bloom's and Prinz's conception of empathy is not sufficient for Batson's conception of empathy either: for example, observing a nervous passenger sitting next to her on an aeroplane in rough weather might cause Anna to feel nervous too, but this does not mean that Anna has empathic concern for the passenger.

Still, it is possible that Batson's conception of empathy and Bloom's and Prinz's conception of empathy are intimately related, at least in typical cases. For example, they might refer to different stages of the same process in which, for example, first Anna feels something qualitatively similar to the pain of a child in Africa (Bloom's and Prinz's empathy), and then this causes the negative emotion, a concern, for example, that Anna feels for the child (Batson's empathy). Alternatively, the distinction between Batson's conception of empathy and Bloom's and Prinz's conception of empathy might be the difference between the *process* of empathy and the *product* of empathy: empathy involves the process of feeling something qualitatively similar to the pain of a hungry child in Africa (Bloom's and Prinz's empathy), and this then produces the negative emotion that Anna feels about the child (Batson's empathy).

Altruism

Following Batson, let us say that behaviour is altruistic if it is motivated by a state (e.g., a desire) 'with the ultimate goal of increasing another's welfare' (Batson 2018, 22). For example, Anna's donation to help suffering children in Africa is altruistic if the act of donating money is motivated by her desire for the increased welfare of children in Africa. In addition, the desire needs to be 'ultimate', 'intrinsic', or 'non-instrumental': for instance, Anna must desire the increased welfare of children in Africa *for its own sake*, rather than it being instrumental in achieving some other goal, such as her selfish goal of feeling good that comes with donating money to charity.

One might think that, given this characterization of altruism, empathy-induced moral behaviour is obviously altruistic. Isn't it obvious that Anna donates money to help children in Africa because she desires an increase in the children's welfare? If we ask her why she donates the money, she will respond by saying that she does it because she cares about increasing the welfare of children in Africa. She might also insist that her desire to increase the welfare of children in Africa is not instrumental to any selfish goal.

But this is too hasty. As we have seen in Chapter 2 and Chapter 3, people have a tendency to confabulate reasons for their own behaviour. Participants in the stockings experiment by Nisbett and Wilson (1977) confabulated about their choice of stockings: their choice was really the product of position effects, but they explained it in a *post hoc* manner in terms of the superior quality of the pair of stockings they chose. Similarly, it is possible that Anna confabulates the reasons for her act of donation: her real motivation is a selfish one (e.g., achieving a good social reputation as a virtuous and compassionate person or feeling better about herself) but she rationalizes the act in a *post hoc* manner in terms of fulfilling some altruistic goal. This means that we need arguments and evidence, rather than relying on mere self-reports, when examining whether people behave altruistically.

Interestingly, a few *a priori* arguments have been put forward to show that altruism is impossible for humans (in which case the empathy–altruism hypothesis has no chance of being true). These arguments are unsuccessful, but discussing them will clarify what altruism actually is and avoid misunderstandings about it.

(1) *My Desire*: The first argument (what we call 'the it's-all-my-desire argument') starts from a seemingly harmless premise that people act on the basis of their desires (and beliefs). Anna acts on the basis of what she wants (and what she believes). According to this argument, this premise immediately leads to the impossibility of genuine altruistic actions. A seemingly altruistic action Anna performs is, ultimately, motivated by some of *her* desires. For example, Anna donating money to help children in Africa, which is seemingly altruistic, is in the end motivated by some of *her* desires. Hence, Anna's action of donating money is not genuinely altruistic.

The problem with the it's-all-my-desire argument is relatively obvious. What is needed for a genuinely altruistic action is that it is motivated by a desire for the well-being of others for its own sake. Now, the problem is that it's-all-my-desire argument confuses two questions: 'Who is the subject of the desire?' and 'Whose well-being is the desire about?' The former has nothing to do with altruistic motivation, whereas the latter does. When Anna donates money to alleviate the suffering of children in Africa, the relevant desire is certainly her desire; the subject of the desire (the person doing the desiring) is Anna. But if the desire is the desire for the well-being of children in Africa for its own sake, then her action of donating money is genuinely altruistic.

The lesson we can learn from (the failure of) the it's-all-my-desire argument is that altruism is not about *who has the desire*, rather it is about *whose well-being the desire is about*.

(2) *My Pleasure*: A related argument (what we call 'the it's-all-my-pleasure argument') also starts from the plausible premise that people act on the basis of their desires (and beliefs), and adds another plausible premise that people feel some pleasure when their desires are satisfied. According to this argument, these premises immediately lead to the impossibility of altruistic actions. A seemingly altruistic action Anna performs is, ultimately, understood as a selfish action – in terms of the selfish concern for the pleasure she receives when her desires are satisfied, rather than the altruistic concern for the welfare of others. For example, Anna's action of donating money to alleviate the suffering of children in Africa is explained by the pleasure she receives when her desires are satisfied. She donates because doing so satisfies her desire (i.e., the desire to improve the welfare of children in Africa), which produces pleasure.

The problem with the it's-all-my-pleasure argument is that even if it is true that the satisfaction of Anna's desires is pleasurable, it does not necessarily follow that pleasure, as opposed to the well-being of the children in Africa, is what she really cares about. Perhaps the pleasure is the by-product of her donation rather than the ultimate aim of it. For example, Anna might really want to improve the welfare of children in Africa, which motivates her to donate money. And, when the well-being of children in Africa is actually improved by her donation (together with the donation of others), her desire might be satisfied, which produces some pleasure as a by-product.

The lesson we can learn from the (failure of the) it's-all-my-pleasure argument is that altruistic behaviour can bring about some pleasure as a by-product without the pleasure being the reason for the behaviour.

(3) *Natural Selection*: The third argument (what we call 'the it's-all-natural-selection argument') appeals to natural selection. The human desire system has been shaped by natural selection, in which the biological and psychological features that enhance the chance of survival and reproduction are selected. Therefore, the desire system is designed to aim at enhancing the chance of one's own survival and reproduction. Hence humans cannot have genuinely altruistic desires.

In its current form, this argument is too crude. It is far from obvious that natural selection completely rules out the possibility of altruism. Perhaps natural selection is compatible with some forms of altruism, such as altruism between genetically related individuals or altruism between individuals who are reciprocally benefiting each other. Thus, the issue here is rather not that natural selection rules out all forms of altruism; the issue is that natural selection does not allow for more than these limited forms of altruism. A more sophisticated version of the it's-all-natural-selection argument might say that, although natural selection is compatible with some limited forms of altruism, it is not compatible with fully fledged altruism, namely altruism that is not necessarily based on genetic connection or reciprocity.

The it's-all-natural-selection argument involves the confusion between *biological* aims or purposes and *personal* aims or purposes (see Chapter 1 for the related discussion of the aim of cognition). It could be argued that the biological aim of a man's sexual desire is reproduction. This is just to say that the psychological system for sexual desire has been selected (via natural selection) to motivate certain organisms to behave in a way that increases their chance of reproduction. But this does not necessarily mean that individual men *aim to* reproduce; men might just want to have pleasurable sexual intercourse. Millikan provides another example to illustrate the distinction between biological purposes and personal purposes:

> Imagine that the eye doctor is trying to put drops in your eye but you keep blinking. You insist you don't mean to blink but that no matter how hard you try, when the eyedropper comes too close, your eye just closes. [...] We say that the eye 'is meant to close automatically' when a foreign object comes too near. The point is to prevent foreign objects

from entering it. That is the purpose of the eye-blink reflex. The difficulty is that you and your eye, or you and your eye-blink reflex, are at cross-purposes. You are trying to let the drops in but the reflex's purpose is to keep them out. (Millikan 2004, 3)

The lesson we can learn from the (failure of the) it's-all-natural-selection argument is that altruism is not about biological aims or purposes but rather about personal desires and goals. Even if the biological aim of the human desire system is egoistic rather than altruistic, this does not necessarily mean that people personally aim to fulfil egoistic goals.

Hereafter, we follow Batson's terminology where 'empathy' refers to the other-oriented emotion elicited by and congruent with the perceived welfare of someone in need, and 'altruism' refers to the behaviour that is motivated by a mental state with the ultimate goal of increasing another's welfare.

5.3 Altruistic Motivation or Aversive-Arousal Reduction?

We will now move on from a philosophical to a psychological investigation of the empathy–altruism hypothesis. Of central importance is a series of experimental studies by Daniel Batson and his colleagues (Batson 1991, 2011, 2018).

The Katie Banks Experiment

Some empirical evidence suggests that empathy does induce helping behaviour that appears to be altruistic. In one such experiment (Coke, Batson, & McDavis 1978), participants first took a capsule (a placebo, in fact) and were told either that the capsule would have the effect of relaxing them (*relaxation* side-effect condition) or that the capsule would have the effect of arousing them (*arousal* side-effect condition). Participants then heard a news report on Katie Banks, who had been suffering and struggling after the tragic loss of her parents in an accident (this news report was, unbeknown to participants, entirely fictional). Participants were then either instructed to imagine how Katie felt about her situation (*imagine-her* condition) or to observe the broadcasting techniques used in the news report (*observe* condition). After hearing the newscast, participants faced an opportunity to help Katie.

The result was that participants in the relaxation side-effect/imagine-her condition were more likely to offer help than those in other conditions (the arousal side-effect/imagine-her condition, the relaxation side-effect/observe condition, and the arousal side-effect/observe condition). This suggests that empathic imagining of Katie's suffering increased the probability of helping behaviour. Participants in the arousal side-effect/imagine-her condition were less likely to offer help, probably because affective arousal (due to empathic imagining) was explained away by the effect of the capsule, and hence it failed to be construed or identified as empathic concern for Katie.

Thus, empathy does induce helping behaviour. The crucial question is whether helping behaviour that is induced by empathy is genuinely altruistic. According to the empathy–altruism hypothesis, helping behaviour is genuinely altruistic. Participants in the relaxation side-effect/imagine-her condition offered help because empathizing with Katie induced the non-instrumental desire to help her. However, the behaviour can also be explained as egoistic rather than altruistic. One such egoistic interpretation is that the helping behaviour was due to the egoistic desire to alleviate the negative emotion or distress that is caused when empathizing with Katie's suffering. By empathizing with Katie's suffering, participants felt a negative-valenced and distressful emotion, which motivated them to get rid of this emotion by helping to alleviate Katie's suffering. This explanation is what Batson calls 'the aversive-arousal reduction hypothesis':

> Becoming empathically aroused by witnessing someone in need is aversive and evokes motivation to reduce this aversive arousal. Rather than empathy evoking altruistic motivation directed toward the ultimate goal relieving the victim's distress, as the empathy–altruism hypothesis claims, the motivation to help evoked by empathy is directed toward the ultimate goal of relieving the helper's own empathic distress. Because relieving the other's need removes the stimulus causing this aversive arousal, helping enables one to reach this egoistic goal. (Batson 1991, 109)

We therefore have at least two possible hypotheses: the empathy–altruism hypothesis and the aversive-arousal reduction hypothesis. Which is correct?

The Elaine Experiment

The empathy–altruism hypothesis and the aversive-arousal reduction hypothesis yield the same prediction in situations in which one has only two options: helping or not helping. However, they give different predictions in situations in which one has one additional option: escaping. If the ultimate goal of participants is the reduction of their own aversive arousal, rather than relieving the suffering of a victim, then simply escaping from the situation could be an easier strategy to achieve that goal. If, in contrast, the ultimate goal of participants is relieving the suffering of a victim, then helping is the only reasonable option; escaping does not solve the problem. In this experiment (Batson et al. 1981), female participants observed a young woman named Elaine (who, unbeknown to participants, was a fictional person) through a TV monitor. Participants watched as Elaine received uncomfortable electric shocks. Participants were informed either that Elaine's values and interests were very similar to theirs (the *similar-victim* condition) or very different (the *dissimilar-victim* condition). It turned out, however, that Elaine was especially sensitive to the shock, and participants were asked to help her by receiving the shock on her behalf. In one condition (the *difficult-escape* condition), participants were told that they had to stay in the experiment and watch Elaine receiving shocks if they did not volunteer to take her place. In the other condition (the *easy-escape* condition), they were told that they could leave if they did not volunteer.

The result suggests that in the similar-victim condition, when empathy was assumed to be activated, ease of escape did not reduce the likelihood of the participant helping Elaine. This contradicts the hypothesis that participants are motivated to reduce their own distress (the aversive-arousal reduction hypothesis), and supports the hypothesis that participants are motivated to increase Elaine's well-being (the empathy–altruism hypothesis). Ease of escape did reduce the likelihood of participants helping Elaine in the dissimilar-victim condition, which can be explained by the fact that participants in this condition had little altruistic motivation to help Elaine; they only had the egoistic motivation to get out of a rather uncomfortable experiment.

One might think that this result is conclusive evidence against the aversive-arousal reduction hypothesis. But this is too hasty. To see why, consider the following famous story about Abraham Lincoln:

Mr Lincoln once remarked to a fellow-passenger on an old-time mud-coach that all men were prompted by selfishness in doing good. His fellow-passenger was antagonizing this position when they were passing over a corduroy bridge that spanned a slough. As they crossed this bridge they espied an old razor-backed sow on the bank making a terrible noise because her pigs had got into the slough and were in danger of drowning. As the old coach began to climb the hill, Mr Lincoln called out, 'Driver, can't you stop just a moment?' Then Mr Lincoln jumped out, ran back and lifted the little pigs out of the mud and water and placed them on the bank. When he returned, his companion remarked: 'Now Abe, where does selfishness come in on this little episode?' 'Why, bless your soul, Ed, that was the very essence of selfishness. I should have had no peace of mind all day had I gone on and left that suffering old sow worrying over those pigs. I did it to get peace of mind, don't you see?' (Sharp 1928, 74–75)

Lincoln explained his own helping behaviour in terms of a form of the aversive-arousal reduction hypothesis when he said 'I should have no peace of mind all day had I gone on and left that suffering old sow worrying over those pigs.' Lincoln did not escape from the scene, according to his own account, not because he really cared about the well-being of the pigs but because a physical escape would not bring a psychological escape or 'peace of mind' for as long as he remembered the pigs in trouble. The same explanation is available when interpreting the results of the Elaine experiment. It is possible that, just like Lincoln, participants in the Elaine experiment did not escape not because they really cared about Elaine's well-being, but because they believed that a physical escape would not bring a psychological escape for as long as they remembered the experiment. Thus, the aversive-arousal reduction hypothesis has not been ruled out yet. It is still possible that the studies by Batson and colleagues can be explained by the aversive-arousal reduction hypothesis together with the idea that people believe that physical escape does not imply psychological escape.

There are, however, some worries about Lincoln's aversive-arousal reduction account of his own behaviour. This account predicts that if Lincoln had believed that he would have forgotten about the pigs in trouble relatively soon after seeing them, then he wouldn't have helped the pigs. But this prediction might not be true, as a relevant study suggests (e.g., Stocks, Lishner, & Decker 2009). Another worry is that there is something strange about Lincoln's explanation of his own behaviour. If Lincoln is a purely egoistic person who only cares about his own well-being, then why can't he achieve peace of mind without helping the pigs? It is likely that Lincoln could not achieve peace of mind without helping the pigs because he is not a purely egoistic person despite his self-diagnosis to the contrary. Indeed, Lincoln's insistence that he would be in persistent psychological distress about the pigs if he did not intervene does not make much sense without him having some altruistic concern for the well-being of the pigs.

So, it would be fair to (tentatively) say that the empathy–altruism hypothesis has some empirical plausibility. This does not, of course, mean that this hypothesis is true. There are many other egoistic hypotheses that have not been ruled out yet. One such hypothesis is that, when a participant empathizes with Elaine, she does not think of herself and Elaine as two distinctive individuals. Empathy merges the participant and Elaine together psychologically. Thus, the participant helping Elaine is not an altruistic act of helping somebody else; it is rather an egoistic act of helping herself, where 'herself' refers to the participant–Elaine hybrid ('self–other merging'; see Batson 2018).

There is a structural problem here that prevents the empathy–altruism hypothesis from being conclusively supported. Batson calls it 'the open-set problem': 'There always may be possibilities other than those we've considered. Although clear contrary evidence can rule out an explanation, supportive evidence is necessarily tentative' (Batson 2018, 143). The open-set problem is a real challenge for defenders of the empathy–altruism hypothesis, but it is fair to say that the studies by Batson and colleagues provide impressive empirical support for the hypothesis.

5.4   The Empathy–Benefit Hypothesis

Empathy and Its Consequences

Let us now move on to the empathy–benefit hypothesis, according to which empathy-induced behaviour has morally desirable consequences.

The former US president Barack Obama is a serious advocate of the political and moral importance of empathy:

> There's a lot of talk in this country about the federal deficit. But I think we should talk more about our empathy deficit – the ability to put ourselves in someone else's shoes; to see the world through those who

are different from us – the child who's hungry, the laid-off steelworker, the immigrant woman cleaning your dorm room. (Obama 2006)

Obama complains about the 'empathy deficit', which he takes to be the source of many political, social, and moral problems in the United States and around the world. Behind Obama's call for more empathy is the assumption that empathy strongly motivates people to behave in morally and socially beneficial ways. This assumption is, in effect, the empathy–benefit hypothesis.

Does empathy-induced behaviour really have morally and socially beneficial consequences? Just like the evaluation of the empathy–altruism hypothesis, the evaluation of the empathy–benefit hypothesis requires philosophical and psychological investigation. Philosophical investigation involves clarifying key concepts in the hypothesis, while psychological investigation involves evaluating the empirical evidence for the hypothesis.

Let us start with the philosophical task. The crucial philosophical question is about the interpretation of the phrase 'morally and socially beneficial consequences'. 'Morally and socially beneficial consequences' is a tricky phrase and it is open to different interpretations that correspond to different theories of morality. To simplify the issue, we will adopt a simplistic utilitarian interpretation of the phrase: 'having beneficial consequences' means 'achieving the greatest happiness for the greatest number', or 'maximizing happiness' for short. Thus, to say that empathy-induced behaviour has morally and socially beneficial consequences is to say that empathy-induced behaviour maximizes happiness. This is nothing but a stipulative interpretation for the sake of simplicity, but philosophical complications on this topic will be largely irrelevant to the main issue of our discussion below.

Thus, the empathy–benefit hypothesis can be understood as the claim that empathy-induced behaviour is happiness-maximizing. This claim is open to different interpretations depending on the different degrees of the strength of the claim. For example, a strong version of this claim is that empathy-induced behaviour is *always* happiness-maximizing. A weaker version is that empathy-induced behaviour *tends to* be happiness-maximizing.

We will now move on to the psychological task. One might think that the studies by Batson and colleagues support not only the empathy–altruism hypothesis but also the empathy–benefit hypothesis. In the Katie Banks experiment, for example, most participants in the relaxation side-effect/imagine-her condition offered help to Katie, which brought with it the morally beneficial consequence of decreasing her suffering (or, more precisely, it would have brought about the morally beneficial consequence if Katie had been a real person). In the Elaine experiment, again, many participants in the similar-victim condition offered help to Elaine, which brought with it the morally beneficial consequence of decreasing her suffering (or, more precisely, it would have brought about the morally beneficial consequence if Elaine had been a real person).

In fact, it is tempting to think that if the empathy–altruism hypothesis is correct, which we tentatively argued in Section 5.3, then it is likely that the empathy–benefit hypothesis is correct too. The thought is that altruistically motivated behaviour is likely to have morally beneficial consequences. Altruistic behaviour is motivated by the goal of increasing someone else's welfare. Such behaviour tends to increase someone else's welfare as a matter of fact, which is a morally desirable consequence.

But this is too hasty. It is a realistic possibility that altruistically motivated behaviour does not have morally beneficial consequences. Think about a different version of the Katie Banks experiment: Katie is suffering but helping her is morally questionable; one can instead help someone else who obviously needs, or deserves, help more than Katie. Helping Katie brings a morally questionable (rather than a morally desirable) consequence. An experiment by Batson and colleagues (1995) actually put participants in a situation of this kind. Participants were told about Sheri Summers, a (fictional) 10-year-old girl who was suffering from a slowly progressing and paralysing disease. Participants who empathized with Sheri helped her by recommending her for immediate treatment ahead of other children who either had a more severe illness than Sheri or had been waiting longer than her.

Note that problems of this kind have a common pattern or structure: the person who attracts our empathic attention is not the person who really deserves the help or who is in the greatest need. Sheri, who attracts our empathic attention, is not the person who really deserved the help (other children had been waiting longer) or who was in the greatest need (other children had more serious conditions). The greatest challenge to the empathy–benefit hypothesis comes from the observation that, due to the morally problematic biases associated with empathy, this kind of mismatch between the person who attracts empathic attention and the person who really ought to be helped is fairly systematic rather than accidental.

Empathy and Its Biases

Both David Hume and Adam Smith point out that empathy (or, strictly speaking, 'sympathy' in their terminology) is subject to morally problematic biases. In particular, they argue that empathy is vulnerable to 'the near-and-dear bias': empathizing with someone who is physically or psychologically close is relatively easy, while empathizing with someone who is not is relatively difficult. For example, Hume says that '[w]e sympathise more with persons contiguous to us, than with persons remote from us: With our acquaintance, than with strangers: With our countrymen, than with foreigners' (Hume 1739/2007, 371). Smith describes a similar issue in vivid detail:

> Let us suppose that the great empire of China, with all its myriads of inhabitants, was suddenly swallowed up by an earthquake, and let us consider how a man of humanity in Europe, who had no sort of connection with that part of the world, would be affected upon receiving intelligence of this dreadful calamity. He would, I imagine, first of all, express very strongly his sorrow for the misfortune of that unhappy people, he would make many melancholy reflections upon the precariousness of human life, and the vanity of all the labours of man, which could thus be annihilated in a moment. [...] And when all this fine philosophy was over, when all these humane sentiments had been once fairly expressed, he would pursue his business or his pleasure, take his repose or his diversion, with the same ease and tranquillity, as if no such accident had happened. (Smith 1759/1976, 136)

The near-and-dear bias poses a serious problem for the empathy–benefit hypothesis. Suppose that you are British and you have some money that you would like to donate. You have a choice: you can donate to a community in Britain to help people who are (mildly) affected by a recent flood, or you can donate to a community in China to help people who are (severely) affected by a catastrophic earthquake. The problem is that, because of the near-and-dear bias, empathy is likely to cause you to choose the first option, which fails to maximize happiness. Thus, it is false that empathy-induced behaviour always maximizes happiness (the strong version of the empathy–benefit hypothesis). Assuming that the near-and-dear bias is systematic rather than accidental, it is also unlikely that empathy-induced behaviour tends to maximize happiness (the weak version of the empathy–benefit hypothesis).

The near-and-dear bias is not the only problem. Empathy is likely to be vulnerable to other biases too. Another example would be 'the identifiable victim bias', which is nicely summarized in the following passage from Thomas Schelling:

> There is a distinction between individual life and statistical life. Let a six-year-old girl with brown hair need thousands of dollars for an operation that will prolong her life until Christmas, and the post office will be swamped with nickels and dimes to save her. But let it be reported that without a sales tax the hospital facilities of Massachusetts will deteriorate and cause a barely perceptible increase in preventable deaths – not many will drop a tear or reach for their check books. John Donne was partly right: the bell tolls for thee, usually, if thou didst send to know for whom it tolls, but most of us get used to the noise and go on about our business. (Schelling 1984, 115)

Schelling suggests that people have the bias of being much more responsive or sensitive to individual (or identified) lives and their losses than to merely statistical lives and their losses. As he points out, this bias seems to have affective or emotional aspects: '[t]o evaluate an individual death requires attention to special feelings', while 'a marginal change in mortality statistics is unlikely to evoke these feelings' (Schelling 1984, 116). Perhaps empathy is vulnerable to this bias: it is easy to empathize with individual (or identified) people, such as the six-year-old girl with a terminal illness, while it is difficult, and perhaps impossible, to empathize with merely statistical people, such as the unidentified future victims of healthcare deterioration in Massachusetts.

The identifiable victim bias poses another problem for the empathy–benefit hypothesis. Suppose that you have a choice: you can donate money to a girl so that she can enjoy her last Christmas, or you can donate money to hospitals in Massachusetts to prevent healthcare deterioration. The problem is that, due to the identifiable victim bias, empathy might cause you to choose the first option, which is unlikely to maximize happiness. Thus, again, it is false that empathy-induced behaviour always maximizes happiness (the strong version of the empathy–benefit hypothesis). Assuming that the identifiable victim bias is systematic rather than accidental, it is also unlikely that empathy-induced behaviour tends to maximize happiness (the weak version of the empathy–benefit hypothesis).

The idea that empathy is particularly vulnerable to morally problematic biases, such as the near-and-dear bias or the identifiable victim bias, has been supported by philosophers and psychologists in recent years. For example, Batson identified some potentially harmful consequences of empathy:

> [Empathy] can be harmful to those in need when acted on without wisdom and sensitivity, or when a cool head is required. It can produce paternalism. It's less likely to be evoked by nonpersonalized, abstract, and chronic needs. It can be a source of immoral action, leading us to show partiality toward those for whom we care even when we know that to do so is neither fair nor best for all. Indeed, when our behavior is public, empathy-induced altruism can pose a more serious threat to the common good than does self-interest. Finally, it can jeopardize our mental and physical health – even our life. (Batson 2018, 250)

Other authors, such as Prinz and Bloom, have expressed even more pessimistic views.

> [E]mpathy is easily manipulated, leading us to give preferential treatment to those who don't deserve it. [...] [E]mpathy is biased: it increases when those in need are salient, similar to ourselves, and close by. We contribute more to a neighbor in need than to the thousands ravaged by a distant tsunami or the millions who die from starvation or disease. Indeed, we often feel greater empathy for cute critters, such as abandoned puppies, than for struggling people. In making policy, we would be better off ignoring empathy. The crucial question is not whose suffering touches us most but who needs us most. (Prinz 2014)

> Empathy is a spotlight focusing on certain people in the here and now. This makes us care more about them, but it leaves us insensitive to the long-term consequences of our acts and blind as well to the suffering of those we do not or cannot empathize with. Empathy is biased, pushing us in the direction of parochialism and racism. It is shortsighted, motivating actions that might make things better in the short term but lead to tragic results in the future. It is innumerate, favoring one over the many. It can spark violence; our empathy for those close to us is a powerful force for war and atrocity toward others. It is corrosive in personal relationships; it exhausts the spirit and can diminish the force of kindness and love. (Bloom 2016, 9)

5.5   Responding to the Challenge

Revising the Hypothesis

Our discussion so far suggests that the empathy–benefit hypothesis is unlikely to be true; empathy is subject to morally problematic biases and empathy-induced behaviour systematically fails to maximize happiness. We will now consider potential responses to the problem. There are roughly two kinds of responses: revising the empathy–benefit hypothesis and biting the bullet. In the revising option, we revise the empathy–benefit hypothesis in one way or another without abandoning the basic idea that empathy can be morally beneficial. In the biting-the-bullet option, we do not revise the hypothesis and insist that empathy-induced behaviour has morally beneficial consequences.

Revising Response 1 (Correcting Empathy)

One option is to revise the empathy–benefit hypothesis such that empathy, *when corrected in one way or another*, has morally beneficial responses.

The idea of correcting empathy can be found in Hume and Smith, who did not only identify the biased nature of empathy but also explored solutions to the problem. They have similar but slightly different ideas about how to correct the near-and-dear bias. Hume proposes that the near-and-dear bias can be corrected by taking the 'general point of view', which amounts to taking the point of view of the 'narrow circle' to which a person belongs. For example, a British person might have difficulty empathizing with a suffering person in China, but they can overcome the difficulty by taking the point of view of the person's 'narrow circle' of friends and associates in China.

> Our servant, if diligent and faithful, may excite stronger sentiments of love and kindness than Marcus Brutus, as represented in history; but we say not upon that account, that the former character is more laudable than the latter. We know, that were we to approach equally near to that renown'd patriot, he wou'd command a much higher degree of affection and admiration. (Hume 1739/2007, 372)

However, Hume's proposal does not seem to be a satisfactory response. In particular, taking the point of view of the narrow circle might result in replacing one bias with another. For example, one might success-fully correct the near-and-dear bias in favour of British people by taking the point of view of a Chinese narrow circle, but in doing so one might acquire another near-and-dear bias in favour of Chinese people. Of course, this new bias will result in maximizing happiness when, say, the happiness-maximizing option is donating money to the Chinese community. But this is simply a lucky case in which the bias happens to result in maximizing happiness. The bias does not result in maximizing happiness in other cases in which donating money to the Chinese community is not the happiness-maximizing option (e.g., the community in Britain that is suffering more than the community in China). Thus taking the point of view of a narrow circle does not lead to the happiness-maximizing behaviour *systematically*.

Let us move on to Smith's proposal. Smith's proposal is somewhat similar to, but still importantly different from, Hume's proposal. Smith's idea is that the near-and-dear bias can be corrected by taking 'the impartial spectator's point of view', which roughly amounts to taking a disinterested third-party point of view. For example, one might overcome one's difficulty empathizing with a suffering person in China by taking a disinterested third-party point of view, which is different from a British point of view or a Chinese point of view. Smith wrote:

> Before we can make any proper comparison of those opposite interests [between 'us' and 'them'], we must change our position. We must view them, neither from our own place nor yet from his, neither with our own eyes nor yet with his, but from the place and with the eyes of a third person, who has no particular connexion with either, and who judges with impartiality between us. (Smith 1759/1976, 135)

Unlike Hume's proposal, Smith's proposal seems to be free from the problem of 'replacing one bias with another'. The impartial specta-tor's point of view is a disinterested third-party point of view that is free from the near-and-dear bias in favour of any relevant parties. The problem, however, is that taking the impartial spectator's point of view might *destroy*, rather than *correct*, the motivating function of empathy. For example, when you take a disinterested third-party point of view, you might not be biased in favour of any party, but at the same time you might not be strongly motivated to help any party either. By holding the disinterested third-party point of view, perhaps you are not strongly motivated to help either British people or Chinese people. To occupy the impartial spectator's point of view is to occupy the point of view of people who are not strongly motivated to help British people or Chinese people. This result is morally worse than the original case with the near-and-dear bias in favour of British people; at least in the original case the outcome is that British people receive help.

Revising Response 2 *(Full Empathy)*

Another option is to revise the empathy–benefit hypothesis such that empathy, *when cultivated or developed into full or real empathy*, has morally beneficial consequences.

Michael Slote expressed an idea of this kind: '[A] full development of the natural human capacity for empathic concern for others might well include strong empathic concern for groups of people one didn't individually know, and even for humanity as a whole' (Slote 2007, 30).

This is certainly an intriguing option, but some worries remain. For example, even if it is true that some problematic features of empathy can be modified by developing full empathy, there should be some intrinsic limits with regard to what can be modified. Maybe the near-and-dear bias can be removed or at least weakened by cultivating one's capacity to be fully empathic. But empathizing with unidentified future victims might be beyond an intrinsic limit of empathy and no amount of development or cultivation might be able to modify empathy to that extent.

Consider the famous claim, often attributed to Stalin, that the death of one person is a tragedy, while the death of millions of people is only statistical. The death of one victim easily triggers empathic attention, while the death of millions of victims does not. This does not seem to be a contingent and revisable feature of empathy; empathizing with millions of victims is likely to be beyond the intrinsic limit of empathy.

Against this, one might agree that there are some intrinsic limits that cannot be overcome by traditional methods of developing or cultivating one's empathic capacities, such as traditional training, education, meditation, and so on, but one might still insist that these limits can be overcome, at least in principle, by non-traditional interventions, such as biomedical moral enhancement (Persson & Savulescu 2012) (i.e., enhancing moral capacity with the help of biomedical technology). For instance, our empathic capacities might be enhanced by prescribing oxytocin, a peptide hormone which has been associated with maternal care, pair bonding, and other prosocial attitudes (Insel & Fernald 2004).

But this proposal faces some problems too. Even biomedical moral enhancement might not overcome the intrinsic limits of empathy (setting aside the issue of the feasibility of moral enhancement in general). For instance, some studies suggest that prescribing oxytocin enhances prosocial and altruistic behaviour (de Dreu et al. 2011), but it only enhances prosocial and altruistic behaviour towards in-group members. In other words, oxytocin does make people more prosocial and altruistic, but it does not modify the bias in favour of in-group members and against out-group members. Back to our example, with oxytocin, British people might be strongly motivated to help British people (mildly) affected by a flood but not Chinese people (severely) affected by a devastating earthquake.

There can of course be other radical biomedical methods of enhancement, such as brain surgery or gene modification, which are free from problems of this kind. However, even these methods face problems: if we overcome the intrinsic limits of empathy with the help of some radical biomedical technology, the resulting mental state might not be empathy anymore; it might be something else. If, for example, you can 'empathize' with millions of people at once after some radical form of biomedical enhancement, perhaps your mental state is not really empathy any more. It is probably a mental state that normal, non-enhanced humans are not capable of. In short, even with radical biomedical enhancement, it is not clear that empathy, rather than some new capacity, has morally beneficial consequences.

Biting the Bullet

Biting the Bullet Response 1 (Maximizing Local Happiness)
Let us move on to the third response, which involves the biting-the-bullet strategy. To bite the bullet here is to admit that empathy is vulnerable to biases, but still insist that the empathy–benefit hypothesis is correct.

A biting-the-bullet strategy is inspired by the following passage by John Stuart Mill:

[I]t is a misapprehension of the utilitarian mode of thought, to conceive it as implying that people should fix their minds upon so wide a generality as the world, or society at large. The great majority of good actions are intended not for the benefit of the world, but for that of individuals, of which the good of the world is made up; and the thoughts of the most virtuous man need not on these occasions travel beyond the particular persons concerned, except so far as is necessary to assure himself that in benefiting them he is not violating the rights, that is, the legitimate and authorised expectations, of anyone else. (Mill 1861/1991, 132)

Mill says that utilitarianism does not recommend the idea of aiming to maximize happiness in the world as a whole; it rather recommends the idea of aiming to maximize the happiness of some particular people around us. The reason for this is that ordinary citizens, as opposed to politicians or billionaires, do not have the capacity to make a significant difference to people's lives in the world as a whole. The best utilitarian contribution we can make is to maximize the happiness of some particular people around us.

From this perspective, then, perhaps the alleged problematic features of empathy are not so problematic. For example, we have difficulty empathizing with people who are not near and dear to us. But perhaps this makes some utilitarian sense: my helping will make a crucial difference to the lives of people who are near and dear to me, but it might not make the same degree of difference to the lives of people who are not. They are not 'near' to us, so helping them might not be very effective due to the physical distance. They are not 'dear' to us, so we do not know much about them, and we do not know what is best for them.

This response raises some interesting points, but it does not solve the problem completely. Mill's claim might have been plausible in the 19th century, when, for example, an ordinary British citizen did not have much power to change the lives of people in China. However, his claim is less plausible in the 21st century. The best thing Mill could have done with his spare money was to use it to help people in the local community. Sending the money to China to alleviate the suffering of earthquake victims was practically impossible due to technological and organizational limitations. But the current world is very different; it is not difficult to make a significant difference to the lives of earthquake victims in China, thanks to the internet, technology, and networks of charity organizations. All it takes is to visit the website of a charity and typing in your credit card number.

Biting the Bullet Response 2 (Partial Obligation)

Here is another biting-the-bullet strategy. The near-and-dear bias might not be as problematic as it first seems. For example, the nearest and dearest people to you are your family members and close friends. But is it really morally problematic for you to be more empathic to your family and close friends than to other people? If a father is especially empathic to his children, isn't he a good father? If a woman is especially empathic to her close friends, isn't she a good friend?

Even Bloom, who emphasizes the harmful consequences of empathy, admits that the role of empathy can be more beneficial in intimate relationships:

> [A]ll the factors that make empathy so problematic in the policy domain, such as how biased it is, might not be problems when things get more personal. In fact they may be advantages. [...] Most of us, I presume, wish to be special in the eyes of those we love and who love us. For that, the spotlight nature of empathy seems just the ticket. (Bloom 2016, 130)

According to Michael Slote, empathy is certainly partial (e.g., subject to the near-and-dear bias) but its partiality corresponds to the partiality of morality itself. The partiality of empathy is not morally problematic; it reflects an important fact about moral obligations: we have stronger moral obligations to the people who are near and dear to us, such as our family members or close friends.

> [E]mpathy also helps account for the greater concern we feel for the welfare of people who are near and dear to us. And here, once again, the difference between our empathic reactions vis-à-vis problems for those we know or are related to and our reactions vis-à-vis problems for people we don't personally know (well) corresponds pretty well to common moral opinion. We think of our moral obligations to (help) near and dear as stronger than our obligations to (help) strangers, mere acquaintances, and unknown others. (Slote 2010, 24)

This biting-the-bullet strategy is certainly attractive as long as we are considering the biases in favour of family members or close friends. There is something to the idea that family or friends are morally relevant social categories – they make a moral difference.

A problem, however, is that empathy would be influenced not only by social categories (such as family or friends) that may be morally relevant, but also by social categories (such as race) that may not be morally relevant. Can we bite the bullet and say that people of a particular race have stronger moral obligations to help people of the same race than to help people of other races?

Even if the biting-the-bullet strategy were a promising response to the problem of the near-and-dear bias, it could not deal effectively with other problems, such as the one of the identifiable victim bias. For example, we cannot bite the bullet and say that we have stronger moral obligations to Sheri Summers than to other children who either have a more severe illness than her or have been waiting longer than her. Again, we cannot bite the bullet and say that we have stronger moral obligations to the six-year-old girl with a terminal illness than to the unidentified future victims of healthcare deterioration in Massachusetts.

5.6 Is Empathy Particularly Problematic?

Our discussion so far has suggested that the empathy–benefit hypothesis is unlikely to be true. Empathy-induced behaviour systematically deviates from happiness-maximizing action. Still, it might not be fair to blame empathy for failing to have morally beneficial consequences because failing to have morally beneficial consequences may well be a general problem rather than a problem for empathy in particular.

Are there any other mental states that are morally better than empathy? One might think that there are other emotional states that are morally superior to empathy. For example, Prinz argues that anger is morally superior:

> Righteous rage is a cornerstone of women's liberation, civil rights, and battles against tyranny. It also outperforms empathy in crucial ways: anger is highly motivating, difficult to manipulate, applicable wherever injustice is found, and easier to insulate against bias. We fight for those who have been mistreated not because they are like us, but because we are passionate about principles. (Prinz 2014)

Prinz is correct that anger can be a source of motivation for moral and political advancements, but sometimes empathy can do the same. Empathy for victims of social injustice can be a source of motivation for moral and political advancements. The problem with empathy is that, even though it can have positive moral and political consequences in some cases, it might have an overall negative moral and political impact. Is anger better than empathy on this issue? Probably not. Just like empathy, anger is vulnerable to the near-and-dear bias: we get angrier at injustices suffered by near-and-dear victims than injustices suffered by other victims. Anger might also be vulnerable to the identifiable victim effect: we get angrier at injustices suffered by identifiable victims than injustices suffered by unidentified and merely statistical victims.

What about appealing to reason instead of empathy, anger, or any other emotional state? Reason, not emotion, could be our best guide to morally beneficial consequences. As Bloom points out:

> Reason [...] at its best can lead to moral insight. It is reason that leads us to recognize, despite what our feelings tell us, that a child in a faraway land matters as much as our neighbor's child, that it's a tragedy if an immunization leads to a child getting sick or if a furlough program leads to rape and assault – but if these programs nonetheless lead to an overall improvement in human welfare, we should keep them until something better comes along. (Bloom 2016, 51)

Appealing to reason is a very attractive option. Against the near-and-dear bias, reason tells us that the life of an earthquake victim in China is just as important as the life of a flood victim in Britain. Against the identifiable victim bias, reason tells us that the life of an identifiable victim is just as important as the life of an unidentified victim. The problem with appealing to reason, however, is that it is far from obvious that reason is sufficiently motivating. Certainly, reason might tell you that the value of the life of an earthquake victim in China is the same as the value of the life of a flood victim in Britain, and that the life of an identifiable victim is just as important as the life of an unidentified victim. But it is far from obvious that these thoughts would strongly motivate you to help earthquake victims in China or to do something for unidentified victims.

Bloom writes of Zell Kravinsky, who donated his kidney to a total stranger on the basis of the mathematical calculation of expected utility, that he 'said that people find this [donating a kidney to a total stranger] unusual only because "they don't understand math." But this isn't quite right – the real problem is that often people don't care about math' (Bloom 2016, 102). So, according to Bloom's analysis, what is peculiar about Kravinsky is not that he is especially smart or that he can do a mathematical calculation that other people cannot. Other people do not follow Kravinsky because they do not care about what mathematics tells them. In other words, mathematics does not motivate them.

Both Prinz and Bloom are aware of these problems and respond to them with the same strategy, namely a hybrid strategy of combining different mental states and processes. Prinz proposes correcting the biases associated with anger by combining anger with reason. This is certainly a sensible proposal, but it does not necessarily show that anger is morally superior to empathy. After all, this sort of combination strategy should also be available to the defenders of empathy. For example, if the biases associated with anger can be corrected by combining anger with reason in some way, then why can't the biases associated with empathy also be corrected by combining empathy with reason?

Bloom proposes compensating for a lack of motivational force by combining reason with compassion, which, he claims, is psychologically and neurologically distinguished from empathy. Unlike empathy, compassion involves a person's 'desire to make his or her distress go away, without any shared experience or empathic distress' (Bloom 2017, 28). This is certainly a sensible proposal, but again it does not necessarily show that empathy is particularly problematic. For example, it is not clear why we cannot combine reason with empathy rather than with compassion.

5.7 Summary

- According to the empathy–altruism hypothesis, empathy-induced behaviour is genuinely motivated by altruism. This hypothesis is supported by experimental studies by Batson and colleagues, such as the Katie Banks experiment, which suggests that empathy motivates helping behaviour, and the Elaine experiment, which suggests that the empathy–altruism hypothesis is more plausible than the aversive-arousal reduction hypothesis.
- According to the empathy–benefit hypothesis, empathy-induced behaviour has morally beneficial consequences (such as maximizing happiness). This hypothesis is in serious doubt. It is likely that empathy-induced behaviour systematically fails to maximize happiness because of the biases it is subject to, including the bias

of preferentially empathizing with near-and-dear people, or the bias of empathizing with identifiable victims more easily than statistical victims.

Further Resources

Articles and Books

Derek Matravers' *Empathy* (2017) and Heidi Maibom's *Empathy* (2020) are both excellent introductions to the philosophical issues of empathy.

On empathy and altruism, the best place to start is Daniel Batson's *A Scientific Search for Altruism: Do We Only Care About Ourselves?* (2018), which is an accessible introduction to his study of empathy and altruistic behaviour. Batson's earlier books, *The Altruism Question: Toward a Social-Psychological Answer* (1991) and *Altruism in Humans* (2011), include a helpful survey of the field, careful arguments, and impressive empirical studies. Also see Stephen Stich, John Doris, and Erica Roedder's overview of the debate on the empathy–altruism hypothesis (2010), and Heidi Maibom's overview of the research of empathy and prosocial action (2012). *Empathy and Morality* (Oxford University Press 2014), edited by Maibom, contains useful discussions of empathy and its role for morality.

Scepticism about the moral importance of empathy has been developed in Jesse Prinz's paper (2011) as well as Paul Bloom's *Against Empathy: The Case of Rational Compassion* (2016). Ingmar Persson and Julian Savulescu (2018) defend empathy from the sceptical challenge.

Online Resources

The *Boston Review* hosted an online forum on Bloom's empathy scepticism (see Bloom 2014), with responses from Peter Singer, Leslie Jamison, Simon Baron-Cohen, Nomy Arpaly, Sam Harris, and Jesse Prinz, among others.

On YouTube you will find Paul Bloom's lecture at College of the Holy Cross (2015) as well as Molly Crockett and Jesse Prinz's debate at University of Cambridge (2015).

Questions

1. How many different senses of 'empathy' are there? How can they be distinguished from each other? How are they related to each other? Which sense of empathy is morally valuable or desirable?
2. We discussed the empathy–altruism hypothesis and the aversive-arousal reduction hypothesis about helping behaviour. What other hypotheses about helping behaviour may be plausible?
3. Can you think of real-life cases in which biased empathy causes morally problematic consequences?
4. Is it possible to reduce or eliminate biases, such as the near-and-dear bias or the identifiable victim bias? If so, how?
5. Can you think of real-life people or fictional characters in movies and books who are morally virtuous but are not empathic?

6

Free Will and Responsibility

6.1 Introduction

Free will is one of the central topics in philosophy. There are two crucial issues in the philosophical discussions of free will: what it takes to be a free and responsible agent; and whether humans are free and responsible agents. Traditionally, philosophical discussions of free will have been associated with physics. One concern is that, if our best theory of physics supports determinism, according to which all events in the universe are determined by the initial state of the universe together with laws of nature, then humans cannot act freely. Human actions are already determined and thus they are not freely chosen. Another concern is that, if our best theory of physics denies determinism and instead implies that all events in the universe arise randomly (i.e., they are not determined by preceding events), then humans cannot act freely. Human actions are random and thus they are not freely chosen. Either way, whether physics supports determinism or denies it, human agents are not free.

Our focus in this chapter is not on physics but rather on psychology and neuroscience. What do they tell us about free will and responsibility? Do psychological and neuroscientific studies advance the debate on free will? Recently, a number of philosophers, psychologists, and neuroscientists have claimed that the idea of free will is simply incompatible with the best scientific account of the human mind and brain. In other words, psychology and neuroscience entail that there is no such thing as free will. The basic idea is that they deny that you can be a free and responsible agent. Psychology reveals that an unconscious part of your mind is responsible for what you do and think, and neuroscience reveals that your brain is responsible for what you do and think. Either way, you, a conscious and psychological agent, are not responsible for your behaviour or your thoughts.

In fact, we have already touched on several considerations that motivate the sceptical stance on free will. In everyday life people uncritically and unreflectively assume that they are free agents who (at least in most cases) consciously and responsively choose and control their actions (where to go, what to do, etc.). Suppose, for example, that we ask participants of the stockings experiment by Nisbett and Wilson (1977) 'Did you freely choose that pair of stockings?' Most (if not all) participants would say 'Yes' (after all, it is exactly what they were instructed to do), and they would explain the reasons for their (free) choice, such as the pair they chose being of superior quality. The problem is that, as we have already seen, participants' explanations of their free choices are *post hoc* rationalizations: their choices were in fact determined by unconscious position effects of which they were not aware, and they simply confabulated about their choices *as if* they were the choices they freely made. Participants thought that they made a free choice based on their evaluation of the quality of the stockings, but that was not the case.

This chapter will review psychological and neuroscientific studies that are directly relevant to free will and responsibility, and it will examine their implications for the idea that humans are free and responsible agents.

Our two main questions are: (1) 'Are humans free agents?' and (2) 'If humans are free agents, how much freedom do they have?' In the end, our answers will be that psychological and neuroscientific studies (1) do not suggest that humans completely lack free will, but (2) do suggest that humans are not as free as we might think.

We begin by discussing a classification of scientific arguments against free will (Section 6.2). Our focus will be on what we call 'the argument from epiphenomenalism', which denies free agency on the grounds that our conscious mental states and processes are epiphenomenal (i.e., they are causally irrelevant to our behaviour). After, we will move on to investigate alleged psychological and neuroscientific evidence for the claim that our conscious mental states and processes are epiphenomenal (Section 6.3). The evidence comes from three distinct lines of research: (a) neuroscientific studies of the timing of decisions ('Libet-style studies'); (b) psychological studies of the influence of situational factors on human behaviour ('situationist studies'); and (c) psychological studies of the phenomenology of conscious will ('Wegner-style studies'). We will conclude that the empirical evidence currently available does not support the idea that consciousness is epiphenomenal, and thus the argument from epiphenomenalism is not empirically supported. That said, psychological and neuroscientific studies suggest that the degree to which humans are free and the scope of their free agency are both limited. Psychological and neuroscientific studies are important not because they reveal that free will is an illusion once and for all but because they teach us about the extent to which humans have free will and in what domains agency can be exercised. We will illustrate this point with a case study on responsibility for implicit biases (Section 6.4).

6.2 Varieties of Free Will Scepticism

Materialism and Determinism

Before examining the relevant empirical studies, it is important to be clear about the nature of the sceptical challenge and distinguish it from other challenges. This is particularly important in the context of the free will debate since free-will sceptics, in particular sceptical scientists, tend not to distinguish between distinct challenges, which is a potential source of confusion.

Psychological and neuroscientific arguments against free will have a common structure (Nahmias 2010):

Premise 1: *P* is true, according to psychology and/or neuroscience.
Premise 2: Free will is incompatible with the truth of *P*.
Conclusion: Therefore, we do not have free will.

We call premise 1 of each argument 'the psychological premise' (because it is primarily subject to psychological and/or neuroscientific scrutiny) and premise 2 'the philosophical premise' (because it is primarily subject to philosophical scrutiny).

The first argument goes as follows:

Argument from Materialism

Premise 1: Materialism is true, according to psychology and/or neuroscience.

Premise 2: Free will is incompatible with the truth of materialism.

Conclusion: Therefore, we do not have free will.

The psychological premise of this argument says that psychology and/or neuroscience support materialism, according to which everything in this world is material or physical and, consequently, immaterial mental substances or souls do not exist. The philosophical premise says that free will is something attributed to an immaterial soul; hence, the idea of free will is incompatible with materialism (since, according to materialism, immaterial souls do not exist). An argument of this kind has been expressed in a passage by P. Read Montague:

> Free will is the idea that we make choices and have thoughts independent of anything remotely resembling a physical process. Free will is the close cousin to the idea of the soul – the concept that 'you', your thoughts and feelings, derive from an entity that is separate and distinct from the physical mechanisms that make up your body. From this perspective, your choices are not caused by physical events, but instead emerge wholly formed from somewhere indescribable and outside the purview of physical descriptions. This implies that free will cannot have evolved by natural selection, as that would place it directly in a stream of causally connected physical events. Consequently, the idea of free will is not even in principle within reach of scientific description. (Montague 2008, R584)

Here is another argument:

Argument from Determinism

Premise 1: Determinism is true, according to psychology and/or neuroscience.

Premise 2: Free will is incompatible with the truth of determinism.

Conclusion: Therefore, we do not have free will.

The psychological premise of this argument says that psychology and/or neuroscience support determinism, according to which all events and actions have already been determined by past events together with the laws of nature. The philosophical premise comes from the 'incompatibilist' account of free will, according to which free will and determinism are incompatible with each other; hence, if determinism is true, free will is denied. An argument of this kind has been expressed by Patrick Haggard:

> [T]he law-like causal nature of brain processes seem to leave no place for freedom. In philosophy, an action is often considered free if the person could have acted otherwise. However, if the action directly results from a set of law-like events in the person's brain, as claimed by neuroscience, the person presumably could not have acted otherwise, and is therefore not free. (Haggard 2011, 220)

We will not discuss in detail the two arguments above, the one from materialism and the one from determinism. The reason is that the philosophical premise in each argument is highly controversial. Most contemporary philosophers think that free will is compatible with materialism and many ('compatibilist') philosophers think that free will is compatible with determinism. Of course, these issues are far from being settled: for example, an interesting development in recent years is the research in 'experimental philosophy' of the intuition people have of the compatibility between free will and materialism and between free will and determinism. However, discussing these will take us too far away from the main issues in this chapter.

Another reason why we will not discuss the argument from materialism and the argument from determinism is that their psychological premises are questionable. It is questionable that materialism and determinism are true *according to psychology and/or neuroscience.* After all, there are no particular psychological or scientific studies that show that materialism or determinism is true. Of course, it is conceivable, perhaps for some sociological reasons, that psychologists tend to accept materialism or that neuroscientists tend to accept determinism. But this does not mean that they justify materialism or determinism in terms of psychological or neuroscientific studies. Typically, their justification comes from their commitment to physics and not to psychology or neuroscience.

Epiphenomenalism

We will focus on the following argument:

Argument from Epiphenomenalism
Premise 1: Epiphenomenalism is true, according to psychology and/or neuroscience.

Premise 2: Free will is incompatible with the truth of epiphenomenalism.
Conclusion: Therefore, we do not have free will.

The psychological premise of this argument says that psychology and/or neuroscience support epiphenomenalism, according to which conscious mental states and processes (e.g., a conscious decision to do something, a conscious thought about what to do, a conscious deliberation about what is to be done, etc.) do not play a significant causal role in producing behaviour. The philosophical premise says that if conscious states and processes have nothing to do with how people behave, and if all people's behaviour is determined by unconscious psychological or neural processes in the brain, then there is no interesting sense in which people as conscious agents are free.

The philosophical premise sounds plausible. If people's behaviour is determined by unconscious psychological or neural processes in the brain – which bypass their conscious decisions, conscious thoughts, conscious deliberations, etc. – then it is difficult to see how they can be regarded as having free will or being responsible for their behaviour.

Our focus will be on the psychological premise, according to which epiphenomenalism is strongly supported by psychology and/ or neuroscience. There are roughly two possible kinds of epiphenomenalism: *metaphysical* and *scientific*.

Metaphysical epiphenomenalism says that conscious states are epiphenomenal because the neural correlates of consciousness (i.e., neural states and processes that are correlated with conscious states and processes) play all relevant causal roles in producing action. Hence, metaphysically speaking, there is no causal role left for conscious states and processes. For example, when you consciously decide to raise your right hand, the neural correlate of the conscious decision plays all the causal roles in initiating the physiological processes resulting in you raising your right hand. There is no causal role left for your conscious decision itself. Thus, your conscious decision is epiphenomenal. We call this 'metaphysical epiphenomenalism' because it relies on the metaphysical principle that neural correlates of consciousness *exclude* consciousness from being causally relevant ('the principle of causal exclusion' as in Kim 2005). Metaphysical epiphenomenalism is of interest not only to philosophers but also to neuroscientists. For instance, Haggard seems to be committed to metaphysical epiphenomenalism or something similar in the following passage:

[T]he material nature of the brain seems to leave no room for conscious decision. The standard everyday concept of free will suggests that people consciously choose a particular action, and then consciously cause the action by an act of conscious will. Neuroscience, however, rejects the idea of person-level, brain-independent consciousness. Therefore, if conscious thought is conceived as brain-independent, it cannot cause actions or any other neural or physical event. (Haggard 2011, 220)

We will not address metaphysical epiphenomenalism. Instead, we will focus on what we call 'scientific epiphenomenalism'. Scientific epiphenomenalism appeals to some empirical findings in psychology and neuroscience to show that conscious decisions, conscious thoughts, conscious deliberations, and so on, have no role to play in determining behaviour. Scientific epiphenomenalism does not appeal to the causal exclusion principle or other metaphysical principles. It says that consciousness is epiphenomenal not because the relevant causal role is played by neural correlates but because (according to psychological and neuroscientific findings) neither conscious states nor their neural correlates play a relevant causal role. Hereafter, 'epiphenomenalism' means 'scientific epiphenomenalism'.

The next section will introduce some relevant empirical studies and examine whether they genuinely support epiphenomenalism. Before examining these studies, let us be clearer about what the empirical studies need to show in order to support epiphenomenalism.

If epiphenomenalism supports scepticism about free will, then it has to imply that conscious mental states either have no causal role to play whatsoever or play a negligible role. To support such a strong claim, we need some relevant evidence that rules out any significant causal role for conscious mental states. We call this 'the causal irrelevance condition'.

Again, if epiphenomenalism supports scepticism about free will, then it has to be a general claim about all forms of human behaviour rather than a local claim about some forms of human behaviour. To support such a general claim, we need relevant evidence that can be generalized to all forms of behaviour. We call this 'the generalizability condition' for evidence of epiphenomenalism.

Our question is whether there are any psychological or neuroscientific studies concerning epiphenomenalism that satisfy both the causal irrelevance condition and the generalizability condition. This will be the topic of the next section.

6.3 Empirical Evidence for Epiphenomenalism?

Libet-Style Studies

We will now examine three sets of empirical studies: Libet-style studies of the timing of decisions; situationist studies of the influence of situational factors on human behaviour; and Wegner-style studies of the experience of conscious will.

Let us begin with Libet-style studies. We call these 'Libet-style studies' because they follow an experimental paradigm set by Benjamin Libet (1985, 2004; Libet et al. 1983). Although they are different in their approach, they collectively support the common idea that preparatory brain activities precede conscious decisions or conscious choices. These studies can be taken to show that a decision is already made unconsciously in the brain, and there is no causal role left for conscious decision (which only comes after). Thus, according to Haggard:

> Libet's result seems to raise profound problems for the concept of human voluntary action by which we live our everyday lives. In particular, if 'I' do not cause my actions by my conscious decisions and intentions, but rather my actions are determined by unconscious brain processes, how can I be held responsible for what I do? (Haggard 2011, 221)

The Libet Experiment

The pioneering experiment by Libet (1985, 2004; Libet et al. 1983) examined the time when a person forms the conscious intention to perform a simple motor act as well as the time when the person's brain exhibits preparatory activities. The task was simple: participants performed a sudden flick of their wrist whenever they wanted. The timing of preparatory brain activities was measured by the so-called 'readiness potential', an electrical charge recordable on the scalp at the vertex. The timing of conscious intention was estimated on the basis of self-report: participants observed a fast-moving clock on a screen, and reported when they first became aware of their conscious intention to act. The result suggests that readiness potential (roughly 550 milliseconds before the act) was reliably observed before the reported conscious intention (roughly 200 milliseconds before the act). This result seems to suggest that conscious intention comes too late to initiate the chain of behavioural processes. Libet summarizes his findings as follows:

> Onsets of RPs [readiness potentials] regularly begin at least several hundred ms before reported times for awareness of any intention to act in the case of acts performed ad lib. It would appear, therefore, that some neuronal activity associated with the eventual performance of the act has started well before any (recallable) conscious initiation or intervention is possible. This leads to the conclusion that cerebral initiation even of a spontaneous voluntary act of the land studied here can and usually does begin unconsciously. [...] Put another way, the brain 'decides' to initiate or, at least, to prepare to initiate the act before there is any reportable subjective awareness that such a decision has taken place. (Libet 1985, 536)

More recent studies using the Libet paradigm report more impressive results. An experiment by Chun Siong Soon and colleagues (2008) makes progress on three counts. First, the original Libet study uses non-invasive EEG recording, which provides indirect and weak signals of brain activities. In contrast, Soon and colleagues obtain more informative data of brain activities using fMRI. Second, the original Libet study reveals preparatory brain activities that occur 550 milliseconds before the act. In contrast, Soon and colleagues reveal preparatory brain activities 10 seconds before the act. Third, the original Libet study reveals brain activities that are temporarily prior to conscious intentions. Soon and colleagues, in contrast, reveal brain activities that not only are temporarily prior to a conscious intention to act but also statistically predict how participants act.

Do these studies successfully establish epiphenomenalism? Do they threaten free will? Let us carefully examine Libet-style studies in terms of the causal irrelevance condition and the generalizability condition, beginning with the former.

Interestingly, Libet himself does not think that his experimental result satisfies the causal irrelevance condition. He argues that although conscious states occur too late to initiate a physiological process, which seems to be the implication of his study, they are still able to veto or intervene in the process.

> The role of conscious free will would be, then, not to initiate a voluntary act, but rather to control whether the act takes place. We may view the unconscious initiatives for voluntary actions as 'bubbling up' in the brain. The conscious-will then selects which of

these initiatives may go forward to an action or which ones to veto and abort, with no act appearing. (Libet 1999, 54)

Libet's idea reminds us of the default-intervention model in the dual-process theory (see Chapter 3 and Chapter 4): Type-1 processes make the default judgment and Type-2 processes often let that judgment go unchallenged. When necessary, however, Type-2 processes can veto or intervene in that judgment. Similarly, according to Libet, unconscious processes in the brain make the default decision, and conscious processes often let that decision go unchallenged. When necessary, however, conscious processes can veto or intervene in that decision.

However, Libet's view is not very popular, and other neuroscientists tend to dismiss his proposal about vetoing. They tend to accept something analogous to the lawyer–client model according to which the job of conscious processes is not to veto or intervene in unconscious decisions but only to confabulate about them in a *post hoc* manner, just like in the case of the stockings experiment.

But even setting aside the idea of vetoing, there are other problems concerning the causal irrelevance condition. Libet-style studies show that preparatory brain activities precede conscious decisions, but this does not necessarily entail that conscious states play no significant role. For example, perhaps conscious decisions do play a significant causal role but preparatory brain activities are among the causes of conscious decisions. Note that it is not surprising at all that conscious decisions have unconscious or physical causes. After all, conscious decisions have some causes, and these causes have further causes, and so on. And when we trace back these chains of causes, we will inevitably find some causal *relata* that are unconscious or physical.

Similarly, as Alfred Mele (2008) has suggested, preparatory brain activities can be understood as an inclination or an urge to do something. An inclination or urge can influence, but not determine, behaviour. Determining behaviour is the job of conscious decision. This interpretation is consistent with the finding that preparatory brain activities do predict behaviour (inclinations or urges do *predict* one's behaviour), but the correlation is far from perfect (inclinations or urges do not *determine* one's behaviour).

Let us move on to the generalizability condition. Libet's study involves a simple and rather trivial kind of action where there is no reason to prefer one option over the other (i.e., flicking one's wrist whenever one likes). All options are basically equivalent (e.g., there is no significant difference between flicking one's wrist in one moment and flicking it 10 seconds later), and the decision does not make any difference to the lives of the participants. As Adina Roskies points out, 'Arbitrary action [in Libet's experiment] is, at best, a degenerate case of freedom of the will, one in which what matters about freedom fails to hold' (Roskies 2011, 18).

It is certainly interesting if it turns out that consciousness does not play an important role in arbitrary and trivial actions, but it is far from obvious that this result can be generalized for other kinds of actions, including actions with non-equivalent options or actions that really matter, such as deciding where to spend one's next holiday or choosing which university to attend. People consciously contemplate and deliberate in those choices and decisions, and it is hard to imagine that their conscious contemplation and deliberation do not have significant roles to play in how people choose and decide.

The upshot is that neither the causal irrelevance condition nor the generalizability condition is satisfied by Libet-style studies.

Situationist Studies

The second body of evidence for epiphenomenalism comes from situationist studies. The studies are all distinct but collectively support a common idea: the external situation plays a bigger role in determining people's behaviour than one might think. These studies show that behaviour is largely determined by external situations; that external situations have an impact on unconscious and automatic processes; and that there is not much of a role left for conscious processes. Thus, according to John Bargh:

> [T]he more we know about the situational causes of psychological phenomena, the less need we have for postulating internal conscious mediating process to explain these phenomena. [...] [I]t is hard to escape the forecast that as knowledge progresses regarding psychological phenomena, there will be less of a role played by free will or conscious choice in accounting for them. (Bargh 1997, 1)

The Good Samaritan Study

A classic study by John Darley and Daniel Batson (1973) was inspired by the parable of the Good Samaritan in the Bible in which a priest did not help a suffering stranger on a road, while a Samaritan did. Darley and Batson investigated the role of the external situation in people's helping behaviour. Participants – who were seminary students – first answered personality questionnaires concerning their religious beliefs and commitments and then were asked to move to another building in which they were supposed to do the next task. The next task was to express their thoughts either on the jobs in which seminary students would be effective (the *task-relevant* condition) or on the parable of the Good Samaritan (the *helping-relevant* condition). Some participants were told to move to another building quickly because they were late (the *high-hurry* condition), while others were told that they were ahead of schedule (the *low-hurry* condition). When participants passed through an alley to the other building, they encountered a man who was in need, sitting in a doorway, head down, not moving, coughing and groaning.

The result of the study indicates that participants in the low-hurry condition were more likely to offer help than participants in the high-hurry condition. In contrast, other factors, such as thinking about the parable of the Good Samaritan (the helping-relevant condition) or types of religious personality (e.g., being committed to religion for its own sake rather than as means to another end), did not predict helping behaviour. This result seems to show that what is most relevant to helping behaviour is the situation in which the agents find themselves, such as whether participants are in the high-hurry situation or the low-hurry situation. Personality or conscious thoughts (even those that are directly relevant to helping) did not influence helping behaviour. Darley and Batson note that this conclusion is consistent with the parable of the Good Samaritan: the priest who did not offer help (while the Samaritan did) was probably busier than the Samaritan (for other situationist studies, some of which are now ethically controversial, see Box 6A).

Do situationist studies satisfy the generalizability condition and the causal irrelevance condition?

It is not clear that the causal irrelevance condition is really satisfied by the results of situationist studies. Remember that Bargh said in the quote above that 'the more we know about the situational causes of psychological phenomena, the less need we have for postulating internal conscious mediating process to explain these phenomena', but this does not necessarily rule out the possibility that conscious processes play at least some causal role.

BOX 6A: Influential Situationist Studies

(1) *The bystander effect by Latané and Darley (1968)*: In an emergency situation, participants were much more likely to intervene and offer help if they were on their own. The presence of bystanders inhibited intervention.

(2) *Obedience to authority by Milgram (1963)*: The behaviour of participants was influenced by the instructions of an experimenter who appeared to be an authority figure, to the point that participants acted against their best judgment and contrary to their personal values (albeit reluctantly).

(3) *Stanford prison experiment by Haney, Banks, and Zimbardo (1973)*: In an experiment requiring participants to behave as either guards or prisoners, their behaviour was heavily influenced by the arbitrarily assigned roles, e.g. guards abused their power over prisoners.

Situationist experiments reveal that situational factors influence people's behaviour, but these factors do not seem to *fully determine* behaviour. After all, not all people behave in the same way in a particular situation. For example, not all participants in the high-hurry condition failed to help, and not all participants in the low-hurry condition offered help.

The Good Samaritan study suggests that consciously thinking about a parable where a stranger in trouble receives help (the helping-relevant condition) does not significantly increase the likelihood of actually helping a stranger. But this does not necessarily mean that all forms of conscious thinking have no effect on behaviour. For example, even if consciously thinking about a parable where a stranger in trouble receives help does not increase the likelihood of helping, the conscious and explicit intention to help a stranger might increase the likelihood of helping.

The results of situationist studies do not seem to satisfy the generalizability condition either. Remember that Libet-style studies mainly look at rather uninteresting and trivial actions such as randomly flicking one's wrist, which invites worries about its generalizability. Relevant actions in situationist studies are not as uninteresting and trivial as the ones in Libet-style studies, but a similar worry can be raised. For instance, the Good Samaritan study put participants in the high-hurry condition in a situation in which they needed to make a decision (e.g., helping a person in need) rather quickly, with little time for careful deliberation. In a sense, it is not surprising that conscious and slow processes (or Type-2 processes) do not play a significant role when people do not have enough time to deliberate. The crucial question is not whether conscious and slow processes have roles to play when people do not have time for careful deliberation, but whether they have roles to play when people do have the time. People usually spend a relatively long time examining and evaluating options before making important decisions in their lives, such as decisions concerning their career or marriage. Is the role of conscious decision-making in these important decisions as small as the role of conscious decision-making in the urgent decision about whether to help a stranger in need? Are these important decisions influenced by situational factors as strongly as the urgent decision about whether to help a stranger in need?

Our conclusion is that situationist studies do not satisfy either the causal irrelevance condition or the generalizability condition.

Wegner-Style Studies

Further evidence for epiphenomenalism comes from Wegner-style studies of the experience of conscious will. We call them 'Wegner-style studies' because Daniel Wegner is the central figure in this line of research (Wegner 2002; Wegner & Wheatley 1999). Both Libet-style studies and situationist studies aim to identify some causal factors (i.e., preparatory brain activities or situational factors) that explain human behaviour, and thereby deny or at least deemphasize the relevance of conscious processes. Wegner-style studies, in contrast, have a rather different aim. The target of these studies is the experience of conscious will (i.e., feeling as if one is consciously willing an action) as responsible for the occurrence of the action. Wegner-style studies reveal that 'conscious will is an illusion' in the sense that 'the experience of consciously willing an action is not a direct indication that the conscious thought has caused the action' (Wegner 2002, 2).

The I Spy Experiment

In one study, Daniel Wegner and Thalia Wheatley (1999) revealed an illusory experience of conscious will. A participant was teamed up with another participant (who was in fact a confederate), and they were asked to jointly move a cursor on a screen that was filled with various objects (taken from the book *I Spy* by Jean Marzollo and Walter Wick). They controlled the cursor by moving a square board attached to a computer mouse and stopped every 30 seconds or so. In some cases, the confederate knowingly exerted influence to stop the cursor at a particular object (the *forced stop* condition). In other cases, the confederate let the participant stop the cursor without exerting any influence (the *unforced stop* condition). At each stop, the participant was asked to indicate the degree of personal intentionality concerning the stop using a scale with 'I allowed the stop to happen' at one end and 'I intended to make the stop' at the other. During the experiment, the participant listened to some words through headphones and was told that the words were random distractors. It turned out, however, that the words were manipulated; in particular, in the forced stop condition in which the confederate intentionally forced the cursor to stop on an object (e.g., a swan), there was a corresponding word heard by the participant through their headphones (e.g., 'swan') that primed that result.

The result suggests that, in the forced stop condition, the rating of intentionality was influenced and manipulated by the priming words and when they were heard. The rating was relatively low when the word was heard 30 seconds before the forced stop or 1 second after it, while the rating was relatively high when the word was heard immediately before (1 second before or 5 seconds before) the forced stop. For example, if a participant heard 'swan' 1 second before the confederate forced the cursor to stop at a swan on the screen, the participant judged the stop to be their own intentional action. These are the cases in which, according to Wegner and Wheatley, the participant went through an illusory experience of conscious will: '[T]he experience of will can be created by the manipulation of thought and action in accord with the principle of priority, and this experience can occur even when the person's thought cannot have created the action' (Wegner 2002, 78).

This is certainly an interesting result, but does it support epiphenomenalism? Wegner-style studies seem to have a problem with the generalizability condition. These experiments do show that experiences of conscious will are illusory in special cases (e.g., in the *I Spy* experiment), but it would be far-fetched to conclude from this that experiences of conscious will are illusory all the time. The inductive argument from 'conscious will is illusory in some cases' to 'conscious will is illusory in all cases' does not seem to be compelling.

Indeed, Wegner himself acknowledges that cases like the *I Spy* experiment are not typical. With respect to the experience of conscious will, he distinguishes four cases: (1) normal voluntary action (where X performs an act A and X has the conscious experience of willing A); (2) normal inaction (where X does not perform A and X does not have the conscious experience of willing A); (3) automatism (where X performs A and does not have the conscious experience of willing A); and (4) illusion of control (where X does not perform A and has the conscious experience of willing A; the *I Spy* experiment belongs to this category). It is certainly true that the conscious experience of will is illusory in the fourth category, but it does not seem to be illusory in the first category, into which, Wegner admits, 'most of the things we do in everyday life seem to fall' (Wegner 2002, 11).

The results of Wegner-style studies do not satisfy the causal irrelevance condition either. Wegner takes his studies to show that the processes that are responsible for producing the experience of conscious will are distinct from the processes that are responsible for producing actual behaviour. The processes that produce action are unconscious and automatic processes (we call this 'the automaticity thesis'), while the processes that are responsible for the experience of conscious will are the processes that compare thoughts and actions. In particular, for the experience of conscious will, the thought 'should occur before the action, be consistent with the action, and not be accompanied by other potential causes' (Wegner 2002, 69). We call this 'the matching model' of conscious will (see Bayne 2006).

We agree that Wegner-style studies support the matching model. In the *I Spy* experiment, for example, the experience of conscious will was produced because a priming word ('swan') was heard just before the act of stopping the cursor on a swan on the screen. However, it is not clear how Wegner-style studies support the automaticity thesis. Note that the automaticity thesis and the matching model are different claims, and the former does not follow from the latter. Wegner's matching model is perfectly consistent with the idea that conscious thoughts play a significant causal role (Bayne 2006). If the results of the Wegner-style studies do not support the automaticity thesis, then the causal irrelevance condition is not met. In fact, when it comes to the automaticity thesis, Wegner appeals to other studies such as situationist and automaticity studies. But then Wegner-style studies do not constitute a new challenge to free will, distinct from the situationist challenge discussed above.

Thus, neither the causal irrelevance condition nor the generalizability condition is satisfied by Wegner-style studies.

6.4   Implicit Bias and Responsibility

Implicit Bias: A Case Study

Let us summarize the discussion so far. We have yet to see any good empirical evidence for epiphenomenalism. We have discussed three kinds of empirical research – Libet-style research, situationist research, and Wegner-style research – none of which satisfies the causal irrelevance condition and the generalizability condition simultaneously.

The argument for epiphenomenalism is therefore not supported by the available evidence from psychology and neuroscience, at least for now. But this does not mean that those engaged in philosophical discussions about free will cannot learn anything from psychology and neuroscience. Although we could not find good evidence for radical scepticism about free will, studies in psychology and neuroscience provide us with good reasons to accept a partial or moderate form of scepticism according to which we are not as free and responsible as we might have thought.

Moderate scepticism has at least two dimensions. First, people's freedom is limited in the sense that they are free and responsible *in fewer cases* than we might have thought. For instance, Libet-style studies show that people are not free with respect to some simple behaviours such as flicking their wrists. This falls short of a general form of epiphenomenalism, but it is still an interesting finding. Without Libet's experiment, we might have continued to think that people can flick their wrist freely and spontaneously whenever they like.

Second, people's freedom is also limited in the sense that they are free and responsible *to a lesser degree* than we might have thought. Situationist studies, for example, show that agents are not fully free and responsible for all their actions and choices. That is because behaviour may be influenced by factors that are not known to them, as in the case of agents failing to stop and help a stranger in need when they are in a hurry. This does not amount to fully fledged epiphenomenalism, but it is still an interesting finding. Without the Good Samaritan experiment, we might have continued to think that agents were mostly responsible for all their actions and choices.

If moderate scepticism is correct, our question about free will and responsibility is not 'Are humans free/responsible?', but rather 'What are the cases in which humans are free/responsible?' and 'To what degree are we free/responsible in those cases?' These questions should be discussed on a case-by-case basis with the results of the relevant psychological and neuroscientific studies taken into account.

The most interesting questions are those concerning borderline cases, namely those cases in which it is not obvious that agents possess freedom and responsibility given the empirical data and the philosophical consensus, but it is not obvious that agents lack freedom and responsibility either. As a case study, we will now discuss responsibility for implicit biases. Remember the case of Elsa (mentioned in the Introduction to this volume). Elsa thinks of herself as an egalitarian person who respects everybody and treats people equally, irrespective of ethnic origin or skin colour. It turns out, however, that she has been implicitly biased in a systematic manner. Some of her everyday behaviours are not coherent with her self-image: she tends to ignore her Nigerian secretary, avoids sitting next to Asian passengers on public transport, and so on.

Implicit biases can be ethically problematic. For example, Elsa might be responsible for hiring people in the company where she works, and if her evaluations are implicitly biased, this could have serious consequences for the candidates and their career. She might evaluate the CV of a white candidate as stronger than the CV of a black candidate, although the CVs are just as strong. Alternatively, Elsa might be an armed police officer and her reaction to a suspect might be implicitly biased, which could have serious and even fatal consequences for the suspect and people in the community. If a stranger on the street holds an object that cannot be identified immediately, Elsa might be quicker to regard the object as a gun if it is held by a black suspect than if it were held by a white suspect.

Implicit biases are 'implicit' in a psychological sense: they are not accessible via introspection and people do not have peculiar access to them (Chapter 2). Elsa does not have introspective or peculiar access to her biases. Implicit biases are 'implicit' also in a methodological sense: they are studied by implicit measures and tests, such as the Implicit Association Test (more on this below), that do not rely on self-report. Implicit biases are 'biases' in a descriptive sense: implicitly biased behaviour deviates from what people take themselves to be. Elsa thinks that she is ethnically and racially egalitarian, but her actual behaviour says otherwise. Implicit biases are also 'biases' in a normative sense: implicitly biased behaviour deviates from the way people ought to behave. Elsa ought to treat her Nigerian secretary in the same way that she treats her white colleagues, but she fails to do so.

'Implicit bias' can refer to implicitly biased behaviour (e.g., Elsa's implicitly discriminatory behaviour towards her Nigerian secretary). It can also refer to underlying psychological processes (e.g., the under-lying psychological processes that give rise to Elsa's discriminatory behaviour). Similar (but not synonymous) expressions are 'implicit attitudes' (e.g., Elsa's implicit negative attitude towards black people) and 'implicit associations' (e.g., Elsa's implicit association between black people and violence).

The Implicit Association Test
Implicit biases (or implicit associations) are often measured with the Implicit Association Test (IAT), developed by Mahzarin Banaji and Tony Greenwald. The best way to understand this test is to take it yourself online at Project Implicit. In the race version of the IAT (there are many other versions too, including one about age, one about gender, and one about disability), for example, words appear one by one at the centre of a screen. Your first task is to assign words (by pressing keys) to one of two categories as quickly and accurately as possible: assign a word to the right-hand side of the screen if the word means something *good*, and assign a word to the left-hand side if it means something *bad*. For example, when the word 'pleasure' appears, you should assign it to the right-hand side. The next stage is similar but slightly different. Photos of faces appear one by one at the centre of the screen, and your task is to assign the faces to one of two categories: assign a photo to the right-hand side of the screen if it is the face of a *white* person, and assign a photo to the left-hand side of the screen if it is the face of a *black* person. For example, when the face of somebody who looks like Denzel Washington appears, you

should assign it to the left-hand side. Next comes the crucial part of the test where the previous two tasks are combined. Some words or photos of faces appear one by one at the centre of the screen and your task is to assign them to one of two categories: assign it to the right-hand side of the screen if it is either a *good* word or a *white* face, and assign it to the left-hand-side of the screen if it is either a *bad* word or a *black* face. You then do almost the same task except that the word–face pairs are switched: assign it to the right-hand side of the screen if it is either a *good* word or a *black* face, and assign it to the left-hand side of the screen if it is either a *bad* word or a *white* face. The IAT calculates your score on the basis of the speed and accuracy of your performance.

Many people find the task after the switch (with the good/black pair and the bad/white pair, or the 'GBBW task' for short) more difficult than the previous task (with the good/white pair and the bad/black pair, or the 'GWBB task' for short). People are slower and make more mistakes in the GBBW task than in the GWBB task. In fact, some vividly feel the difficulty of the GBBW task as well as a slowdown in their performance while undertaking it. Greenwald recalls his own experience of the first IAT (which was about flowers and insects rather than about white people and black people):

> I had to press the left key for flower names or unpleasant words, and the right one for insect names or pleasant words. Within a few seconds, I could see that this was difficult. After (slowly) completing a series of fifty key presses at this task, I assumed that I would soon overcome this difficulty by practicing the task another few times. Wrong! I repeated the task several times – I did not improve at all. Then I tried just forcing myself to respond rapidly to each word. The result was frustration. I made frequent errors – pressing the wrong key. (Banaji & Greenwald 2013, 40)

The fact that the GBBW task is more difficult than the GWBB task for many people is explained by their implicit mental associations. They implicitly associate black people with bad things and white people with good things, which explains why the GWBB task is natural and easy while the GBBW task is unnatural and difficult.

The IAT is influential in the implicit bias literature, but there are several things to be said about it. First, the IAT is not the only game in town. There are some other measures of implicit processes, and they can yield different results. For example, the results of these other measures can conflict with one another, which challenges the assumption that implicit bias is a single and unitary state of mind. Second, the IAT measures implicit mental associations (e.g., Elsa's mental association between black people and bad things), but it does not measure implicitly biased behaviour (e.g., Elsa's biased behaviour toward her Nigerian secretary). It is an empirical question whether the IAT score of a person is correlated with their implicitly biased behaviour. IAT scores seem to be correlated with some behaviour or micro-behaviour (e.g., eye-contact, blinking, etc.), but there is controversy over whether the race IAT scores successfully predict significant implicit racist behaviour or attitudes in real life (e.g., Oswald et al. 2013).

Awareness and Control

It is tempting to think that Elsa is not responsible or blameworthy for her implicit biases towards her Nigerian secretary (or, at the very least, the degree of her responsibility is very small). On the implicit biases about sex, Jennifer Saul writes:

> A person should not be blamed for an implicit bias of which they are completely unaware that results solely from the fact that they live in a sexist culture. Even once they become aware that they are likely to have implicit biases, they do not instantly become able to control their biases, and so they should not be blamed for them. (Saul 2013, 55)

This passage contains at least two arguments for the view that people are not responsible or blameworthy for their implicit biases. First, biases are implicit and hence people are not aware of their biases. They cannot be responsible for something of which they are not aware. Let us call this 'the argument from awareness'. Second, biases work automatically and are thus beyond a person's control. They cannot be responsible for something over which they do not have control. Let us call this 'the argument from control'.

The argument from awareness and the argument from control are open to different interpretations, depending on what is meant by 'awareness' and 'control'. One might be able to distinguish direct awareness/control from indirect awareness/control. 'Direct awareness' means introspective or peculiar awareness without observation of behavioural cues (Chapter 2). 'Indirect awareness' means any other form of awareness that is not direct. Crucially, indirect awareness includes scientific awareness, such as how one can be aware of one's own biases by taking a test, such as the IAT, or by reading a news article about the pervasive impact of racial implicit biases. 'Direct control' means immediate and voluntary control, namely the kind of control one has over one's intentional bodily actions. 'Indirect control', in contrast, means any other form of control that is not direct. Crucially, indirect control includes scientific interventions, such as those kinds of interventions that have been studied in the psychological literature (more on this below).

With the direct/indirect distinction, we can formulate two versions of each argument (cf., Holroyd 2012; Holroyd, Scaife, & Stafford 2017).

Argument from Direct Awareness
Premise 1: People lack direct awareness of their implicit biases.
Premise 2: Responsibility for implicit biases is incompatible with the lack of direct awareness of them.
Conclusion: Therefore, people are not responsible for their biases.

Argument from Direct and Indirect Awareness
Premise 1: People lack direct and indirect awareness of their implicit biases.
Premise 2: Responsibility for implicit biases is incompatible with the lack of direct and indirect awareness of them.
Conclusion: Therefore, people are not responsible for their biases.

Argument from Direct Control
Premise 1: People lack direct control of their implicit biases.
Premise 2: Responsibility for implicit biases is incompatible with the lack of direct control of them.
Conclusion: Therefore, people are not responsible for their biases.

Argument from Direct and Indirect Control
Premise 1: People lack direct and indirect control of their implicit biases.
Premise 2: Responsibility for implicit biases is incompatible with the lack of direct and indirect control of them.

Conclusion: Therefore, people are not responsible for their biases.

We call premise 1 of each argument 'the psychological premise' and premise 2 of each argument 'the philosophical premise'.

We will examine each of these arguments below. Our conclusion will be that none of them succeeds in establishing the conclusion that people are not responsible for their biases. Due to limitations of space, however, we will not examine all premises of each arguments one by one. Instead, we will focus on one premise in each argument (except for the argument from direct and indirect awareness), namely the premise that we take to be particularly problematic.

Let us begin with the argument from direct and indirect control. This argument is problematic because of its psychological premise (that people lack direct and indirect control of their implicit biases). We can grant, for the sake of argument, that people do not have direct control over their implicit biases (e.g., Elsa is not able to control her biases in the same way that she controls her imagination when she is mentally combining parts of different creatures – such as the head of a lion and the body of a chimpanzee – to form a fictional creature). But it is far from obvious that people do not have indirect and scientific control over them. An active line of research in the empirical literature is investigating how to effectively intervene in implicit biases, and several questions are raised about how effective different types of interventions can be, how long their effects last, and which one is the most effective. Perhaps Elsa's implicit biases could be reduced when, before visiting the office, she looks at some stereotype-discordant images, such as viewing a photo of Oprah Winfrey or Nelson Mandela (cf., Dasgupta & Greenwald 2001). Elsa's implicit biases could also be reduced when, before visiting the office, she explicitly says to herself 'If my secretary is in the same conversation as I am, I will pay close attention to what she says' (cf., Gollwitzer & Sheeran 2006).

The argument from direct control is problematic because of its philosophical premise (that responsibility for implicit biases is incompatible with the lack of direct control over them). Even if Elsa is not able to directly control her implicit biases, there might be some indirect and scientific interventions readily available to her (such as looking at the photo of Oprah Winfrey or Nelson Mandela). Suppose also that these interventions are reasonably effective in reducing implicit biases. It turns out, however, that Elsa fails to use any of these interventions and keeps behaving in the same way towards her Nigerian secretary. Now, should we say that Elsa is not responsible for her biases just because she lacks direct control over them? We find this counterintuitive. It seems to us that directness does not really matter in this context; the crucial question here is whether Elsa has some kind of control over biases, regardless of whether her control is direct or not. As far as control is concerned, Elsa can be said to be responsible if she has some kind of control over her biases.

The argument from direct awareness is problematic because of its philosophical premise (that responsibility for implicit biases is incompatible with the lack of direct awareness of them). Again, think about Elsa, but let us add some more assumptions about awareness: Elsa does not have direct and introspective awareness of her biases, but she nonetheless has indirect and scientific awareness of them (e.g., she took the IAT herself and read some news articles about implicit biases). Now, should we say that Elsa is not responsible for her biases just because she lacks direct awareness of them? We find this counterintuitive. Directness does not matter; the crucial question here is whether Elsa has some kind of awareness, not whether the awareness is direct. As far as awareness is concerned, Elsa can be said to be responsible if she has some kind of direct or indirect awareness of the biases.

The last argument we will consider is the one from direct and indirect awareness, which we will examine more carefully than the other arguments. Its psychological premise says that people lack direct and indirect awareness of their biases. This premise is problematic because, even if we grant for the sake of argument that people do not have direct and introspective awareness of their implicit biases (which could be controversial, though, for doesn't Greenwald in the quote above have some introspective access to his implicit associations at work?), an immediate objection can be raised about indirect access: many people seem to have indirect and scientific awareness of their implicit biases. Appetite for implicit bias research is growing not only in academia but also in the media, industry, and so on, and so we can expect that many people have some indirect and scientific awareness of their biases.

The philosophical premise says that responsibility for implicit biases is incompatible with the lack of direct and indirect awareness of them. This premise is problematic too. To see this, let us revise our Elsa case once more: Elsa lacks not only direct and introspective awareness but also indirect and scientific awareness of her biases. For example, she is not a big fan of science-related articles in the news and she has not read about implicit biases. Now, let us suppose that she is not indirectly and scientifically aware of her biases, but she *ought to be*. For example, her company, which is seriously committed to racial equality in the workplace, often circulates emails and documents about the danger of racial biases and discrimination, all of which she neglects to read. The company also holds obligatory seminars on the topic; she attended one seminar but she did not pay attention and only pretended to listen while responding to emails on her laptop. Now, should we say that Elsa is not responsible for her biases just because she is not (directly or indirectly) aware of her biases? Probably not. The crucial question here is whether she *ought to be* aware of her biases rather than whether she *is* actually (directly or indirectly) aware of them. Elsa can be said to be responsible if she ought to be aware of her biases, even if she is not actually aware of them.

Thus, just like the other arguments, the argument from direct and indirect awareness fails. But some worries remain. In particular, there is a sense in which the objections leave out many people. For example, against the psychological premise we said that many people have some indirect and scientific awareness of their biases through the IAT or news articles. This is certainly true, but it leaves out other people (arguably, the majority of people in our society) who do not have indirect awareness of their biases.

Again, against the philosophical premise we said that Elsa is responsible for her biases and her responsibility has something to do with the fact that she ought to be aware of her biases; she is expected to be aware of her biases given the information and opportunities available to her. Even if this is correct, however, it is uncertain whether the same thing can be said about other people in our society. In other words, it is unclear how many people in our society have sufficient information about biases and opportunities to become aware of them.

One might think that Elsa's case is exceptional. After all, not many employers are as serious about equality and inclusivity as hers. Most people in our society are not directly or indirectly aware of their biases, and they are not even expected to be aware of them. If they are not expected to be aware of their biases, they are not to be held responsible for them.

However, Elsa's case is not so exceptional. People can be expected to be aware of their biases even if they do not have much information available to them or many opportunities to learn about biases. As we have already noted, implicit bias research is increasingly popular both inside and outside academia, and perhaps this will be sufficient for awareness of biases to become more common.

6.5 Summary

- According to the argument from epiphenomenalism, which was the main focus of this chapter, we do not have free will because (1) epiphenomenalism is true according to psychology and/or neuroscience (the psychological premise) and (2) free will is incompatible with the truth of epiphenomenalism (the philosophical premise).
- The psychological premise, however, is not plausible. We examined three bodies of empirical evidence for epiphenomenalism – Libet-style studies, situationist studies, and Wegner-style studies – none of which satisfy the two conditions required of epiphenomenalism: the causal irrelevance condition, according to which the evidence rules out the causal relevance of conscious states and processes; and the generalizability condition, according to which the evidence is generalized to all forms of actions.
- Although psychological and neuroscientific studies do not support fully fledged scepticism about free will, they do support a moderate form of scepticism according to which people are free to a lesser degree than they might think. Moderate scepticism opens up questions about borderline cases, such as the cases of implicit biases, in which it is not clear whether people are free and responsible.

Further Resources

Articles and Books

We recommend two accessible introductory books by Alfred Mele: *A Dialogue on Free Will and Science* (2013) and *Free: Why Science Hasn't Disproved Free Will* (2014). For a more detailed discussion, see his *Effective Intentions: The Power of Conscious Will* (2009).

Informative interdisciplinary discussions of free will are included in *Are We Free? Psychology and Free Will* (2008), edited by John Baer, James Kaufman, and Roy Baumeister, and Volume 4 (*Free Will and Moral Responsibility*, 2014) of the *Moral Psychology* series from MIT Press, edited by Walter Sinnott-Armstrong.

To learn more about the studies that we discussed or mentioned in this chapter, we recommend *Mind Time: The Temporal Factor in Consciousness* by Benjamin Libet (2004), *The Illusion of Conscious Will* by Daniel Wegner (2002), *Obedience to Authority* by Stanley Milgram (1974), and *The Lucifer Effect: Understanding How Good People Turn Evil* by Philip Zimbardo (2007).

On implicit biases, *Blindspot: Hidden Biases of Good People* by Mahzarin Banaji and Anthony Greenwald (2013) is the best place to start.

For philosophical discussions of implicit biases, including a discussion of moral responsibility for implicit biases, *Implicit Bias and Philosophy* Volume 1 (*Metaphysics and Epistemology*, 2016a) and Volume 2 (*Moral Responsibility, Structural Injustice, and Ethics*, 2016b), both edited by Michael Brownstein and Jennifer Saul, are the most useful resources available at the moment.

Online Resources

'Closer to truth – Big questions in free will' (2016), available on YouTube, contains interviews with leading psychologists, neuroscientists, and philosophers working on free will.

Michael Brownstein's *Stanford Encyclopedia of Philosophy* entry on implicit bias (2019) contains a useful overview of relevant empirical studies and philosophical discussions. On *Analysis*, a BBC 4 Radio programme, you will find a 30-minute podcast on implicit bias (2017) including several philosophers who specialize in bias and prejudice.

Anyone can try the Implicit Association Test at the Project Implicit website (*https://implicit.harvard.edu/implicit/*). Taking the test is the best way to learn how it works, but we do not recommend it to those who may be adversely affected by the possibility that they might learn some uncomfortable truths about their own biases. See the Ethical Considerations section on the website.

Questions

1. What is the role of psychology and neuroscience in the debate on free will and responsibility? How can psychologists and neuroscientists contribute to the debate?
2. How can philosophers, psychologists, and neuroscientists work together in a fruitful and productive manner to investigate free will and responsibility?
3. Can people be free and responsible in a world in which determinism, materialism, or epiphenomenalism is true? What is your intuitive answer?
4. What does a society without free will look like? How might social and legal systems be changed if free will turns out to be an illusion?
5. Can you think of real-life cases in which implicit biases might cause morally and socially problematic consequences?
6. In what circumstances are people responsible for their implicit biases? Why?

7

Delusion and Confabulation

7.1 Introduction

This chapter and the next chapter will discuss the philosophical and scientific issues raised by the study of unusual behaviours, often characterized as signs of pathological or neurodivergent conditions. We think this is important for three reasons. First, the vulnerability of human agents to unusual behaviour needs to be taken into account when seeking a realistic (rather than idealized) conception of the mind. Second, some unusual behaviours are philosophically important in their own right. They raise philosophical questions that are worth serious attention; the kind of questions that might not be asked if we confine our discussion to statistically normal phenomena. Third, unusual behaviours provide us with useful data for thinking about mind and cognition in general. As we will see, they provide new insights into many of the topics we have already discussed in this book, including rationality, self-knowledge, mindreading, empathy, moral judgment, and moral behaviour. Among many different kinds of unusual psychological and behavioural phenomena, this chapter will discuss *delusion* and *confabulation*, which are characterized by people misrepresenting reality and are considered as symptoms of mental disorders. In Chapter 8, we will discuss two neurodivergent conditions: *autism*, which is characterized by people exhibiting atypical communicative and social interactions; and *psychopathy*, which is characterized by people engaging in atypical moral and pro-social behaviour.

It is tempting to think that delusions and confabulations are distinctive in how they distort reality. Definitions of delusion and confabulation in psychology and psychiatry tend to characterize them as beliefs with evident epistemic faults: for instance, as beliefs that are false or irresponsive to evidence. Suppose that Judy has the delusion that she is harassed and harmed by envious co-workers when, as a matter of fact, her co-workers are sympathetic to her and supportive (*persecutory delusion*). Suppose that Jacob reports that he walked on the beach with his mother this morning, but his mother died 30 years ago (*distorted memory*). It is tempting to think that Judy's delusion and Jacob's confabulation are false and irrational in a distinctive way.

Chapters 1 and 2 provided numerous examples of beliefs that are false and irrational in non-clinical contexts. Many people's beliefs are false and irrational: for example, some of those that are produced by heuristic processes (e.g., the belief that Linda is more likely to be a feminist bank teller than a bank teller in the Linda experiment reported by Tversky & Kahneman 1983). Many of the explanations that people offer for their attitudes and choices are also inaccurate and not grounded in evidence (e.g., the claim that the stockings were chosen for their superior quality in the stockings experiment by Nisbett & Wilson 1977). However, we might think that the distortions of reality present in delusions and confabulations are different from those we find in everyday beliefs and explanations.

One possibility is that the irrationality of Judy's delusion about being harassed and harmed by envious co-workers is *different in kind* from the irrationality of the belief that Linda is more likely to be a feminist bank teller than a bank teller. The inaccuracy of Jacob's report about his morning walk with his mother is *different in kind* from the inaccuracy of people's explanations of their consumer choices.

Another possibility is that the irrationality of delusions and the inaccuracy of confabulations are *different in degree*, not in kind, from the irrationality and inaccuracy of everyday beliefs. Delusions and confabulations fall short of the relevant standards – of rationality and accuracy – to a greater extent. Judy's delusion about being harassed and harmed by envious co-workers is significantly *more* irrational than the everyday irrational belief about Linda being more likely to be a feminist bank teller than a bank teller. Jacob's report of his walk with his mother is *more* obviously inaccurate than people's everyday inaccurate explanations of their consumer choices.

A competing possibility is that delusions and confabulations are not distinctive in their epistemic faults – they are neither epistemically faulty in a distinctive way nor more epistemically faulty than everyday beliefs and explanations – but they appear so because they are unusual and less widespread.

After an introductory overview of the phenomenon of delusion, we briefly review the literature on delusion formation and discuss what empirical findings and theories tell us about the process through which delusions are formed and maintained. We then examine a series of arguments for the conclusion that delusions are too irrational to be regarded as beliefs. We focus on two of these arguments: that delusions are not responsive to evidence (*epistemic irrationality*) and that they do not consistently drive action (*agential irrationality*) (Section 7.2). This discussion will lead to some general considerations about the nature of belief.

We then examine the irrationality of delusions in more detail (Section 7.3). We first focus on whether people who have delusions reason in a less rational way than people who do not have delusions. Although delusions may exhibit several kinds of irrationality, none of those kinds of irrationality uniquely and distinguishes delusions from non-clinical irrational beliefs.

Next, we turn to confabulation (Section 7.4). We begin by discussing its definition and sketching the most influential theories about the mechanisms responsible for its occurrence. Then, we turn to whether the distortion of memory reports in confabulation is distinctive or whether it can also be observed in everyday memory reports. We will see that distorted memories are a very common occurrence. This discussion will lead to some general considerations about the nature and function of human memory: should we conceive of remembering as retrieving accurate information about the past or as developing a coherent story from a number of clues by using the capacities involved in inference and imagination?

7.2 Delusion

What Are Delusions?

In the literature we review in this chapter, the term 'delusion' refers to a clinical phenomenon, and in particular to an observable symptom of schizophrenia, delusional disorders, dementia, amnesia, and other psychiatric disorders (see Box 7A for issues concerning the language we use to talk about mental health).

There is no universally accepted definition of delusion (see Box 7B for the standard definition of delusions in the *Diagnostic and Statistical Manual of Mental Disorders* produced by the American Psychiatric Association) but, generally, a delusion can be understood as a belief that is held despite obvious counter-evidence and that is not explained by the person's social, cultural, or religious background. For example, Samir firmly believes that God has an important mission for him, communicated via the movement of a dog raising its paw in front of the town church. Not only is Samir's belief unusual, implausible, and not supported by his existing beliefs, it is also an idiosyncratic belief; other people – even people from his religious community – do not share his belief.

Delusions can have a variety of themes (some common delusional themes are listed in Box 7C). Delusions can occur *monothematically* or *polythematically*. In a monothematic case, a person is delusional about one particular topic. A monothematic delusion has been described as 'an island of irrationality within a sea of rationality' (Stone & Young 1997). In a polythematic case, in contrast, a person is delusional about multiple topics, and the person typically ends up with a delusional *belief system*. Delusions due to brain damage (such as stroke or brain injury) tend to occur monothematically, while delusions in schizophrenia can occur polythematically.

Here are two cases to illustrate the distinction. The first is a case of polythematic delusion involving delusions of persecution, reference, and grandiosity. The second is a case of monothematic delusion in which the person has delusional anosognosia concerning her left hand.

[*CASE 1*] A Thirty-One-Year-Old Woman with Chronic Schizophrenia. The patient had been ill for seven years. At the time of the interview, she reported olfactory and somatic hallucinations but no auditory or

BOX 7A: The Language We Use to Talk About Mental Health

Mental health debates in philosophy and psychology are lively and political, and participants disagree on the best language to use. It is important to be aware of the choices we make when we talk about people who experience mental health problems, such as people with delusions and confabulations.

- Authors who believe that there are disorders that can be primarily physical or primarily mental and that there is an analogy between them are happy to use phrases such as *mental illness* or *mental disorder*. Authors who reject a medical view of distress avoid using phrases such as mental *illness* or mental *disorder*. They may talk instead about *mental difference* or *psychological distress*.
- Some believe that calling people who experience mental health issues *schizophrenics*, *depressives*, and so on, is to be avoided because in doing so we identify people with their psychiatric diagnoses and leave behind the idea that there is more to people than their mental health issues. Calling people *schizophrenics* is to identify them with their symptoms, which is problematic, especially as the validity of diagnostic labels such as *schizophrenia* is contested.
- The term *patient,* as in mental health *patient*, is also controversial as it suggests a state of passivity on behalf of the person who seeks medical attention. It has been replaced by terms such as *service user* or *client* in some contexts. *Service user* and *client* are also criticized for suggesting that the person who seeks medical attention has more power than is the case in the dynamic of the relationship with health care professionals.
- When in doubt, it is advisable to talk about *people who experience mental health issues* or *people with a diagnosis of schizophrenia, depression,* and so on. This is respectful of the fact that the person is not entirely defined by their mental health issues and neutral with respect to the legitimacy of their diagnostic label.

BOX 7B: Definition of Delusion in Diagnostic and Statistical Manual of Mental Disorders, 5th Edition (*DSM-5*)

Delusion: A false belief based on incorrect inference about external reality that is firmly held despite what almost everyone else believes and despite what constitutes incontrovertible and obvious proof or evidence to the contrary. The belief is not ordinarily accepted by other members of the person's culture or subculture (i.e., it is not an article of religious faith). When a false belief involves a value judgment, it is regarded as a delusion only when the judgment is so extreme as to defy credibility. Delusional conviction can sometimes be inferred from an overvalued idea (in which case the individual has an unreasonable belief or idea but does not hold it as firmly as is the case with a delusion). (American Psychiatric Association 2013, 819)

BOX 7C: Some Delusional Themes

Delusions are usually classified in terms of their themes or topics:

- In the *delusion of persecution*, a person reports that other people are hostile and intend to cause them harm.
- In the *delusion of reference*, a person reports that other people or objects are somehow referring to her (people are talking about her, objects convey messages to her, etc.).
- In the *delusion of grandiosity*, a person reports that she has special powers or talents that other people do not recognize.

Other delusions involve more bizarre themes:

- In *delusional anosognosia*, people deny an illness or impairment that is obvious to everyone else (such as the paralysis of a limb).
- In the *Capgras delusion*, a person reports that someone close to her (her spouse or a family member) has been replaced by an imposter.
- In the *Cotard delusion*, a person reports that she is disembodied or dead.

visual hallucinations. She noticed an occasional unexplained powdery smell about her body – something like the smell of baby powder – and was distressed by the experience of physical blows raining down on her head on a daily basis. Marked paranoia was present; she avoided all contact with her family, believing that they would harm her if they knew of her location. She also avoided public places, being generally distrustful of other people. She believed that people followed her with their eyes and gossiped about her whenever she went out in public. The only places that she was prepared to frequent on a relatively regular basis were the gym (at times when other people were unlikely to be present) and a local church that she had started attending. [...] She also described a special freckle on her body; this was a freckle that God had made especially for her to mark her as his chosen. She believed that she had a special relationship with God; God had stepped in to save her from her enemies, and this was because she had a mission. That was why she had returned to the church: to find out about her mission for God. (Davies et al. 2001, 135)

[*CASE* 2] Patient L.A.-O (clinical record NA 472, 1980) was a 65-year-old, right-handed woman who was admitted to the emergency department of our hospital on the evening of 2 July 1980. Shortly before admission she had suddenly developed left hemiplegia without loss of consciousness. Alert and cooperative, she claimed that the reason for her hospitalization was sudden weakness and annoying paresthesia of the *right* limbs; her narrative, supplied in a mild state of anxiety, was indeed accompanied by sustained massage of the allegedly hyposthenic right inferior limb. She also claimed that the left hand did not belong to her but had been forgotten in the ambulance by another patient. On request, she admitted without hesitation that her left shoulder was part of her body and *inferentially* came to the same conclusion as regards her left arm and elbow, given, as she remarked, the evident continuity of those members. She was elusive about the forearm but insisted in denying ownership of the left hand, even when it had been passively placed on the right side of her trunk. She could not explain why her rings happened to be worn by the fingers of the alien hand. (Bisiach & Geminiani 1991, 32–33)

How Are Delusions Formed?

How does a person come to believe, for example, that her family members would harm her if they knew of her location (CASE 1) or that her left hand did not belong to her (CASE 2)?

In research of the delusion formation process, a widespread idea is that delusions (or at least most of them) are formed in response to an abnormal experience. Brendan Maher (1974) is an influential advocate of this view. Maher contrasted two accounts of delusion formation: the *reasoning abnormality* account (or the 'thought disorder' account) and the *perceptual abnormality* account. He argues that available evidence supports only the latter account. According to Maher, delusions are explanations of abnormal experiences. The reasoning involved in generating and adopting the explanation (i.e., delusion) is 'the operation of normal cognitive processes', which 'is essentially indistinguishable from that employed by non-patients, by scientists, and by people generally' (Maher 1974, 103).

But what kind of abnormal experience do people with delusions have? Hadyn Ellis and Andrew Young (1990), who studied people with the Capgras delusion, argue that the delusion is formed in response to an abnormal experience of familiar faces. It is known that typical individuals exhibit stronger autonomic responses (measured by skin conductance response) when perceiving a familiar face than when perceiving an unfamiliar face. However, the asymmetry in autonomic responses is missing in people with the Capgras delusion (Ellis et al. 1997). This finding seems to suggest that, when seeing a familiar face, a person with the Capgras delusion visually recognizes the familiar features of a face but is not able to feel an affective form of familiarity: '[T]hey receive a veridical image of a person they are looking at, which stimulates all the appropriate overt semantic data held about that person, but they lack another, possibly confirming, set of information which [...] may carry some sort of affective tone', and in facing such an abnormal experience, people 'adopt some sort of rationalisation strategy in which the individual before them is deemed to be an imposter, a dummy, a robot, or whatever extant technology may suggest' (Ellis & Young 1990, 244).

Multiple Factors

We saw that the Capgras delusion results from the abnormal experience of seeing a familiar face but not feeling the affective response that usually comes with it. So far, this is consistent with Maher's view. However, Tony Stone and Andrew Young (1997) go on to argue that the abnormal experience is not sufficient to explain the Capgras delusion. In addition to the abnormal experience, a reasoning bias is necessary. Their main argument is that the mere presence of an abnormal experience does not account for the adoption of such a bizarre explanation: 'Why does the patient form such a bizarre belief to explain their anomalous experience and not adopt what Maher calls "the more natural explanation" by simply saying that things seem strange and stopping there?' (Stone & Young 1997, 341).

Stone and Young therefore propose a multi-factorial account of the Capgras delusion in which the contributing factors include not only the abnormal experience of seeing a familiar face without feeling the affective response usually associated with it, but also a form of reasoning bias which they call a 'bias towards observational adequacy'. A healthy belief change requires maintaining an appropriate balance between two conflicting imperatives: incorporating new observations into one's belief system ('observational adequacy') and keeping existing beliefs as long as possible ('doxastic conservatism'). Observational adequacy ensures that a person's beliefs reflect reality, while doxastic conservatism ensures that the person has a stable worldview. According to Stone and Young, people with the Capgras delusion have a bias towards the former imperative. This is why, when a person has the abnormal experience of a familiar face, he does not hesitate to revise his existing belief that the woman is his real wife and come to the conclusion that she is not his real wife, which does incorporate the new observation (i.e., the abnormal experience of seeing a familiar face).

Max Coltheart and colleagues (Coltheart 2007; Coltheart, Langdon, & McKay 2011) propose a general theory of (monothematic) delusion, known as 'the two-factor theory'. Two-factor theorists follow Stone and Young in rejecting the idea that an abnormal experience is sufficient for the development of a delusion. In addition to an abnormal experience or abnormal data (which is the first factor), there has to be another factor. The main argument for the second factor in the formation of the Capgras delusion goes as follows: just like people with the Capgras delusion, people with damage to the ventromedial prefrontal cortex (VMPFC) fail to show the asymmetrical autonomic responses between familiar and unfamiliar faces (Tranel, Damasio, & Damasio 1995), which suggests that people with the Capgras delusion and those with VMPFC damage have a similar abnormal experience of seeing familar faces. However, people with VMPFC damage do not develop the Capgras delusion. The best explanation of this is that the abnormal experience is not sufficient for the development of the Capgras delusion, and the second factor explains why people with the Capgras delusion, but not those with VMPFC damage, develop a delusional belief. Similar arguments about other monothematic delusions have also been presented (see Coltheart 2007; Coltheart, Langdon, & McKay 2011).

There are different proposals among two-factor theorists concerning the nature of the second factor. Ryan McKay (McKay 2012; Miyazono & McKay 2019), for instance, follows Stone and Young's suggestion that the inferential step from the first factor (e.g., an abnormal experience of seeing familiar faces) to the delusional belief (e.g., 'this woman is not my wife') involves a bias towards observational adequacy. And this bias is the second factor. Max Coltheart, Peter Menzies, and John Sutton (2010), in contrast, claim that the inferential step from the first factor to the delusional belief is not biased. The second factor is thus not a biased inference from the experience to the delusional belief. According to Coltheart and colleagues, once the delusional belief has been adopted, people with a delusion irrationally maintain the delusional belief despite counter-evidence. Such resistance to counter-evidence, which is described as a deficit in belief evaluation, is the second factor.

Prediction Errors

The disagreement between Maher on one hand and Stone and Young on the other hand is whether an abnormal experience is sufficient for delusion formation or whether a reasoning bias or deficit is also necessary. One might think, however, that the debate is based upon a dubious assumption, namely that there is a sharp dichotomy between experiential factors and reasoning factors. In discussing Maher's proposal, Richard Bentall, for example, says that 'the clear distinction made between perception and inference [...] is in reality oversimplistic and perception is to some extent belief-driven' (Bentall 1990, 40).

The prediction-error theory (Corlett et al. 2010; Fletcher & Frith 2009) rejects a sharp distinction between perceiving and reasoning (or believing), at least at the neurophysiological level. Paul Fletcher and Chris Frith write:

> The boundaries between perception and belief at the physiological level are not so distinct. An important principle that has emerged is that both perception of the world and learning about the world (and therefore beliefs) are dependent on predictions and the extent to

which they are fulfilled. This suggests that a single deficit could explain abnormal perceptions and beliefs. (Fletcher & Frith 2009, 51)

The prediction-error theory of delusion is based on a general theory of the brain and its functions that is known as the 'predictive coding' theory or the 'predictive processing' theory (Clark 2013; Friston 2010; Hohwy 2013). The predictive coding theory explains the functions of the brain, including perceptual functions and reasoning functions, in a unified manner in terms of minimizing prediction errors (i.e., the mismatch between an expectation and an actual input). Applying this general framework to delusions, prediction-error theorists argue that delusions can be explained, without a sharp perceiving/reasoning distinction, in terms of an abnormality in processing prediction errors.

A remarkable study (Corlett et al. 2007) suggests that the processing of prediction errors is indeed abnormal in people with delusions in the context of schizophrenia. In the study, two groups of subjects, people with delusions due to schizophrenia and non-clinical controls, were tested in a task involving learning and predicting a person's allergic reactions to food items. The activity of the right prefrontal cortex (rPFC) (which had been identified as a reliable marker of prediction-error processing in previous studies) was monitored with fMRI. Results showed that, in the control group, the rPFC activity was much greater in cases where their predictions were disconfirmed than in the cases where they were confirmed, as if their brains were 'surprised' when their predictions were disconfirmed but not when they were confirmed. In the delusional group, the asymmetry in the rPFC activity was diminished with respect to the control group, as if their brains were 'surprised' not only when their predictions were disconfirmed but also when they were confirmed.

This finding might suggest that people with delusions are constantly surprised by events that others would consider irrelevant or insignificant. So, they attach some special meaning or significance to those events, and delusions eventually arise as an explanation of their meaning or significance:

[U]nder the influence of inappropriate prediction error signal, possibly as a consequence of dopamine dysregulation, events that are insignificant and merely coincident seem to demand attention, feel important and relate to each other in meaningful ways. Delusions ultimately arise as a means of explaining these odd experiences. (Corlett et al. 2009)

Are Delusions Beliefs?

So far, we have been assuming that delusions are beliefs. For example, the woman with schizophrenia in CASE 1 *believes* that her family members would harm her if they knew of her location, and L.A.-O in CASE 2 *believes* that her left hand does not belong to her. Whether delusions are beliefs, however, has been the focus of a recent philosophical debate.

We will review two approaches to the nature of delusions. The first approach defends the common assumption that delusions are beliefs (*doxasticism*). Doxasticists agree that delusions are beliefs (Bayne & Pacherie 2005; Bortolotti 2010; Miyazono 2018), but they may disagree about whether delusions are rational or irrational beliefs and about whether they are continuous with, or categorically different from, non-delusional beliefs.

The second approach is to regard delusions as something other than beliefs (*anti-doxasticism*). Anti-doxasticists agree that characterizing delusions as beliefs is unsatisfactory, but they disagree about the positive account that best captures the nature of delusions. Although some argue that delusions are empty utterances with no meaning (Berrios 1991), most anti-doxasticists defend the view that delusions are mental states of a non-doxastic or non-exclusively doxastic nature, including: acts of imagination (Currie & Ravenscroft 2002); perceptual inferences (Hohwy & Rajan 2012); states in-between beliefs and non-beliefs (Schwitzgebel 2012; Tumulty 2011); states in-between beliefs and imaginings (Egan 2008); attitudes towards mental states (Stephens & Graham 2004); acceptances (Frankish 2012); or thoughts expressing the content of default processes (Gerrans 2014).

We will review two arguments against the claim that delusions are best understood as beliefs. In response to these anti-doxastic arguments, we will argue that, if we adopt a psychologically realistic view of the relationship between beliefs and evidence and acknowledge the role that affective and motivational states play in driving action, anti-doxasticism can be resisted.

The first argument against doxasticism concerns epistemic irrationality and we call it 'the argument from responsiveness to evidence':

Premise 1: It is a constitutive feature of beliefs that they are responsive to evidence.

Premise 2: Delusions are not responsive to evidence.
Conclusion: Therefore, delusions are not beliefs.

To evaluate this argument, we need to consider the plausibility of the two premises.

Let us start with premise 2. Are delusions responsive to evidence? On some definitions of delusions, resistance to counter-evidence is the main feature of delusions (Gilleen & David 2005). This feature is also an important diagnostic criterion for delusions. According to *DSM-5*, delusions are 'fixed beliefs'. It would be unwise to claim that all delusions are equally impervious to revision, but empirical evidence speaks in favour of the view that most delusions are not responsive to counter-evidence. For instance, in a case report, a woman with erotomania (the delusion that one is loved by another person, usually a person of higher status) continued to believe that a man was in love with her and intended to propose to her, even after she talked to him on the phone and he told her that he was not in love with her and could barely remember who she was (Jordan & Howe 1980). This does not mean that delusional beliefs are completely insensitive to evidence, though. People tend to argue for the content of their delusions when they encounter challenges. Moreover, their conviction in their delusions may fluctuate, and sometimes it does so as a result of experience, reflection, or external challenges.

Let us now consider premise 1. Do beliefs need to be responsive to evidence? There are several philosophical and psychological accounts of what constitutes a belief, but there is very little agreement on the necessary and sufficient conditions for belief. Thus, it is hard to argue for or against the doxastic nature of delusions on the basis of what we take beliefs to be. Many accounts converge on the fact that responsiveness to evidence is a key feature of beliefs; it is a feature that, for instance, distinguishes beliefs from acts of imagination or wishful thinking. It is, however, debatable whether responsiveness to evidence is a criterion of belief or an ideal to which rational beliefs aspire. We seem to categorize some attitudes as beliefs even if they are not responsive to evidence. In some circumstances, we form beliefs and uphold them independently of whether the evidence supports them. In other circumstances, we form beliefs based on evidence, but we do not promptly update or reject them when counter-evidence emerges. Examples include prejudiced, superstitious, and religious beliefs (see Rusche & Brewster 2008 on table-side racism), beliefs in scientific theories to which we are committed (see Chinn & Brewer 2001 on data evaluation), and beliefs about ourselves in general, including beliefs about our traits, talents, weaknesses, and ideological convictions (see, e.g., Pyszczynski, Greenberg, & Holt 1985 on biased evaluation of personal information).

Thus, the argument from responsiveness to evidence does not seem to be conclusive as an argument against the doxastic nature of delusions. Doxasticists may respond to the argument by acknowledging that delusions tend to be resistant to counter-evidence, while also pointing out that other instances of belief can be resistant too. This puts pressure on anti-doxasticists to either provide additional reasons to doubt the doxastic nature of delusion or conclude that other attitudes commonly described as beliefs are not genuine instances of beliefs due to their resistance to counter-evidence. Anti-doxasticists can respond to this challenge, but we will not examine this debate further (see Bortolotti 2010).

The second argument against doxasticism concerns agential irrationality and we will call it 'the argument from action guidance':

Premise 1: It is a constitutive feature of beliefs that they guide action.
Premise 2: Delusions do not guide action.
Conclusion: Therefore, delusions are not beliefs.

To evaluate this argument, we need to consider the plausibility of the two premises.

Let us start with premise 2. Do delusions really fail to guide action? It is a diagnostic criterion for delusions that they lead to action, and thus it is implausible to claim that delusions generally fail to guide action. People have been known to engage in risky behaviour, stop contacting their family, move cities, abandon their studies, and change their job as a result of their delusion. But some philosophers have commented on the phenomenon of *double-bookkeeping* that seems to apply to at least some delusions. Double-bookkeeping refers to the presence of conflicting commitments within an agent and is usually exemplified by people who make verbal reports that are not reflected in their non-verbal behaviour. For instance, a man claims that the nurses in the hospital in which he is a patient want to poison him, but he eats the food they give him regardless (Gallagher 2009). In such circumstances, it is legitimate to ask whether the man is serious in his allegations against the hospital nurses.

What about premise 1? Action-guiding is an important feature of beliefs and, just like responsiveness to evidence, it may help us distinguish beliefs from other attitudes. Believing that an untamed lion is in the room may lead us to run away, whilst imagining a lion in the room may not have the same effect. That said, as with responsiveness to evidence, not all beliefs share the same action-guiding potential. Some beliefs have a direct impact on behaviour and some do not. Some beliefs are acted on in some circumstances and not in others. The psychological literature on everyday instances of hypocrisy shows that cases of double-bookkeeping are by no means confined to delusions.

One important consideration is the role played by motivation in turning beliefs into action. Even the most strongly held belief may not be acted on if independent factors inhibit motivation, such as an agent lacking confidence, fearing a sanction, or missing the opportunity to act. In psychiatric disorders characterized by delusions, and especially in schizophrenia, motivation is negatively affected. This might mean that genuine beliefs can generate the appropriate intentions to act but fail to play their action-guiding role. As a result, such intentions are not carried out and are not converted into action. This phenomenon provides some explanation for the apparent lack of commitment to some delusional states observed in the literature on double-bookkeeping (Bortolotti & Broome 2012).

The arguments we reviewed may not be convincing on their own, but they have been powerfully combined in the work of some influential anti-doxasticists. If delusions fail to be responsive to evidence and they also fail to guide action in the relevant circumstances, one may deny that they have the same causal roles as beliefs and wonder whether it is helpful to regard them as beliefs at all. Two options emerge: revisionism and conservatism about belief.

Revisionism recommends that we should change our terminology. 'Beliefs' are only those attitudes that are responsive to evidence and guide action (i.e., that play the causal roles of beliefs) and we should find some other term to refer to those attitudes that share many of the features of beliefs but which are less responsive to evidence and less influential on action than typical beliefs. Authors who pursue this strategy in different ways include Greg Currie, Andy Egan, Keith Frankish, Dominic Murphy, and Eric Schwitzgebel. The worry with this particular revisionist strategy is that it does not necessarily lead to a philosophy of belief that is more compatible with psychological science or our everyday experience of believers. Instead, it is an attempt to preserve an idealized notion of belief that applies only to attitudes that conform to norms of rationality for beliefs. If followed through, this move would make the category of belief much less populated.

Conservatism recommends that we should not change our terminology and that we should continue to use the term 'belief' quite liberally. The category of belief needs to somehow be demarcated but it should not be required of all attitudes to be responsive to evidence and to be action-guiding to count as beliefs. Those who are conservative about the notion of belief have no reason to doubt the doxastic nature of delusions. Just like other attitudes that are resistant to evidence or that fail to guide action, delusional states can count as beliefs. After all, ascribing delusions often serves the same purpose as ascribing beliefs: it allows agents to predict and understand other agents' behaviour, coordination, and cooperation.

Both revisionism and conservatism can be plausibly defended, and the budding literature on the topic shows that philosophers can make sense of many features of delusions independently of the strategy they choose. One thing that cannot be ignored is that, whether we regard delusions as beliefs or as something else, many of their epistemic features are shared by attitudes that are widespread in the non-clinical population, which suggests a continuity between so-called 'normal' and 'abnormal' cognition.

7.3 Delusion and Irrationality

Is Delusional Reasoning Irrational?

We will now turn to the irrationality of delusions. According to the standard picture, rationality consists in reasoning in accordance with logico-mathematical rules such as the conjunction rule or Bayes' rule. In Chapter 1, we saw that humans systematically and predictably deviate from logico-mathematical rules of reasoning. Our question here is whether people with delusions reason differently from people with no psychiatric diagnosis and, in particular, whether people with delusions reason more irrationally than people with no psychiatric diagnosis.

According to Eilhard von Domarus (1944), delusions involve a distinctive failure of deductive reasoning. For example, a person might acquire the delusion that he is Napoleon on the basis of the following faulty reasoning:

Premise 1: Napoleon was exiled and incarcerated.
Premise 2: I have been exiled and incarcerated.
Conclusion: Therefore, I am Napoleon.

If von Domarus' hypothesis is correct, it strongly supports the view that the deductive reasoning of people with delusion is significantly more irrational than the deductive reasoning of people without known pathologies. People without known pathologies exhibit some errors and biases, including the deductive errors shown in the Wason selection task (discussed in Chapter 1) and deductive biases such as the belief bias (discussed in Chapter 3), but they do not make these obvious errors in syllogistic reasoning.

Von Domarus' hypothesis, however, is not widely accepted, mainly due to a lack of empirical support (see Garety & Hemsley 1997). In fact, the ability to reason deductively does not seem to be especially impaired in people with delusions. For example, consider the following case of a person with anosognosia (the delusional denial of illness), P.R., concerning the paralysis of the left side of his body:

> On one occasion, the examiner placed P.R.'s left hand on the bedclothes, between his own hands and asked the patient whose hands they were: Unhesitatingly, P.R. replied that they were the examiner's hands. Questioned as to whether he had ever met a three-handed man, P.R., pointing to the three arms in front of him, answered that because the examiner had three arms he also must have three hands. (Bisiach & Geminiani 1991, 34)

P.R. came to the delusional conclusion that the examiner had three hands. Their reasoning seems to be as follows:

Premise 1: The examiner has three arms.
Premise 2: Anyone with three arms has three hands.
Conclusion: Therefore, the examiner has three hands.

This looks like a reasonable piece of deductive reasoning (although this reasoning can be a *post hoc* justification of P.R.'s denial of the ownership of the hand). The problem is not P.R.'s reasoning, it is rather their acceptance of an implausible premise (the premise that the examiner has three hands).

But even if von Domarus' hypothesis is wrong, there may still be doubts about Maher's strong claim that the reasoning of people with delusions is completely normal and 'essentially indistinguishable from that employed by non-patients, by scientists, and by people generally' (Maher 1974, 103). There is in fact a strong body of evidence suggesting that probabilistic reasoning abnormalities, rather than deductive reasoning abnormalities, are associated with delusions. The most famous finding concerns the jumping-to-conclusion bias.

The Jumping-to-Conclusion Bias

In a well-known study (Huq, Garety, & Hemsley 1988), three groups of participants (a group with schizophrenic delusions, a group with a psychiatric condition but without delusions, and a group with no psychiatric conditions) were asked to observe a jam jar with 100 coloured beads in it and identify whether it was Jar *A* (containing 85 pink beads and 15 green beads) or Jar *B* (containing 15 pink beads and 85 green beads) on the basis of the beads drawn from it. The result revealed that participants in the delusional group tended to 'jump to the conclusion': they required less evidence (observing 2.22 beads on average) before coming to a conclusion than participants in the non-delusional group (observing 4.58 beads on average) and participants in the non-clinical group (observing 3.60 beads on average).

One might think, then, that the jumping-to-conclusion bias clearly shows that people with delusions are significantly more irrational than non-clinical people in the sense that they do not wait to acquire sufficient evidence before reaching a conclusion in a probabilistic judgment. This is, however, too hasty. To see this, we need to clarify the notion of 'bias'. The term 'bias' can mean different things in different contexts. First, it can mean a deviation from some rational norms such as logico-mathematical rules. Let us call those deviations 'irrational biases'. Base-rate neglect, which we saw in Chapter 1, is an irrational bias and a deviation from Bayes' rule. Second, 'bias' can mean a deviation from statistically normal performance. Let us call such deviations 'abnormal biases'. The jumping-to-conclusion bias is an abnormal bias; what studies have revealed is that people with delusions reach a conclusion more quickly than non-clinical people.

The jumping-to-conclusion bias is an abnormal bias (a deviation from normal performance). But here is the crucial question: 'Is the jumping-to-conclusion bias also an irrational bias (a deviation from normative standards)?' The answer is probably 'No'. In the beads experiment, those with delusions required 2.22 beads on average before reaching a conclusion, which means that they reached a conclusion when the probability of the conclusion (e.g., the conclusion that it was Jar *A* rather than Jar *B*) was over 0.97 according to Bayesian statistics. Endorsing a hypothesis whose probability is over 0.97 would be rational. For example, it would be rational for you to judge that it will rain today and take an umbrella with you when you go outside if reliable weather forecasts indicate that there is a 97% chance of rain today. People without delusions, who required 3.60 beads on average, reached a conclusion when the probability of the hypothesis was even higher. Hesitating to endorse a hypothesis whose probability is 0.97 can be regarded as irrational in some contexts. For example, it would be irrational for you to doubt that it will rain today and fail to bring an umbrella with you if reliable weather forecasts indicate that there is a 97% chance of rain today.

Thus, the finding about the jumping-to-conclusion bias does not show that people with delusions *irrationally jump* to a conclusion; instead, it shows that people without delusions *irrationally hesitate* to accept a conclusion. From a logico-mathematical point of view, it is the people without delusions, not the people with delusions, who are biased in the sense that their performance deviates from standards of rationality. This is why Huq, Garety, and Hemsley write that 'it may be argued that the deluded sample reached a decision at an objectively "rational" point. It may further be argued that the two control groups were somewhat over-cautious' (Huq, Garety, & Hemsley 1988, 809).

Interestingly, however, Huq, Garety, and Hemsley continued:

> Although the deluded sample's responses on two of the measures appears more 'Bayesian', being less subject to the 'conservatism' bias than normals, it is not possible to conclude that deluded people are better reasoners. [...] Conservatism of this type may, in certain circumstances, be ecologically valid serving as a useful general strategy under conditions of uncertainty. (Huq, Garety, & Hemsley 1988, 810)

In effect, Huq, Garety, and Hemsley appeal to the ecological picture of rationality (which we discussed in Chapter 1), and argue that people with delusions could be irrational according to the ecological conception of rationality (although they are rational according to the standard picture of rationality). The reasoning performance of non-clinical participants is somewhat conservative from a logico-mathematical point of view, but it makes sense ecologically because excessive caution is often beneficial for the purposes of survival and reproduction. If Huq, Garety, and Hemsley are correct, then delusion is another case in which the standard picture and the ecological picture have different implications for rationality.

In any case, the suggestion that those with delusions are (in the standard picture) more rational than those without delusions is surprising, but it is consistent with other empirical findings. For example, a similar pattern emerges when people with delusions are tested in the reasoning tasks of the heuristics and biases programme.

In one study, Rhiannon Corcoran and colleagues (2006) examined the probabilistic reasoning of those with persecutory delusions using the reasoning tasks in the heuristics and biases programme. For example, one of the tasks was a version of the base-rate neglect task by Tversky and Kahneman (1974). Participants first read the following personality description and then answered whether Barry is a builder or a street robber.

> Barry is a skinny rough-looking individual who keeps himself to himself. He is quite a selfish person and is not very considerate towards other people. Nonetheless, Barry has a high level of awareness for what is going on around him and his reflexes are very fast.

Just like in the original study by Tversky and Kahneman, different base-rate information is provided in different conditions. In one condition, it is said that Barry was randomly selected from 100 descriptions, where 70 of them are builders and 30 of them are street robbers. The base-rate information is reversed in the other condition (i.e., 30 builders and 70 street robbers). The result was that people without delusions largely neglected the base-rate information, just like in the original study, while those with persecutory delusions were significantly more sensitive to base-rate information. This shows that people with persecutory delusions are more rational, and less biased, than people without delusions.

Let us summarize our discussion so far. At this moment it is not clear that the (deductive or probabilistic) reasoning of people with delusions is significantly more irrational than the reasoning of people without delusions and without a psychiatric diagnosis. Indeed, some evidence suggests that people with delusions can perform better than people without delusions and without a psychiatric diagnosis as far as the rationality of reasoning is concerned.

Are Delusions Irrational in a Distinctive Way?

We saw that people do not need to reason irrationally to adopt delusional beliefs, but there may be some other aspect of the adoption or maintenance of delusions which suggests that something is amiss.

Let us start with *procedural rationality*. Procedural rationality concerns the relationship between a person's beliefs and their other intentional states. Procedurally rational beliefs are well integrated in a largely coherent system and mutually support each other. Are delusions procedurally irrational? Some seem to be. A person with the Cotard delusion who states that she is dead might agree that typically dead people do not talk or move, and recognize that she does talk and move, but remain convinced that she is dead (McKay & Cipolotti 2007). The beliefs the person has (1. dead people do not talk; 2. I talk; 3. I am dead) do not hang together well. We could say that they conflict with one another and contribute to an incoherent set of beliefs.

We might be tempted to think that procedural irrationality is a distinctive feature of delusions and sets them apart from other beliefs. It is not uncommon for people to have implausible beliefs, but it is rare to hear people endorse in the same conversation claims that clash with one another. However, there are pervasive and significant failures of procedural rationality in non-delusional beliefs as well – this means that procedural rationality is not a distinctive feature of delusions. For instance, people who work in the police force or in hospital emergency services tend to believe that more accidents happen during nights of a full moon even though their experience and background knowledge should speak against a full moon being a causal factor of accidents.

Let us move on to *epistemic rationality*. Epistemic rationality concerns the relationship between a person's beliefs and the evidence available to that person, before and after adopting the belief. As we have seen, delusions are often defined in terms of their violation of norms of epistemic rationality – they are defined as beliefs that are ill grounded and resistant to counter-evidence. However, there is an interesting debate in philosophy about whether delusions actually are epistemically irrational, and to what extent. As we have seen, some authors argue that a person adopting delusions is just endorsing an explanation of their anomalous experience, where such experience is evidence for the delusional belief. Similarly, it is undeniable that delusions are resistant to counter-evidence, but it is widely acknowledged that people with delusions are sensitive to evidence; they often have some insight into the implausibility of their delusions and defend their delusions from external challenges with arguments that involve presenting evidence for the delusion.

Again, we might be tempted to think that epistemic irrationality is a distinctive feature of delusions and sets them apart from other beliefs. It is not uncommon for people to have beliefs that are not well supported by evidence and to hold on to their beliefs strenuously, but it is rare for people to hold on to beliefs that they themselves recognize as implausible to the same extent that people with delusions hold on to their delusions. However, psychological evidence about biases in the formation and revision of beliefs (e.g., how prejudiced and superstitious beliefs are adopted on flimsy evidence and how difficult it is for people to relinquish those beliefs despite an abundance of counter-evidence) suggests that there are widespread and systematic failures of epistemic rationality in non-delusional beliefs as well.

Finally, let us consider *agential rationality*. Agential rationality concerns the relationship between beliefs and behaviour. This notion bridges the traditional divide between theoretical and practical rationality. We expect rational beliefs to be reflected in an agent's behaviour and to guide action in the relevant circumstances. We know that people reporting delusions do not consistently act on their delusions in the appropriate circumstances. In a classic example by Eugen Bleuler (1911), a woman claimed to be the queen but did not behave like royalty.

Agential irrationality seems to set delusions apart from other beliefs. People may not always act on their beliefs, but it is rare for people to report beliefs with the same conviction with which people with delusions report their delusions, and then show no commitment to such beliefs in their behaviour. However, the evidence on attitude–behaviour inconsistencies undermines the suggestion that agential rationality is a distinctive feature of delusions. For instance, in Elliot Aronson's influential work on cognitive dissonance, we find that people are hypocritical by endorsing general principles and then denying that such principles apply to their own conduct (Aronson 2019). One example is college students' attitudes to safe sex in the United States. College students are likely to endorse the principle that one should always practise safe sex but recognize that they often do not practise safe sex. The fact that they acknowledge their own conduct as violating that principle does not lead them to revisit their endorsement of the general principle.

In summary, delusions are continuous with non-delusional beliefs and they are not irrational in a distinctive way. This means that their being pathological (their being considered symptoms of mental disorders) cannot be accounted for by their irrationality alone. What, then, distinguishes delusions from other irrational beliefs? For example, what distinguishes the delusion that one is being harassed and harmed by envious co-workers from the irrational belief that Linda is more likely to be a feminist bank teller than just a bank teller? Is the former more harmful than the latter? Or is the former caused by a distinctive brain dysfunction? Or should we just reject the assumption that there is a principled distinction between delusions and other irrational beliefs?

7.4 Confabulation

What Is Confabulation?

When the term 'confabulation' is used in a clinical context, it refers to a symptom of disorders involving severe memory impairments, such as dementia and amnesia. In this section, we will focus on clinical confabulation, also called *narrow* confabulation, where an inaccurate or ill-grounded claim is made as a result of a memory impairment. As in the case of delusion, there are controversies about the best definition of confabulation – see Box 7D for two popular definitions, characterizing confabulation as either a *fabricated or distorted* memory or a *false* belief; and Box 7E for a list of key features of confabulation. What most definitions have in common is that they describe confabulation in terms of an epistemic fault and make no specific reference to underlying mechanisms.

Here is an example of confabulation: HW, who has memory impairments due to frontal damage, correctly reports that he is

BOX 7D: Definitions of Confabulation

'An extreme form of pathological memory distortion is confabulation, i.e. the production of fabricated, or distorted memories about one's self or the world, without the conscious intention to deceive' (Fotopoulou et al. 2008, 1429).

'Confabulations are typically understood to represent instances of false beliefs: opinions about the world that are manifestly incorrect and yet are held by the patient to be true in spite of clearly presented evidence to the contrary' (Turnbull, Jenkins, & Rowley 2004, 6).

BOX 7E: Features of Confabulation (Cherry 2020)

- Lack of awareness that the memory report is false or distorted.
- No attempt to deceive or lie.
- The story is usually drawn from the person's memory.
- The story can be either coherent and plausible or incoherent and unrealistic.

married and that he has four children. When he is asked how long he has been married, he incorrectly replies 'four months' instead of '30 years'. When he is asked how it is that he has four children after only four months of marriage, he claims that his children were adopted, even though they are in fact his natural children (Moscovitch 1995). Not only are HW's reports about his autobiographical past incorrect, he is also resistant to challenges from his interlocutors.

Different types of confabulation have been identified, and differences occur in either form or content. The form of confabulations can be *spontaneous* or *provoked* (Kopelman 1999; Schnider 2003). Spontaneous confabulations (usually associated with a frontal dysfunction) are unsolicited reports, whereas provoked confabulations are answers to direct questioning that may occur in the absence of an identified impairment. The content of confabulations can be *fantastic* or *mundane* (Berlyne 1972). Spontaneous confabulations tend to be fantastic and provoked confabulations tend to be mundane. A further distinction can be made between *primary* and *secondary* confabulations. Primary confabulation is an initial inaccurate report about the past; secondary confabulation is a further report that is offered to support the primary confabulation.

There are competing accounts of the way confabulations arise. On some accounts of confabulation motivational factors are key (see Turnbull, Jenkins, & Rowley 2004), and on other accounts cognitive neuropsychological factors prevail. The former may involve embellishing a memory report to feel better about oneself: for instance, to feel that one is more skilled or more independent than one actually is. The latter may involve: a deficit in retrieval strategies (e.g., an inability to access relevant memories); a confusion of the temporal order of remembered events (e.g., an inability to determine chronology); a deficit in the construction of memories (e.g., exaggerated memory reconstruction); or poor source monitoring (e.g., something imagined is reported as something remembered). Several researchers have argued that to understand how confabulations arise we need to combine neuropsychological and motivational factors (e.g., Fotopoulou et al. 2007; Metcalf, Langdon, & Coltheart 2007).

One suggestion is to apply the two-factor theory we saw in our discussion of delusions to the case of confabulation (Aimola Davies & Davies 2009). The first factor would be responsible for the presence of the confabulation in the first place and the second would explain why the confabulation is accepted as true. In the case of confabulation, similar to the case of delusion, the second factor would be a failure to inhibit explanatory hypotheses or memories that are implausible or ill grounded, and would occur in all instances of confabulation. The first factor would be the neuropsychological factor, potentially different in different pathologies.

Indeed, it is unlikely that a single deficit underpins all pathological cases of confabulation since confabulation is associated with pathologies that have different neurobiological bases (including amnesic syndromes, damage to the anterior cerebral artery, traumatic brain injury, neglect, delusions of misidentification, dementia, and anosognosia). Confabulation can also occur in the absence of any known pathology. We saw in Chapter 2 that instances of confabulation where no deficit is observed are common; the stockings experiment is an example, where people offer explanations for their consumer choices that are not well grounded (Nisbett and Wilson 1977).

Does Confabulation Distort Reality in a Distinctive Way?

Now that we better understand the phenomenon of clinical or narrow confabulation, we can turn to the question of whether memory distortions that are displayed in confabulatory reports are distinctive. In confabulation, the content of memory reports does not match reality – the resulting beliefs may be false and ill grounded as the person lacks autobiographical evidence on which to base their claims due to the memory impairment. Past events are reported differently from how they were experienced. In some cases, the distortion reflects a bias: the person may deny an unpleasant event such as a family fall-out or exaggerate past personal achievements. Also, in confabulation, the content of memory reports may be inconsistent with other things people believe or remember, which causes tension. This means that for people who confabulate due to a clinical impairment, memory reports may at the same time fail to match reality and lack internal coherence.

We may think that a lack of correspondence with the facts and inconsistencies are distinctive features of memory reports and are the result of serious memory impairments. However, recent psychological research suggests that there are widespread everyday memory distortions. Daniel Schacter's work has been very influential in this area (see Schacter 1999). He talks about seven common 'sins of memory' (see Box 7F). Sins of omission occur when people forget something that they should be able to remember. Sins of commission occur when people believe that they remember more than what they actually experienced or report an event differently from how they experienced it. When we look more closely at Schacter's seven sins of memory, we realize that the distortions described are not different in kind from those we observe in clinical confabulations.

The most common sources of memory distortion are *misattribution* and *bias*. Here are some memory distortions that have been studied in some detail. In *imagination inflation*, people who imagine an event that never occurred subsequently falsely recall that the event did occur. In the *Deese–Roediger–McDermott (DRM) effect*, people presented with a list of words falsely believe that some items that are semantically related to the words on the list were also on the list

BOX 7F: Schacter's 'Seven Sins of Memory'

Sins of omission:

1. *Transience*: the accessibility of memories decreases over time (normal with ageing and decay).
2. *Absent-mindedness*: attention lapses and one forgets to do things ('Where are my car keys?').
3. *Blocking*: some stored information is temporarily inaccessible (tip-of-the-tongue syndrome).

Sins of commission:

4. *Suggestibility*: misinformation is integrated into memory due to deception or the way questions are asked.
5. *Bias*: retrospective distortions are produced by one's current state of mind (if one is unhappy with one's relationship now, one thinks of it as being less successful than it was in the past).
6. *Persistence*: information that one does not want to recall persists nonetheless (intrusive memories of trauma).
7. *Misattribution*: memories are attributed to incorrect sources (one believes that one remembers something that was only inferred or imagined).

– this experimental paradigm was developed by Deese (1959) and was revised by Roediger and McDermott (1995). In the *post-information effect*, people seemingly remember details of an experienced event (e.g., a summer ball in their college), but not some detail of that event (e.g., their friend dancing the waltz). This detail was learnt from another source at a later stage (e.g., from the friend who talked about it the next day) and incorporated it into the memory report.

The misrepresentation often fits with what the person wishes to believe: after taking a study skills class, people asked about their performance exaggerated how bad it was before the class and exaggerated how good it was after the class to lend support to the view that the class had helped them improve their skills (Conway & Ross 1984). Indeed, people's present beliefs, feelings, and opinions affect the way they remember past events. For instance, the so-called *consistency bias* occurs when people interpret the past in the light of the present. People were asked to rate their attitudes towards major social issues, such as whether drugs should be legalized, whether women should be treated equally, and whether ethnic minorities should be helped. Nine years later, the same participants were asked to rate their attitudes again and to report what their attitudes had been the first time around. Participants remembered their past attitudes as much closer to their current attitudes than they actually were (Markus 1986).

In the context of dementia and other neuropsychological disorders, memory beliefs are vulnerable to both misattribution and bias. One instance of misattribution is when salient life events are not reported in the right chronological order or are ignored altogether. In this case, it is harder to identify systematic connections among life events. In our earlier example of Jacob reporting that he had been on a walk with his mother that very morning, when in fact the event had taken place several years earlier, Jacob's memory is not entirely fabricated, it is just given the wrong 'time tag'. This might make it harder for Jacob to identify links between individual events and things he knows: he might see himself as a young man when he is actually in his seventies; and he might expect his mother to be still alive, even though she has long passed away.

As in everyday instances of bias, recollections of the past are distorted in patients with brain damage in such a way as to present their past selves in a better light. Stories that depart from reality are not accepted by the person's close social circles and may create tension there (Fotopoulou 2008), but self-enhancing memories can have positive effects on mood regulation. By putting a positive spin on their experiences, people feel better about themselves, and this brings with it some clinical and pragmatic advantages too. Optimistically biased memories are generally correlated with reduced stress and good physical and psychological health, but there are also possible costs, such as when people underestimate risk.

On some occasions, people do not change the past to fit the present, but rather change the present to fit the past. This is known as 'a failure in updating'. People describe their present selves as much more similar to their past selves than they actually are. For instance, people developing a chronic or degenerative disease may continue to view themselves as they were before the onset of the disease and may not acknowledge some of their physical or psychological changes.

People with dementia experience a shift in personality as a result of their condition, becoming more aloof, introverted, unassured, and submissive (Rankin et al. 2005). However, they do not necessarily have awareness of such changes and tend to underestimate how unassured and submissive they have become. This lack of awareness ensures that their concept of self remains largely coherent. Both the principles of internal coherence and correspondence with the facts apply to autobiographical memory (Conway 2005): memories are sometimes altered to preserve a coherent self as the past is rewritten to make sense of the current self-concept (*consistency bias*) or the present is redescribed in a way that makes it more continuous with the past (*updating failure*).

In summary, in this section we have suggested that distortions of memory in clinical confabulation are not different in kind from distortions of memory in everyday life and that in both contexts distortions present themselves as instances of common sins of memory. As the debates on delusions have inspired a renewed interest in the nature of belief, the pervasiveness and the adaptiveness of memory distortions have informed the lively debate about the function of human memory. Is memory supposed to contribute to knowledge of the past or to ensure that agents maintain a coherent sense of self?

How Do We Remember?

If memory distortion does not occur exclusively in disordered minds, but is a much more common phenomenon than we might have initially suspected, how can we explain the widespread fallibility of human memory capacity? How does the frequency of memory errors change the way we think about human memory? One influential view is that the memory distortions we discussed, both the everyday ones and the ones we encounter in clinical confabulation, are due to the reconstructive nature of autobiographical memory.

According to some psychologists (see, e.g., the work of Loftus 2003; Schacter & Addis 2007; Tulving 2002), memory distortions suggest that there is more than one memory system in humans and that such systems operate differently. Whereas semantic memory (memory of a fact that has not been experienced, such as remembering that Rome is the capital of Italy or that World War II ended in 1945) is mostly *reproductive*, episodic memory (memory of a fact that is first-personally experienced) is mostly *reconstructive*. When memory is reproductive, stored information is retrieved at a later time and becomes the content of a belief about the past. Reproductive memory is often described using the analogy of a library or a store-house. When memory is reconstructive, stored information is used to construct a belief about the past. Reconstructive memory is often described as the work of a detective who works through limited clues to arrive at a solution to a mystery (Salvaggio 2018). In a reproductive memory system, there can be gaps and errors when stored information is not properly encoded or cannot be retrieved. But, in a reconstructive memory system, there can also be distortions when the memory of the event that is inferred from the stored information 'makes sense' but does not correspond to how the event was experienced in the past. The reconstructive nature of autobiographical memory and episodic memory would explain the memory distortions we reviewed in both clinical and non-clinical contexts.

What are the implications of episodic memory being reconstructive? A reconstructive memory system can be seen as a disadvantage (if inference is necessary, then distortions can occur), but it can also be seen as an advantage. For instance, in a move that reminds us of Gigerenzer's attempt to describe heuristics as a manifestation of ecological rationality (which we considered in Chapter 1), Schacter argues that memory distortions are not simply epistemic failures; memory distortions reveal the adaptiveness of memory mechanisms. Schacter's claim is not that it is adaptive to have distorted memories, but that it is adaptive to have a memory system that results in the occasional distorted memory:

> While it is tempting to conclude that memory distortions point to fundamental flaws in the nature or composition of memory, a growing number of researchers have argued that, to the contrary, many memory distortions reflect the operation of adaptive processes – that is, processes that contribute to the efficient functioning of memory, but as a consequence of serving that role, also produce distortions. (Schacter, Guerin, & St Jacques 2011, 467)

Let us see how this would work for some of the memory distortions we considered in the previous section. For instance, the DRM effect (when people remember certain items as being on a list of words because the items are semantically related to words on the list) is an obvious distortion leading to an inaccurate memory report (e.g., that the word 'bread' was on a list with 'flour', 'dough', and 'yeast' on it).

However, it also reveals associative processes that benefit the organization and retention of information and facilitate inference (Schacter, Guerin, & St Jacques 2011; Puddifoot & Bortolotti 2019). It is good for people to be able to associate semantically related items as it saves cognitive effort in a number of circumstances. If one goes shopping for the ingredients of a recipe for baking bread, associations between semantically related items ('flour' and 'yeast') make it easier for one to remember what to buy.

Similarly, imagination inflation can be viewed in a positive light. Consider Iyla coming to believe that she broke her arm when she was five, when this is just something she only imagined. Iyla has false beliefs about her past ('I broke my arm') and is also likely to form further beliefs that are consistent with the false memory report and equally fail to reflect reality (such as 'I had to wear a cast' or 'I missed a day at school'). But the fact that people integrate some imagined events into their autobiographical memories also suggests that the same mechanisms are sometimes involved in both remembering the past and imagining the future (Schacter & Addis 2007), and this allows for flexibility of thought, for instance when making plans for the future based on past experience.

> [The] capacity to combine traces of information in different ways [...] enables agents to make predictions about novel future events, facilitating flexible predictions about the future that draw on a diversity of information about the past. (Puddifoot & Bortolotti 2019, 764)

7.5 Summary

- Delusions are defined as irrational beliefs. They can have various themes and can be more or less widespread in a belief system. On most accounts, delusions are formed in response to anomalous experience, but it is controversial whether reasoning deficits or biases also contribute to the formation of delusions.
- When it comes to standards of good reasoning, it is not clear that people with delusions reason irrationally. Evidence suggests that people with delusions reason *differently* from people without a psychiatric diagnosis, but it does not show that the former reason *more irrationally* than the latter.

- Delusions are certainly irrational in several ways, but the irrationality of delusions is not different in kind from the irrationality of non-delusional beliefs. The pathological nature of delusions therefore cannot be accounted for by their irrationality alone.
- In a number of mental disorders and in several everyday contexts, human memory fails and memory reports are distorted. Distortions can have different forms and different causes, from memory impairments to biases.
- There is considerable continuity between distortions in clinical and non-clinical contexts, and many everyday memory reports turn out to be distorted. This suggests that some human memory systems operate reconstructively, where the report is the result of an attempt to fill gaps in information with plausible inferences.

Further Resources

Articles and Books

There are a number of monographs on delusions worth reading which expound competing views of the nature of delusions: Lisa Bortolotti's *Delusions and Other Irrational Beliefs* (2010), which defends the view that delusions are irrational beliefs (doxasticism); Jennifer Radden's *On Delusion* (2010), which contains an interesting discussion of collective delusions; Philip Gerrans' *The Measure of Madness: Philosophy of Mind, Cognitive Neuroscience, and Delusional Thought* (2014), which defends the view that narratives of delusion accommodate anomalous experiences; Peter McKenna's *Delusions: Understanding the Un-understandable* (2017), which is written from the perspective of a clinician; and Kengo Miyazono's *Delusions and Beliefs: A Philosophical Inquiry* (2018), which argues that delusions are malfunctioning beliefs. For a brief summary of recent developments in the philosophical literature on delusions, you can read our own paper in *Philosophy Compass* (Bortolotti & Miyazono 2015).

We also recommend two edited collections: *Delusions in Context* (edited by Lisa Bortolotti, 2018), which encompasses four distinct disciplinary backgrounds; and *Delusion and Confabulation* (edited by Robyn Langdon and Martha Turner, 2010), which discusses the overlapping features of the two puzzling phenomena.

For an introduction to the philosophy of memory, you can look at Sven Bernecker and Kourken Michaelian's *Routledge Handbook of Philosophy of Memory* (2017).

More specifically on clinical confabulation and everyday distortions of memory, there are open-access papers by Lisa Bortolotti and Ema Sullivan-Bissett (2018) and Kathy Puddifoot and Lisa Bortolotti (2019).

Online Resources

There are many useful online resources on delusions: Bortolotti's *Stanford Encyclopedia of Philosophy* entry (2019) is a good place to start, together with her podcast for the *Radical Philosophy* radio programme (3CR 2017). We also recommend Kourken Michaelian and John Sutton's *Stanford Encyclopedia of Philosophy* entry on memory (2017).

On YouTube, there are three useful interviews on delusions by Raj Persaud with philosopher and psychiatrist Matthew Broome (2015a), neuroscientist Philip Corlett (2015b), and psychologist Richard Bentall (2015c). On the *Philosophers on Medicine* podcast series, there is an interview with Matthew Parrott on the nature of delusions (CMAJ Podcasts 2019).

Questions

1. How do you define delusions? What are necessary conditions for a belief to be delusional? What are sufficient conditions for a belief to be delusional?
2. List some examples of everyday irrational beliefs you (or someone you know) have (or used to have) and compare them with delusions. How are they similar? How are they different?
3. A delusion is considered as a pathological mental state, while the false belief that Linda is more likely to be a feminist bank teller than a bank teller is not. Why?
4. Richard Dawkins calls the religious belief in God the 'God Delusion' and endorses Robert Pirsig's statement: 'When one person suffers from a delusion, it is called insanity. When many people suffer from a delusion it is called Religion' (Dawkins 2006, 28). Do you agree with Dawkins? How are religious beliefs and delusions similar? How are they different?

8

Autism and Psychopathy

8.1 Introduction

This chapter continues our discussion of unusual psychological conditions. In the previous chapter, we discussed philosophical issues concerning delusion and confabulation, which are regarded as symptoms of mental disorders such as schizophrenia and dementia. In this chapter, we shift our focus to autism and psychopathy. There are some important issues surrounding how people talk about autism and psychopathy which we review in Box 8A (see also Box 7A in the previous chapter for general considerations about the language used in mental health debates).

In this chapter, we are interested in what characterizes autism and psychopathy. In a nutshell, autism is often characterized by unusual social and communicative behaviour and psychopathy is often characterized by unusual patterns of anti-social behaviour. What explains autism and its characteristic social communicative behaviour? What explains psychopathy and its characteristic anti-social behaviour?

According to Simon Baron-Cohen (2011), both autism and psychopathy involve problems with empathy. He argues that problems with empathy are severe and extreme in these conditions: autism and psychopathy involve 'zero degrees of empathy' (Baron-Cohen 2011, 16).

BOX 8A: Neurodiversity or Disability?

There is some controversy as to how we should understand conditions such as autism which has implications for how we talk about people diagnosed with those conditions. Is autism an illness, a disability, or merely a psychological and neurological difference? (Similar considerations apply to psychopathy.)

- The neurodiversity movement argues that autism should not be pathologized, arguing that it is not something that people have but a central part of the person's identity. If we see autism as a pathology, we devalue people who are autistic. The idea is that non-autistic people are not 'normal' in a normative sense (i.e. they function as they should) but are 'normal' in a statistical sense (i.e. the way they function characterizes the majority of people). In the neurodiversity movement, the preferred way to describe people is *autistic* (as opposed to *neurotypical*) rather than *people with autism*.
- Some disagree with the neurodiversity movement (especially those who care for people with very severe forms of autism) and argue that neurodiversity trivializes the challenges that autistic people experience. The preferred model is a medical model of autism instead where autism indicates suboptimal performance in a number of domains and is something that needs to be prevented and treated. Among those who see autism as a disease or a disability, the preferred way to describe people is *people with autism* rather than *autistic people* as autism is not seen as a central part of the person's identity.

Note that Baron-Cohen uses the term 'empathy' in a very broad sense here. He defines empathy as being constituted by two components: the ability to 'identify what someone else is thinking or feeling' and the ability to 'respond to their thoughts and feelings with an appropriate emotion' (Baron-Cohen 2011, 11). Baron-Cohen's distinction between *identifying* and *responding* corresponds to the distinction (which we mentioned in Chapter 5) between 'cognitive empathy' (or 'mindreading', 'theory of mind', or 'mentalizing') and 'affective empathy'. The former refers to the cognitive process of attributing mental states to somebody else and the latter refers to the affective process of emotionally responding to somebody else in need. Hereafter, we will use the term 'empathy' instead of 'affective empathy' and we will use 'mindreading' instead of 'cognitive empathy'.

Following this terminological distinction, one might think of autism as primarily a disorder of mindreading and psychopathy as primarily a disorder of empathy. In fact, autism is often associated with mindreading deficits, and psychopathy is often associated with empathy deficits. More precisely, autism is characterized by social and communicative problems, which are often associated with mindreading deficits. Psychopathy is often characterized by anti-social behavioural tendencies, which are often associated with empathy deficits.

The main aim of this chapter is to examine the role of mindreading deficits in autism (Section 8.2), and the role of empathy deficits in psychopathy (Section 8.3). Our main claim will be that both autism and psychopathy are complex phenomena, which cannot be fully captured by essentialist views, such as the view that mindreading deficits are the essence of autism, or the view that empathy deficits are the essence of psychopathy. Mindreading deficits are an important factor in autism, but they might not be the essence of it. Again, empathy deficits are an important factor in psychopathy, but they might not be the essence of it.

We will revisit some topics that we discussed in earlier chapters. For instance, in Chapter 2, we discussed the idea of peculiar, non-observational self-knowledge. The assumption was that you do not have to observe your own behaviour to know what you think and feel, while you do need to observe the behaviour of your friends to know what they think and feel. But we have not yet said enough about what you need to do in order to know other minds. This is, in effect, a question about how mindreading works (Section 8.3).

We also discussed moral judgment and the role of emotion in it (Chapter 4), as well as moral behaviour and the role of empathy in it (Chapter 5). If emotion is crucial for making moral judgment, we should expect changes in how emotions are felt to cause changes in moral judgment. Again, if empathy is crucial for engaging in moral behaviour, we should expect changes in empathy to cause changes in moral behaviour. As we will see, psychopathy is an informative test case to examine such predictions about moral judgment (Section 8.4) and moral behaviour (Section 8.3).

8.2   Autism and Mindreading

Autism

'Autism spectrum disorder' (ASD) refers to a spectrum of conditions, including: classic autism, which was first introduced by Leo Kanner and is characterized by a triad of impairments, often called 'Wing's triad of impairment' (Wing & Gould, 1979), that affect social inter-action and communication, and lead to a narrow and repetitive range of activities; and Asperger's syndrome, which was first introduced by Hans Asperger and is characterized by similar symptoms to classic autism but also other symptoms and less severe linguistic delays (Box 8B).

Let us now consider the classical case of Donald T., reported by Kanner (1943). Donald exhibited some unusual behaviour in infancy when it was observed that 'he was happiest when left alone, almost never cried to go with his mother, did not seem to notice his father's homecomings, and was indifferent to visiting relatives' (Kanner 1943, 218). At the age of 3, Donald was placed in a tuberculosis preventorium, where he exhibited a 'disinclination to play with children and do things children his age usually take an interest in' and '[a]n abstraction of mind which made him perfectly oblivious to everything about him' (Kanner 1943, 218). He was first examined at the age of 5, when examiners observed some peculiar patterns of behaviour:

> There was a marked limitation of spontaneous activity. He wandered about, making stereotyped movements with his fingers, crossing them about in the air. He shook his head from side to side, whispering or humming the same three-note tune. He spun with great pleasure anything he could seize upon to spin. [...] Beyond this he showed no initiative, requiring constant instruction (from his mother) in any form of activity other than the limited ones in which he was absorbed. Most of his actions were repetitions carried out in exactly the same way in which they had been performed originally. If he spun a block, he must always start with the same face uppermost. (Kanner 1943, 219)

Linguistic and communicative anomalies were observed too.

> He seemed to have much pleasure in ejaculating words of phrases, such as 'Chrysanthemum'; 'Dahlia, dahlia, dahlia'; 'Business'; 'Trumpet vine'; 'The right one is on, the left one is off'; 'Through the dark

BOX 8B: Autism Spectrum Disorder in *DSM-5* (American Psychiatric Association 2013, 50–51)

A. Persistent deficits in social communication and social interaction across multiple contexts, as manifested by the following, currently or by history:

1. Deficits in social-emotional reciprocity, ranging, for example, from abnormal social approach and failure of normal back-and-forth conversation; to reduced sharing of interests, emotions, or affect; to failure to initiate or respond to social interactions.
2. Deficits in nonverbal communicative behaviors used for social interaction, ranging, for example, from poorly integrated verbal and nonverbal communication; to abnormalities in eye contact and body language or deficits in understanding and use of gestures; to a total lack of facial expressions and nonverbal communication.
3. Deficits in developing, maintaining, and understanding relationships, ranging, for example, from difficulties adjusting behavior to suit various social contexts; to difficulties in sharing imaginative play or in making friends; to absence of interest in peers.

B. Restricted, repetitive patterns of behavior, interests, or activities, as manifested by at least two of the following, currently or by history:

1. Stereotyped or repetitive motor movements, use of objects, or speech (e.g., simple motor stereotypes, lining up toys or flipping objects, echolalia, idiosyncratic phrases).
2. Insistence on sameness, inflexible adherence to routines, or ritualized patterns of verbal or nonverbal behavior (e.g., extreme distress at small changes, difficulties with transitions, rigid thinking patterns, greeting rituals, need to take same route or eat same food every day).
3. Highly restricted, fixated interests that are abnormal in intensity or focus (e.g., strong attachment to or preoccupation

(cont'd)

with unusual objects, excessively circumscribed or persever-
ative interests).
4. Hyper- or hypo-reactivity to sensory input or unusual
interest in sensory aspects of the environment (e.g., apparent
indifference to pain/temperature, adverse response to specific
sounds or textures, excessive smelling or touching of objects,
visual fascination with lights or movement).

C. Symptoms must be present in the early developmental period
(but may not become fully manifest until social demands exceed
limited capacities, or may be masked by learned strategies in
later life).

D. Symptoms cause clinically significant impairment in social,
occupational, or other important areas of current functioning.

clouds shining'. Irrelevant utterances such as these were his ordinary
mode of speech. He always seemed to be parroting what he had heard
said to him at one time or another. He used the personal pronouns for
the persons he was quoting, even imitating the intonation. When he
wanted his mother to pull his shoe off, he said: 'Pull off your shoe.'
When he wanted a bath, he said: 'Do you want a bath?' [...] He
paid no attention to persons around him. When taken into a room,
he completely disregarded the people and instantly went for objects,
preferably those that could be spun. [...] His mother was the only
person with whom he had any contact at all, and even she spent all
of her time developing ways of keeping him at play with her. (Kanner
1943, 219–220)

The case of Donald nicely illustrates Wing's triad of impairments:
impaired social interaction (e.g., lack of interest in other children),
impaired communication and language use (e.g., peculiar usage of
personal pronouns), and narrow interests and repetitive behaviour
(e.g., repetitively spinning objects).

As we noted above, autism is often associated with mindreading
difficulties (e.g., Baron-Cohen 1995), where mindreading is understood as the ability to explain and predict a person's behaviour by
attributing mental states, such as beliefs or desires, to that person. It
is now well established (by a series of experiments) that mindreading
capacity is significantly compromised in autistic people. The most

well-known evidence of this mindreading impairment, which we will see below, comes from studies using so-called 'false-belief tasks'.

False-belief tasks examine the mindreading ability of a person in terms of the person's ability to *attribute false beliefs to others* or *understand the false beliefs of others*. Of course, mindreading ability is not just the ability to understand the beliefs of others. Understanding desires, emotions, values, character traits, and so on, is an important part of mindreading ability. But understanding the beliefs of others is a particularly important component of mindreading ability: without understanding the beliefs of another person, you would fail to understand how that person represents the world and, as a result, you would be unable to accurately predict that person's behaviour.

But why *false* beliefs rather than *true* beliefs? To see the logic behind false-belief tasks, let us first ask what it takes to demonstrate that a person has mindreading ability. Suppose that you are a clinician in charge of Donald and your job is to examine whether he is capable of explaining and predicting the behaviour of his mother (e.g., she goes to the kitchen) by attributing beliefs (e.g., the belief that a box of chocolates is in the kitchen) and desires (e.g., the desire to eat chocolate) to her? It is not sufficient to show that Donald can predict his mother's behaviour accurately. After all, it is possible for Donald to predict his mother's behaviour without attributing beliefs and desires to her. Donald might simply make an inductive inference on the basis of the pattern of his mother's behaviour in the relevant situation (e.g., she habitually goes to the kitchen when there is a box of chocolates in the kitchen) without attributing any mental states to her, in the same way that he can inductively predict that the sun will rise tomorrow morning on the basis of the pattern of the sun's behaviour each morning without attributing any mental states to the sun.

To solve this problem, we need to make sure that the mother's behaviour, which Donald is supposed to predict, cannot simply be inferred on the basis of how she tends to behave in the relevant situation. Daniel Dennett (1978) proposes an elegant solution, which is to make sure that the relevant belief is false. For example, Donald attributes to his mother the belief that there is a box of chocolates in the kitchen *when there is no such box in the kitchen*. We can then rule out the possibility that Donald predicts his mother's visit to the kitchen simply because that's what she tends to do when there is a box of chocolates in the kitchen; after all, there is no box of chocolates there.

Thus, one can test Donald's mindreading ability by examining whether he can predict his mother's behaviour on the basis of her false beliefs. This is the basic idea behind false-belief tasks.

The Sally–Anne Experiment

Baron-Cohen and colleagues used a false-belief task, known as the Sally–Anne task, to test the mindreading ability of autistic children (Baron-Cohen, Leslie, & Frith 1985). The participants were three groups of children: autistic children (mean age: 11 years, 11 months), children with Down's syndrome (mean age: 10 years, 11 months), and neurotypical children (mean age: 4 years, 5 months). The mean mental age (verbal mental age and non-verbal mental age) of the autistic group was the highest among all groups. Participants watched the following story of two doll protagonists, Sally and Anne. Sally first placed a marble into her basket and then left the scene. Anne came in and, unbeknown to Sally, moved the marble from the basket to a box. When Sally returned to the scene, the experimenter asked the question: 'Where will Sally look for her marble?' Note that correctly answering this question requires recognizing Sally's false belief that the marble is in the basket, not in the box, and predicting her behaviour on the basis of this false belief. It turned out that the majority of autistic children failed in this task (i.e., they pointed at the box and not the basket), while most neurotypical children and most children with Down's syndrome successfully completed the task (i.e., they pointed at the basket and not the box). This result cannot be explained by a general cognitive delay. Children with Down's syndrome performed the tasks as successfully as neurotypical children. In addition, the mental age of the autistic group was the highest among the three groups. Thus, the result of the experiment points to a specific failure of mindreading in autistic people. Baron-Cohen and colleagues conclude:

> Our results strongly support the hypothesis that autistic children as a group fail to employ a theory of mind. We wish to explain this failure as an inability to represent mental states. As a result of this the autistic subjects are unable to impute beliefs to others and are thus at a grave disadvantage when having to predict the behaviour of other people. (Baron-Cohen, Leslie, & Frith 1985, 43)

Simulation and Theory

Philosophers have been interested in the failures of mindreading in autism which were exhibited in the Sally–Anne experiment. The main reason for this interest is that mindreading in autism is expected to shed light on how mindreading works in general.

One view, known as 'the theory theory' (e.g., Gopnik & Wellman 1992), says that mindreading abilities are grounded in an implicit theory (so-called 'folk psychology') of mental states and their roles, analogous to the implicit theory of physical objects and their movements (so-called 'folk physics'). The theory theory is often contrasted with a different account of how mindreading works, known as 'the simulation theory' (e.g., Goldman 2006). According to the simulation theory, mindreading ability is grounded in the imaginative simulation of other people's mental states.

To see the difference between the theory theory and the simulation theory, let us think about the following example. Suppose that Mark knows that his wife, Naomi, believes that a box of chocolates is in the kitchen and also that she wants to eat some chocolate. On the basis of these pieces of knowledge, Mark predicts that Naomi will go into the kitchen to get some chocolate from the box. How does Mark know this? How does he predict Naomi's visit to the kitchen? According to the theory theory, he infers this on the basis of a theoretical generalization about people's beliefs and desires, which might look like this: 'If X wants to have something, O, and X believes that O is in a place, P, then X will visit P to get O.' The theoretical inference might look like this:

Premise 1: Naomi wants to have chocolate.
Premise 2: Naomi believes that chocolate is in a box in the kitchen.
Premise 3: If X wants to have something, O, and X believes that O is in a place, P, then X will visit P to get O.
Conclusion: Therefore, Naomi will visit the kitchen to get some chocolate from the box.

In contrast, according to the simulation theory, Mark does not rely on such an inference. What he needs to do is just imaginatively simulate Naomi's mind. So, for example, he might think about what he will do if, putting himself in Naomi's shoes, he believes that a box of chocolates is in the kitchen and wants to eat some chocolate. This simulation process is much simpler than the inferential process in the theory theory: the capacity for simulation would 'yield the same result [of successful prediction] far more parsimoniously' and thus it is 'a vastly more plausible hypothesis' (Goldman 2006, 180).

The two theories, the theory theory and the simulation theory, can have different accounts of the failure of mindreading in autism. The theory theory might account for the failure in terms of a lack of theoretical knowledge or a failure to apply knowledge: 'According to theory theory [...] autism is centrally a deficiency of knowledge, or at any rate of belief. [...] [T]here are some propositions the autistic person doesn't know – and perhaps could not even formulate' (Currie 1996, 243).

The simulation theory, in contrast, might account for the failure in terms of a compromised capacity for imagination and simulation: 'Simulation theory says that autism is a deficiency of imaginative capacity – the capacity to project the self imaginatively into a situation other than its own current, actual position' (Currie 1996, 243). This hypothesis is coherent with some other features of autism, such as the absence of pretend play or inflexible thought and behaviour, which could involve some form of imaginative deficits.

A theoretical worry, however, has been expressed about the simulation theory and about the very idea of a debate between the simulation theory and the theory theory. Pure simulation without theory seems to be useless for the purpose of successful mindreading; the simulation, if successful, needs to be supplemented by some theoretical assumptions. Thus, the simulation theory collapses into a form of the theory theory (this problem is often called 'the threat of collapse').

In fact, it is obvious that simulation in general needs some theoretical assumptions. Simulation without theory is simply hopeless. Think, for example, about simulation processes in the context of engineering. Suppose that you are involved in designing a new energy-efficient passenger aircraft. Your main job is to make the aircraft as light as possible without compromising safety. You think about the possibility of using new carbon fibre composites for the aircraft, which you expect will make the aircraft 5% lighter than the previous model of the same size made of aluminium. To test the safety of the aircraft with carbon fibre composites, you do a computer simulation to assess whether all crucial parts of the aircraft are strong enough in all expected situations (including a bumpy landing, storm, etc.). Now, this simulation would be hopeless without theoretical assumptions: the simulation will provide inaccurate results if it does not have access to basic assumptions about physics, chemical assumptions about the behaviour of carbon fibre, meteorological assumptions about wind and air, and so on.

The same thing is true about simulation of other minds. Suppose that Naomi experiences postnatal depression, and tends to stay in bed for a long time every day. She does not appear to be very happy when taking care of the baby. It is obvious that Mark, when he tries to simulate Naomi's mind, needs some background knowledge. Without sufficient background knowledge of postnatal depression, Mark can easily reach a wrong conclusion when he simulates Naomi's mind. Putting himself in Naomi's shoes, he might conclude that Naomi stays in bed because of her laziness, or that she does not appear to be happy because of her lack of interest in the baby.

The threat of collapse is certainly a serious problem for a pure form of the simulation theory, but we do not necessarily endorse the strong conclusion that the simulation theory fails or that mindreading has nothing to do with simulation. Rather, we take the threat of collapse as suggesting that the solution might lie in a hybrid account, according to which mindreading depends on both simulation-based processes and theory-based processes.

One might think of the hybrid account of mindreading analogously to how we thought of the dual-process theory, which we discussed in Chapters 3 and 4. Simulation could be understood as a form of heuristic (Type-1) process. For example, representational heuristics involve replacing a probability judgment (e.g., 'How probable is it that Linda is a bank teller?'), which is difficult, with a judgment about how similar a person is to a stereotype (e.g., 'How similar is Linda to a stereotypical bank teller?'), which is relatively easier. Similarly, we might say that 'simulative heuristics' involve replacing a judgment about somebody else's mind and behaviour (e.g., 'What will Naomi feel?'), which is rather difficult, with a judgment about one's own mind by putting oneself in the person's shoes (e.g., 'How would I be feeling if I were in Naomi's situation?'), which is relatively easier.

Simulation-based (Type-1) mindreading might be useful and efficient when we try to understand someone who is considered to be similar to us or who is considered to be in-group (i.e., belonging to the same social group). In contrast, theory-based (Type-2) mindreading might be needed when we try to understand someone who is considered to be different from us or who is considered to be out-group (i.e., belonging to a different social group). So, perhaps Mark needs theory-based mindreading rather than simulation-based mindreading to understand Naomi when she is experiencing postnatal depression. It is theory, not simulation, that tells him that many women can be depressed after having a baby.

The relationship between simulation-based (Type-1) process and theory-based (Type-2) process could be understood in terms of the parallel-competitive model (in which two processes compete with one another as rivals), the default-intervention model (in which simulative processes are the default, but possibly intervened in by theoretical processes), or the lawyer–client model (in which theoretical processes confabulate about the product of simulative processes in a *post hoc* manner).

Do Problems with Mindreading Explain Autism?

Let us now discuss the role of mindreading in autism. One might think that the mindreading failure, which is exemplified in poor performances in false-belief tasks (and related tasks), is the essence or central cause of autism in the sense that all symptoms of autism are somehow related to, or derived from, a mindreading impairment. Let us call this 'the essentialist mindreading impairment hypothesis'.

The essentialist mindreading impairment hypothesis, however, is not popular among researchers; most, if not all, researchers now agree that autism involves varieties of symptoms including those that are not related to mindreading deficits. Perhaps we need to adopt ideas from other theories of autism in order to account for those symptoms. In fact, there are other important theories of autism that capture different aspects of the condition.

For example, according to 'the executive dysfunction account' of autism (Hill 2004), autistic people have a fault in the executive system in the (frontal lobes of their) brain, resulting in difficulty controlling and prohibiting their own behaviour. This theory nicely captures repetitive and stimulus-driven behaviour in autism (e.g., Donald might find it difficult to prohibit his repetitive behaviour of spinning objects). According to 'the weak central coherence account' of autism (Happé & Frith 2006), autistic people tend to focus on minute details rather than the larger picture or the context of a situation. This theory of autism nicely captures some excessive abilities exhibited by autistic people, such as the ability to memorize the details of an object, scene, or picture in fine detail, or the ability to complete a jigsaw puzzle upside down without the help of a picture.

Thus, it is not plausible that a mindreading impairment is the essence of autism. We need a weaker claim about the role of mindreading failures in autism. For example, a mindreading impairment does not explain everything there is to know about autism, but it is still responsible for the most salient features of it (i.e., social and communicative problems). All social and communicative problems are somehow related to, or derived from, a mindreading impairment. Let us call this 'the non-essentialist abnormal mindreading impairment hypothesis'.

The non-essentialist mindreading impairment hypothesis is attractive because it is likely that mindreading ability is so central to social and communicative skills that mindreading failures are expected to lead to a variety of social and communicative problems. Baron-Cohen and colleagues write: 'The ability to make inferences about what other people believe to be the case in a given situation allows one to predict what they will do. This is clearly a crucial component of social skills' (Baron-Cohen, Leslie, & Frith 1985, 39). Similarly, Currie writes: '[I]f you don't understand other people's beliefs, desires and intentions you won't relate to them well, since that requires co-ordinating your mental states with theirs, and you won't be able to communicate with them to the extent that you won't be able to figure out speaker's meaning as distinct from semantic meaning' (Currie 1996, 250).

The non-essentialist mindreading impairment hypothesis states, first, that autistic people have significant difficulty when they read other minds and, second, that this difficulty is responsible for social and communicative problems. We will call the former 'the impairment thesis' in the non-essentialist mindreading impairment hypothesis and the latter 'the causality thesis' in it. As we will see, however, both impairment and causality theses are subject to empirical and theoretical complications (e.g., Frith & Happé 1995).

Let us start with the causality thesis. Even those who deny the essentialist version of the mindreading impairment hypothesis tend to think that mindreading difficulty is responsible for social and communicative problems. However, looking closer, the relationship between mindreading and social and communicative skills appears more complicated.

There are some puzzles about the causality thesis. For example, some (high-functioning) autistic children successfully complete false-belief tasks but nonetheless exhibit social and communicative problems. Baron-Cohen and colleagues admit this in their paper on the Sally–Anne experiment: 'There is, however, also a suggestion of a small subgroup of autistic children who succeeded on the task and who thus may be able to employ a theory of mind. These children who, by definition, nevertheless exhibit social impairment, would certainly deserve further study' (Baron-Cohen, Leslie, & Frith 1985, 43). Moreover, many autistic children who initially fail do eventually successfully complete false-belief tasks (Happé 1995), but their social and communicative problems still persist. This raises a puzzle for the causality thesis. How can an autistic person's social and communicative problems be explained by mindreading failures if they can successfully complete false-belief tasks?

Let us move on to another problem with the causality thesis. In the early stage of development, before the age of 4, autistic children and neurotypical children equally fail in mindreading tasks such as the Sally–Anne task. But they are not equal in their social and communicative behaviour. Typically, the social and communicative problems of autism are already present before the age of 4. Remember, for example, that at the age of 3 Donald exhibited a 'disinclination to play with children and do things children his age usually take an interest in' and '[a]n abstraction of mind which made him perfectly oblivious to everything about him' (Kanner 1943, 218). This raises another question for the causality thesis. How can the mindreading impairment explain social and communicative problems if the latter arise earlier than the former?

In short, here is the puzzle about the causality thesis: social and communicative problems start before the presence of the mindreading delay, and these problems persist after the successful completion of false-belief tasks. These facts seem to suggest that the relationship between mindreading failures and social and communicative problems is not a straightforward one.

Let us move on to the impairment thesis, which says that autistic children display impairments in mindreading. Neurotypical children can complete false-belief tasks at roughly the age of 4 (Wellman, Cross, & Watson 2001), whereas autistic children at the same age cannot. This observation suggests a rather simplistic idea that mindreading is a unitary capacity, and it is compromised in autism. However, this simplistic idea has been questioned by a series of studies involving non-verbal mindreading tasks.

The Eye-Tracking Mindreading Study

A remarkable study of mindreading in infancy by Kristine Onishi and Renée Baillargeon suggests that neurotypical children much younger than 4 can complete a non-verbal false-belief task involving eye-tracking (Onishi & Baillargeon 2005). This experiment relies on the violation-of-expectation method, which has been used in research into the cognitive abilities of infants. The basic idea of the method is simple: an infant looks at an object or person longer when the object or person does not behave in an expected manner than when the object or person behaves in an expected manner. When relying on this principle, it is expected that if, for example, an infant attributes Sally with the false belief that the marble is in the basket and thus predicts that she will go to the basket rather than the box when searching for the marble, then the infant will look at Sally longer when Sally goes to the box to search for the marble (and thus the expectation is violated) than when she goes to the basket (and thus the expectation is met). Onishi and Baillargeon (2005) tested 15-month-old infants with a task of this kind. They found that the infants reliably look at an agent longer when she does not behave in the way that is expected on the basis of her false belief about a toy (and thus the expectation is violated) than when she does behave in the way that is expected on the basis of her false belief (and thus the expectation is met). Onishi and Baillargeon conclude: '[W]e propose that the present results suggest that 15-month-old infants expect an actor to search for a toy where she believes, rightly or wrongly, that it is hidden. Such an inter-pretation calls into question the notion that preschoolers undergo a fundamental change from a nonrepresentational to a representational theory of mind' (Onishi & Baillargeon 2005, 257).

This result goes against the simplistic assumption that mindreading is a unitary or single capacity. The ability to succeed in non-verbal mindreading tasks and the ability to succeed in verbal mindreading tasks can be dissociated: a person can have the former ability without having the latter.

Do autistic people have the ability to succeed in non-verbal mindreading tasks? In another experiment, Atsushi Senju and

colleagues tested adults with Asperger's syndrome; they successfully completed a verbal task but failed at a non-verbal task (Senju
et al. 2009). This suggests that the ability for non-verbal tasks and
the ability for verbal tasks can be dissociated in the other direction
too: people with Asperger's syndrome have the latter ability without
having the former. From this, Senju and colleagues concluded that
'our data raise the surprising possibility that an early developing form
of the cognitive ability to mentalize, evident in spontaneous looking
behaviour, is not a necessary precursor of the later developing form
of mental-state attribution, which supports explicit reasoning' (Senju
et al. 2009, 885).

An alternative interpretation of the results of Senju and colleagues'
experiment would be that those with Asperger's syndrome do not
really have the usual ability for verbal tasks. They can successfully
complete verbal mindreading tasks, without acquiring the usual
ability for verbal tasks, in an atypical way by employing some kind
of compensatory learning. Uta Frith suggests that the successful
completion of false-belief tasks by autistic children is due to a form
of compensatory learning, which is not the same as spontaneous
mindreading ability. Her view is that 'there is a gulf between mentalizing learned the hard way and mentalizing learned effortlessly in the
neurotypical way' (Frith 2012, 2085).

This possibility is nicely illustrated in the novel *The Curious
Incident of the Dog in the Night-time* by Mark Haddon (2004), which
is known for its vivid descriptions of autism. Christopher Boone, the
15-year-old autistic narrator, used to fail at a verbal false-belief task
but ends up being able to solve it just like he can solve mathematical
puzzles (which he is very good at). Christopher can complete verbal
false-belief tasks, but only in a highly atypical, intellectual way.

> [W]hen I was little I didn't understand about other people having
> minds. And Julie [Christopher's teacher when he was little] said to
> Mother and Father that I would always find this [verbal false-belief
> task] very difficult. But I don't find this difficult now. Because I decided
> that it was a kind of puzzle, and if something is a puzzle there is always
> a way of solving it. (Haddon 2004, 116)

Either way, these findings about non-verbal mindreading tasks suggest
the following intriguing possibility: performance in a non-verbal
mindreading task is more important for explaining autism than
performance in a verbal mindreading task. As Frith notes, '[I]t is the

early-appearing, implicit form of [mindreading] that points to a core problem in ASD' (Frith 2012, 2085).

Frith's suggestion is plausible and attractive. As we have seen, there is a puzzle with the causality thesis: social and communicative problems start before the presence of the developmental delay in verbal mindreading tasks and they persist after the successful completion of verbal mindreading tasks. This seems to suggest that performance in verbal mindreading tasks has little to do with social and communicative problems. Perhaps it is performance in non-verbal tasks that is more closely related to social and communicative problems in autistic people. This nicely explains the fact that social and communicative problems start before the presence of the developmental delay in the verbal task (because the developmental problem in non-verbal tasks is already manifested in early infancy). It also explains the fact that social and communicative problems persist after a successful performance in verbal mindreading tasks (because autistic adults who successfully complete a verbal mindreading task might not be able to complete a non-verbal mindreading task: Senju et al. 2009).

8.3   Psychopathy and Empathy

Psychopathy

We will now turn to psychopathy. We use the term 'psychopathy' to refer to a condition in which a person demonstrates a remarkable tendency to engage in anti-social behaviour, which is often diagnosed according to the Psychopathy Checklist-Revised (PCL-R) by Robert D. Hare (Box 8C). Psychopathy is similar to 'antisocial personality disorder' in *DSM-5* (American Psychiatric Associations 2013), but their diagnostic criteria are somewhat different. 'Sociopathy' could be used as another name for psychopathy, but the term 'sociopathy' accompanies an emphasis on the social aspect of this condition.

Many psychopathic people are dangerous and violent (such as Ray in the case below), and many psychopathic people end up in prison. But this is not always the case. There are 'white-collar psychopaths' (Hare 1993) or 'snakes in suits' (Baibak & Hare 2006) who are not in prison but rather work in business offices, banks, law offices, and so on.

> **BOX 8C: Items in the Psychopathy Checklist-Revised (PCL-R)**
>
> *Interpersonal*: glibness/superficial charm, grandiose sense of self-worth, pathological lying, conning/manipulative.
> *Affective*: lack of remorse or guilt, shallow affect, callous/lack of empathy, failure to accept responsibility for own actions.
> *Lifestyle*: need for stimulation/proneness to boredom, parasitic lifestyle, lack of realistic, long-term goals, impulsivity, irresponsibility.
> *Anti-social*: poor behavioural control, early behavioural problems, juvenile delinquency, revocation of conditional release, criminal versatility.

Consider the case of Ray, reported by Robert Hare in *Without Conscience* (Hare 1993). Hare was a psychologist at the British Columbia Penitentiary when he met Ray, who was an inmate at the time. On Hare's first day at the prison, Ray showed up in his office with a knife in his hand, apparently to test how cooperative the new psychologist would be. After that encounter, Ray constantly manipulated Hare into doing things for him. On one occasion, he asked him to recommend a transfer from the machine shop (where he was working at the time and where he had probably prepared his knife) to the kitchen. Ray successfully convinced Hare that he could be a good cook. It turned out that after Ray's transfer to the kitchen, he and other inmates used the ingredients available there to distil alcohol beneath the floor, which was later discovered when one of the pots exploded. Hare describes Ray's personality in the following way:

> Ray had an incredible ability to con not just me but everybody. He could talk, and lie, with a smoothness and a directness that sometimes momentarily disarmed even the most experienced and cynical of the prison staff. When I met him he had a long criminal record behind him (and, as it turned out, ahead of him); about half his adult life had been spent in prison, and many of his crimes had been violent. Yet he convinced me, and others more experienced than I, of his readiness to reform, that his interest in crime had been completely overshadowed by a driving passion in – well, cooking, mechanics, you name it. He lied endlessly, lazily, about everything, and it disturbed him not a whit whenever I pointed out something in his file that contradicted one of his lies. He would simply change the subject and spin off in a different direction. (Hare 1993, 12–13)

Psychopathy has been associated with empathy deficits. For example, Ray's violence and manipulation of other people by lying to and deceiving others seem to show that he lacks empathy towards his victims. Thus, Hare talks about 'a deeply disturbing inability to care about the pain and suffering experienced by others – in short, a complete lack of empathy, the prerequisite for love' (Hare 1993, 6).

Mindreading ability does not seem to be particularly problematic in psychopathy. Apparently, psychopathic people tend to be successful at standard false-belief tasks. The fact that Ray could successfully manipulate people seems to suggest an excellent mindreading ability on his part: he is able to grasp what others are thinking, to understand the perspectives of other people, and to figure out the most effective way to influence them.

One might think that an empathy impairment is the *essence*, or the central cause, of psychopathy. In other words, all symptoms of psychopathy are somehow related to, or derived from, empathy impairments. Let us call this 'the essentialist empathy impairment hypothesis'. However, this hypothesis can be challenged for a similar reason for which the essentialist mindreading impairment hypothesis of autism can be challenged. There are many items in the PCL-R that do not seem to be directly related to empathy. For example, it is not clear how items such as 'lack of realistic, long-term goals' or 'impulsivity' can be explained by an empathy impairment. Again, items like 'lack of affect and emotional depth' seem to suggest a general form of affective deficit in psychopathy that is not solely related to empathy. But then it is possible that the real 'essence' of psychopathy is a general affective deficit, of which an empathy impairment is a consequence. It is not surprising that somebody with a general affective deficit is not capable of (affective) emphasizing (Prinz 2011).

So perhaps it is safe to consider a weaker form of the empathy impairment hypothesis: problems of empathy might not explain everything there is about psychopathy, but are nonetheless responsible for the most salient features of it: that is, the tendency to engage in anti-social behaviour. All anti-social behavioural problems are somehow related to, or derived from, an empathy impairment. Let us call this 'the non-essentialist empathy impairment hypothesis'.

Is the non-essentialist empathy impairment hypothesis true? The hypothesis states that, first, psychopathic people have a form of empathy abnormality and, second, it is the primary cause of their tendency to engage in anti-social behaviour. We will call the former 'the impairment thesis' in the non-essentialist empathy impairment hypothesis and the latter 'the causality thesis' in it. We will now discuss both, starting with the former.

Empathy Impairments

It is widely accepted that the abnormality thesis is true: psychopathy involves some form of empathy impairment. However, difficult questions arise concerning the kind of impairment it involves and the severity of it.

Assessing somebody's empathic capacity is not more difficult than assessing somebody's mindreading ability. For one thing, there are empirical difficulties: that is, difficulties about experimenting or operationalizing. Empathy research has been empirically messier than mindreading research. For instance, empathy research has not been fortunate enough to have a counterpart of false-belief tasks. Although there are some empirical measures of empathy (see Maibom 2012 for a useful overview), many of these measures rely on the method of self-reporting, which might not be reliable enough. What if, just like in the stockings experiment by Nisbett and Wilson (1977), people do not have access to how empathic they are and can only confabulate about it?

There are also conceptual difficulties and confusions. Empathy research has been conceptually messier than mindreading research. There is little conceptual confusion about what 'mindreading' is in mindreading research: mindreading is the capacity to attribute mental states to others to predict and explain their behaviour (although different people can adopt different terminology, e.g., 'mindreading', 'theory of mind', 'mentalizing', etc.). In contrast, there is little consensus when it comes to understanding 'empathy'. The term 'empathy' has been used in many different ways. For example, 'empathy' can be occurrent (i.e., empathy as a particular feeling that occurs at a particular time) or dispositional (i.e., empathy as a stable disposition or a character trait). (See Chapter 5 for different senses of empathy.)

How severe are the problems with empathy in psychopathy? The extreme view is that psychopathic people completely lack empathy. In describing psychopathy, for example, Hare talks about the 'complete lack' of empathy (Hare 1993, 6) and Baron-Cohen talks about the 'zero degree' of empathy (Baron-Cohen 2011, 16). The extreme view is certainly a tempting idea, especially when it comes to those psychopathic people who are capable of performing extremely violent and cruel actions.

But is it really true that psychopathic people completely lack empathy? Alternative interpretations are possible as well (and there are surely individual differences among psychopathic people). One such alternative is that empathic capacity is weakened, but not completely diminished, in psychopathic people. Or perhaps they have some empathic capacity, but they do not want to exercise this capacity in some cases probably because empathy with a suffering person can cause distress.

Another alternative is that empathic capacity is only biased, and is not diminished, in psychopathic people (Maibom 2018). In Chapter 5, we saw that empathy is biased in neurotypical populations (e.g., many find it easier to emphasize with those who are near and dear than with those who are not). What psychopathic people exhibit is not something different in kind but rather something different only in degree from the biases in the neurotypical population. Psychopathic people have an exaggerated form of empathy bias. For example, a psychopathic male might find it particularly difficult to empathize with the suffering of female teenagers, but he can perfectly empathize with the suffering of other groups of people such as elderly people or the suffering of non-human animals such as dogs.

Do Empathy Impairments Explain Psychopathy?

What about the causality thesis? Is it really true that psychopathic anti-social behaviour is causally driven by an empathy impairment? One might think that the answer is clearly 'Yes'. After all, psychopathy, which is associated with anti-social behaviour, is diagnosed by the PCL-R, which does include empathy impairments ('callous/lack of empathy'). So, there has to be a causal connection between empathy impairments and psychopathic anti-social behaviour.

This reasoning is, however, too hasty. As we have already pointed out above, empathy impairments are a factor in psychopathy, but they are not the only factor. 'Callous/lack of empathy' is just an item in the PCL-R, among many other items. The diagnosis of psychopathy is given when a person's PCL-R score is more than 30 out of 40, which means that it is possible for a person to receive the diagnosis of psychopathy whilst still possessing empathic capacity. Moreover, even if a psychopathic person exhibits callousness/lack of empathy, it might not be responsible for the person's anti-social behaviour. Other items (e.g., 'impulsivity' and 'poor behavioral control') suggest a lack of self-control, and some other items (e.g., 'parasitic lifestyle' and 'lack of realistic, long-term goals') indicate lifestyle problems. It is not obvious that anti-social behaviour in psychopathy is more strongly associated with empathy impairments than other factors.

A related problem is that psychopathy can be divided into some sub-types, and different sub-types might require different explanations of anti-social behaviour. One distinction is between primary psychopathy (or low-anxious psychopathy) and secondary psychopathy (or high-anxious psychopathy). The former is characterized by callousness, shallow affect, superficial charm, and so on, while the latter is characterized by impulsivity and lack of long-term goals, and so on. It is not at all clear that anti-social behaviour in the two groups should be explained in the same way in terms of empathy impairments. For instance, anti-social behaviour in the secondary group tends to be reactive (e.g., aggression in response to an insult, an attack, or something similar). The anti-social behaviour in this group might be more easily explained by a lack of self-control or lifestyle problems than by empathy deficits (Maibom 2018).

Another challenge to the causality thesis is that the thesis predicts that anti-social behaviour will be seen in another condition which also involves empathy impairments. But this prediction does not seem plausible. For example, it has been suggested that autism involves both mindreading and empathy impairments: 'The person with classic (low functioning) autism often lacks both of these components of empathy [i.e., cognitive empathy and affective empathy]' (Baron-Cohen 2011, 83). But autistic people do not typically exhibit the kind of anti-social behaviour we see in cases of psychopathy. In fact, Baron-Cohen argues that autistic people are 'super moral rather than immoral' (Baron-Cohen 2011, 65): they tend to stick to moral codes in a very strict and inflexible manner. If Baron-Cohen is correct, then the causality thesis faces a *prima facie* problem: empathy impairments do not seem to be sufficient for anti-social behaviour.

We therefore need to know more about what exactly is responsible for anti-social behaviour in psychopathic people. The non-essentialist empathy impairment hypothesis has some intuitive attractiveness, but alternative theories have not been ruled out yet.

8.4 Psychopathy and Moral Judgment

Psychopathy and the Moral–Conventional Distinction

We have talked about the (moral) behaviour of psychopathic people. We will now turn to another aspect of psychopathy, namely the aspect of (moral) judgment. Do psychopathic people have problems with moral judgment? If so, how are their moral judgments problematic?

One might think that people like Ray certainly have problems with moral judgment or moral knowledge. Ray's repetitive violence and manipulation without any remorse or guilt seem to suggest that he does not know that his behaviour is morally wrong. He could pretend to know that his behaviour is morally wrong if needed (e.g., at a parole board interview), but he does not *really* know that it is morally wrong.

But what is missing in moral judgment or moral knowledge in psychopathy? To investigate this issue, let us now consider some relevant empirical evidence. In particular, we will consider the moral judgment in psychopathy with respect to two types of experimental tasks that we discussed in Chapter 4: moral-conventional tasks (e.g., Turiel, Killen, & Helwig 1987) and sacrificial dilemmas (e.g., Greene et al. 2001). As we have already seen, both types of tasks have been used to investigate how moral judgment works in general, but they can also be used to investigate the moral judgment of psychopathic people. We might be able to reveal what is amiss in the moral judgment or moral knowledge of psychopathic people by observing their responses to the tasks.

There is at least some evidence that psychopathic people fail to distinguish moral transgressions from conventional transgressions. In a study by R. J. R. Blair (1995), for example, psychopathic participants (classified by the PCL-R) failed to make a distinction between moral and conventional transgressions, particularly when it came to the authority-dependence/independence of the relevant transgressions. The pattern of the failure is interesting. Psychopathic participants treated all transgressions, including conventional ones, as moral transgressions; they regarded all transgressions, including conventional ones, as authority-independently wrong. So, for example, a young boy wearing a skirt is treated as acting in a wrong way even when an authority figure, say a teacher, says that he can wear what he likes. Blair interprets this as a deceptive response. Psychopathic participants' real reaction is to treat all transgressions as conventional ones; all transgressions, including moral ones, are authority-dependently wrong. However, psychopathic participants are highly motivated to demonstrate their genuine understanding of normative rules and of how bad their violations are, and they deceptively treat all transgressions as being morally wrong, independently of authority.

What does this show? It is tempting to think that this experimental result shows that psychopathic people fail to understand the distinction between moral judgments and conventional judgments. Without understanding the distinction, they are not capable of acquiring genuine moral knowledge or making genuine moral judgments. This does not necessarily mean that psychopathic people do not know that some actions are prohibited, that they invite punishment, that they are perceived as being immoral, and so on; perhaps they do know these things very well. But they fail to know the distinctive wrongness of moral transgressions. If it is true that psychopathic people are not capable of making genuine moral judgments, this can have some philosophically significant implications. Neil Levy, for example, argues that a psychopath's inability to make genuine moral judgments decreases their moral responsibility for their (anti-social) behaviour: '[P]sychopaths do not possess the relevant moral knowledge for distinctively *moral* responsibility; lacking this knowledge, they are unable to control their actions in the light of moral reasons' (Levy 2007, 129; also see Levy 2014).

Does the result of Blair's study really show that psychopathic people are not capable of making genuine moral judgments or acquiring genuine moral knowledge? There are some reasons to be sceptical. First, there are some empirical uncertainties regarding Blair's result. In a study by Eyal Aharoni and colleagues (2012), for example, PCL-R scores of incarcerated offenders did not predict their performance in moral–conventional tasks with a forced-choice method. Participants were told that half of the transgressions they were supposed to evaluate had been pre-rated by members of society to be moral (rather than conventional) and that their job was to identify those transgressions. With this method, we can rule out Blair's worry about the possibility that participants deceptively treat all transgressions as authority-independently wrong for the purpose of demonstrating their understanding of normative rules.

As we have already seen in Chapter 4, the clear distinction between moral transgressions and conventional transgressions is not a universal phenomenon; it is restricted only within some cultural and socio-economic groups. It would be too hasty to conclude that psychopathic people lack moral knowledge just because they fail to draw the line between moral and conventional transgressions in the same way that people in some particular groups (i.e., Western or high socio-economic groups) do.

Remember that, in the study by Jonathan Haidt, Silvia Koller, and Maria Dias (1993), people in lower socio-economic groups exhibited a stronger moralizing tendency (i.e., a tendency to treat transgressions as moral rather than conventional) than higher socio-economic groups. But then it is conceivable that what Blair has found is (at least partially) explained by this tendency: the psychopathic patients in high-security psychiatric hospitals in England (in Blair's study) belong to lower socio-economic groups whose members have a moralizing tendency.

Psychopathy and Sacrificial Dilemmas

Another limitation of Blair's study is that it does not take into account different kinds of moral judgments; in particular, it does not account of the difference between 'deontological' judgments that are driven by emotional processes and 'utilitarian' judgments that are driven by reasoning processes (see Chapter 4). Perhaps psychopathic people are not capable of making 'deontological' moral judgments, probably due to their affective deficits (e.g., their lack of affect and emotional depth), but they might still be capable of making 'utilitarian' moral judgments. This leads us to the second set of experiments with sacrificial dilemmas.

A terminological note: we use the terms 'deontological judgment' and 'utilitarian judgment' in a loose sense, referring to the judgment against the sacrificing option and the judgment in favour of the sacrificing option, respectively. Thus, the judgment in favour of pulling the lever in the trolley case is 'utilitarian'; the judgment against pushing the stranger off the bridge is 'deontological'. We do not presuppose the commitment interpretation (Chapter 4) of 'deontological' and 'utilitarian' judgment. In other words, we do not presuppose that anyone who makes the 'utilitarian' decision to pull the lever is genuinely committed to utilitarian principles, or that anyone who makes the 'deontological' decision to not push the stranger off the bridge is genuinely committed to deontological principles.

Several studies have looked at the relationship between psychopathic traits and their judgments in sacrificial dilemmas, such as the trolley dilemma or the footbridge dilemma (e.g., Bartels & Pizarro 2011; Kahane et al. 2015; Koenigs et al. 2012). Overall, they seem to suggest a correlation between psychopathic traits and the tendency to make 'utilitarian' judgments in sacrificial dilemmas. In one study, for example, Michael Koenigs and colleagues (2012) found that, when compared to non-psychopathic participants, psychopathic participants (who scored 30 or above in the PCL-R) were significantly more likely to endorse a 'utilitarian' judgment in sacrificial dilemmas. Low-anxious psychopathic participants, but not high-anxious psychopathic participants, were significantly more likely to endorse a 'utilitarian' judgment in personal dilemmas, such as the footbridge dilemma.

What are the implications of these results? One possible implication concerns the role of sacrificial dilemmas in the study of moral judgment. Guy Kahane and colleagues (2015) take these results to be a problem for the sacrificial dilemma studies by Joshua Greene and colleagues (2001). These studies are not appropriate for the study of utilitarian thinking since the 'utilitarian' response in the dilemmas seems to track psychopathic thinking (i.e., sacrificing a person's life in order to achieve a goal with no hesitation) rather than genuine utilitarian thinking (i.e., aiming to maximize happiness). These studies do not tell us much about the nature of utilitarianism or the psychological processes of utilitarian thinking. We have already discussed this issue in Chapter 5; here, instead we will focus on the issues concerning psychopathy rather than sacrificial dilemmas.

There is another implication for psychopathy. Studies involving sacrificial dilemmas seem to suggest the following: consistent with affective deficits in psychopathy (particularly in low-anxious psychopathy), a psychopath's capacity to make emotion-based moral judgments seems to be compromised. This explains their tendency to make 'utilitarian' responses: 'deontological' responses tend to be made in emotion-based processes, which is compromised in psychopathic people.

This hypothesis sheds a new light on the nature of the problems with moral judgments in psychopathic people. Their impairments in making of moral judgments have little to do with the content of the judgments they make; in fact, the content of their judgments is the same as the content of judgments by genuine utilitarians, such as John Stuart Mill or Peter Singer, who are explicitly committed to utilitarian principles, at least as far as sacrificial dilemmas are concerned. Problems in moral judgments are rather in the process in which the judgment is formed.

Genuine utilitarians and psychopathic people eventually make the same choice, but their decisions are arrived at through very different processes. For example, genuine utilitarians eventually arrive at the utilitarian response, but they do so only after the initial stage of being pulled in different directions (i.e., the 'utilitarian' direction and the 'deontological' direction). And they feel the pull towards the 'deontological' option even after choosing the 'utilitarian' option. A psychopath's route to the 'utilitarian' response is much more straightforward. They bypass the initial stage of being pulled in different directions. And they lack the feeling of being pulled towards the 'deontological' option after choosing the utilitarian option. In short, psychopathic people do not think of a sacrificial dilemma as being a 'dilemma' in the first place. The choices they make in sacrificial dilemmas are not particularly difficult for them.

This can be nicely captured in the dual-process framework, which posits that Type-1 processes are 'deontological' and that Type-2 processes are 'utilitarian'. Both processes are active and interact with each other when making moral judgments. When confronted with a sacrificial dilemma, two processes pull us in different directions: Type-1 processes pull us in the 'deontological' direction while Type-2 processes pull us in the 'utilitarian' direction. Eventually, we will make a choice depending on which process is generally strongest in us as well as in the particular context. Psychopathic people, on the other hand, have a weak Type-1 system; thus, they simply rely on Type-2 processes and reach the 'utilitarian' conclusion in a very straightforward manner.

When philosophers discuss a sacrificial dilemma, they are mainly interested in the correct response to it (e.g. the 'utilitarian' response that maximizes utility or the 'deontological' response that respects duties and rights). But by focusing on how one does or should respond to sacrificial dilemmas, one can easily miss an obvious but important fact about these dilemmas: they involve difficult choices. They are sacrificial 'dilemmas'; they naturally pull us in different directions. The most salient feature of sacrificial dilemmas is that they puzzle us by pulling us in competing directions. One can even say that agents are *supposed to be pulled in different directions* in a sacrificial dilemma; there is a sense in which the right reaction is to be pulled in two competing directions.

Of course, when forced, agents will make a choice eventually; they will eventually make a 'utilitarian' or 'deontological' decision. But this does not change the fact that they make a choice only after going through the initial stage of being pulled in different directions. Even after making a choice, say the 'utilitarian' one, they still feel the pull to the 'deontological' direction, in a similar way that they still feel the pull to the feminist bank teller hypothesis even after they see that the bank teller hypothesis is more probable than the feminist bank teller hypothesis (cf., the quote from Gould about the Linda experiment in Chapter 3). Psychopathic people, then, can be meaningfully compared to somebody who reaches the (correct) conclusion that the bank teller hypothesis is more probable than the feminist bank teller hypothesis in a straightforward manner, without going through the initial stage of being pulled towards the feminist bank teller hypothesis and without feeling the pull to the hypothesis after making their decision.

8.5   Summary

- The essentialist idea that impaired mindreading is the essence of autism is too simplistic. Autism is a complex phenomenon in which failures of mindreading are at best only a part of the condition (though they might be an important part). Perhaps failures of mindreading have little, if anything, to do with the excellent capacity to identify and remember minute details of a situation or other features of autism.
- The non-essentialist idea that impaired mindreading is responsible for social and communicative problems is promising, but the details relevant to providing a full picture are still unclear.
- The essentialist idea that impaired empathy is the essence of psychopathy is too simplistic. Psychopathy is a complex phenomenon in which problems of empathy are at best only a part of the condition. Perhaps empathy has little, if anything, to do with a lack of self-control or lifestyle problems in psychopathy.
- The non-essentialist idea that impaired empathy is responsible for anti-social behaviour has not been ruled out yet, but there remain important, unanswered questions about how empathy is impaired

in psychopathy and how the empathy impairment contributes to psychopathic anti-social behaviour.

Further Resources

Articles and Books

For an introduction to autism, and for a discussion of some empirical findings, we recommend *Autism: A New Introduction to Psychological Theory and Current Debate* (2019) by Sue Fletcher-Watson and Francesca Happé and *Autism: A Very Short Introduction* (2008) by Uta Frith.

For more on the psychological research of autism, we recommend Frith's *Autism: Explaining the Enigma* (2003), in which the weak central coherence theory is discussed, and Simon Baron-Cohen's *Mindblindness: An Essay on Autism and Theory of Mind* (1997), in which the mindreading abnormality theory (or the 'mindblindness theory') is defended.

To learn more about psychopathy, we recommend Robert Hare's *Without Conscience: The Disturbing World of the Psychopaths Among Us* (1993), which contains plenty of vivid examples. Baron-Cohen's *Zero Degrees of Empathy: A New Theory of Human Cruelty* (2011) contains an accessible introduction to psychopathy, autism, and other related conditions.

For information about the philosophical issues of psychopathy, Heidi Maibom's writings, such as her 'What can philosophers learn from psychopathy?' (2018), are particularly useful and informative. The philosophical implications of psychopathy are discussed in Volume 3 (*The Neuroscience of Morality: Emotion, Brain Disorders, and Development*, 2008) of the *Moral Psychology* series from MIT Press, edited by Walter Sinnott-Armstrong.

Online Resources

Uta Frith's interviews on autism (2016a), theory of mind (2016b) and talents in autism (2017) for *Serious Science* are accessible and informative.

There are useful podcasts on autism and psychopathy, including Ian Hacking on 'Making up autism' (2013), Gary Watson on

'Psychopathy and prudential deficits' (2013), and Neil Levy on 'Psychopathy and responsibility' (2013).

The Stanford Encyclopedia of Philosophy includes relevant entries, including Matthew Talbert (2019) on moral responsibility and Karsten Stueber (2019) on empathy.

Questions

1. Are mindreading and empathy independent of one another? Or are they related?
2. Verbal and non-verbal false-belief tasks capture an aspect of mindreading ability. What are the other important aspects?
3. Think about your own everyday experience and describe how you actually use your own mindreading ability.
4. Is mindreading ability just weakened or completely lacking in autism?
5. How many different kinds of 'empathy' are there? How are they related to each other?
6. Is empathy just weakened or completely lacking in psychopathic people?
7. Thinking of novels or films featuring a character with psychopathic traits, what are the aspects of the condition that are most often presented as problematic? Do they correspond to what we know about psychopathy from psychological science?

Conclusion

The central aim of this book has been to offer an empirically informed picture of the human mind and cognition. Throughout this book, we have claimed that human cognition and agency are 'imperfect' in the sense that they fail to meet some ideal standards of cognitive performance and agency, such as rationality (Chapter 1), self-knowledge (Chapter 2), unity (Chapter 3), and free will and responsibility (Chapter 6). In addition, human cognition and agency can be 'imperfect' in another sense: they can be adversely affected by so-called disorders of the mind, such as schizophrenia (Chapter 7), autism, and psychopathy (Chapter 8).

As we indicated in the Introduction, however, we do not intend to sketch a bleak picture of the human mind. Rather, our claim has simply been that human cognition and agency are 'imperfect', and not that people are 'stupid' or 'dumb'. We do not endorse what John Kihlstrom calls 'the "People are Stupid" school of psychology' (PASSP), summarized in the quote below:

(1) *People are fundamentally irrational*: In the ordinary course of everyday living, we do not think very hard about anything, preferring heuristic shortcuts that lead us astray; and we let our feelings and motives get in the way of our thought processes. (2) *We are on automatic pilot*: We do not pay much attention to what is going on around us, and to what we are doing; as a result, our thoughts and actions are inordinately swayed by first impressions and immediate responses; free will is an illusion. (3) *We don't know what we're doing*:

> When all is said and done, our behavior is mostly unconscious; the reasons we give are little more than post-hoc rationalizations, and our forecasts are invalid; to make things worse, consciousness actually gets in the way of adaptive behavior. (Kihlstrom 2004, 348)

Throughout this book, we have been critical of both unwarranted optimism and unwarranted pessimism about human cognition and agency. For instance, in Chapter 1, we resisted strong optimism about human rationality (i.e., humans are ideally rational), but we did not endorse extreme pessimism about it (i.e., humans are hopelessly irrational) either. In Chapter 2, we rejected strong optimism about self-knowledge being peculiar (i.e., self-knowledge is always peculiar), but we did not endorse strong pessimism (i.e., self-knowledge is never peculiar) either. In Chapter 6, we were sceptical about strong optimism about free will (i.e., humans are fully free and responsible for their actions all the time), but we were also sceptical about strong pessimism (i.e., free will is just an illusion).

We do not think that PASSP is supported by the available evidence. Moreover, PASSP is committed to radical scepticism about rationality, which, as we pointed out in Chapter 3, is self-defeating. If we are so irrational that even our best cognitive performance invites frequent mistakes in basic reasoning problems (such as the Linda experiment), then there is no hope for us to carry out reliable and effective psychological studies, which require the cognitive capacity for solving difficult and complicated problems in reasoning and statistics. But this undermines the trustworthiness of the psychological findings that allegedly support PASSP. Human cognition and agency are not perfect, but they are good enough for many purposes, including the purpose of doing philosophy and psychology through which people can learn about their own limitations.

As Paul Bloom points out, psychological studies exploring limitations in human cognition and agency are in fact an indication of how smart people are:

> [The psychological studies of biases and errors] illustrate irrationality, how things go wrong, how we are limited. But they also illustrate how intelligent we are, how we can override our biases. After all, we know that they are mistakes! [...] It turns out that every demonstration of our irrationality is also a demonstration of how smart we are, because without our smarts we wouldn't be able to appreciate that it's a demonstration of irrationality. (Bloom 2016, 228)

In Chapter 2, we discussed various studies of self-knowledge that cast doubt on the idea that humans are self-knowing creatures. Still, through psychological findings and philosophical argumentation, people can achieve a better understanding of the nature and operation of their mind, such as a better understanding of how self-knowledge works and where its limitations lie. Understanding the limitations of self-knowledge enables people to compensate for those limitations with the tools that philosophy and psychology make available. A person might not know why they made a choice if some of the relevant causal factors are opaque to introspection, but they can fill in the blanks if they learn about common priming effects that are likely to have interfered in their choice.

Something similar is true about responsibility. In Chapter 6, we discussed the idea that people are not fully responsible for their implicitly biased behaviour due to them lacking awareness of their implicit biases. However, this changes when people come to know about their likely biases based on the results of psychological studies. In other words, people can become more responsible for their implicitly biased behaviour after they have had the opportunity to learn about implicit biases they might have. This means that a person's acquisition of philosophical and psychological knowledge about limitations and biases can both improve their self-knowledge and extend their responsibility.

Thus, although the limitations of human cognition and agency are real, it is important not to exaggerate their implications. It is important to remember that we can do something about those limitations, starting from an appreciation of the issues discussed in this book. Philosophical and psychological knowledge of one's limitations might lead to developing ideas about how to overcome the existing constraints on one's cognition and agency.

For instance, people might be able to outsmart their biases after identifying them. Daniel Kahneman describes his own experience of the *halo effect*, which is the tendency to let one's evaluation of a person in one aspect or domain (e.g., being physically attractive) influence subsequent evaluations of that person in other aspects or domains (e.g., being competent as a co-worker). Initially, when grading student essays, Kahneman was reading and evaluating all the essays submitted by a student before moving on to the next student's work. However, he realized that this way of grading can easily be biased by the halo effect:

I began to suspect that my grading exhibited a halo effect, and that the first question I scored had a disproportionate effect on the overall grade. [...] If a student had written two essays, one strong and one weak, I would end up with different final grades depending on which essay I read first. I had told the students that the two essays had equal weight, but that was not true: the first one had a much greater impact on the final grade than the second. (Kahneman 2011, 83)

As a result, Kahneman changed his grading procedure to avoid the halo effect, grading essay one first for all his students before moving to grading essay two. More generally, awareness of what biases a person has and how biases work can be the first step towards a reduction of the effect of those biases on that person's behaviour.

Knowledge of biases can also be advantageous in a distinct way. Instead of outsmarting biases, or compensating for them, people can use those biases to achieve certain ends. The idea of 'nudges' developed by Richard Thaler and Cass Sunstein (2009) is a good example of this strategy. To 'nudge' people is to influence their choice by designing the context ('choice architecture') in which they make choices in a particular way, without resorting to any coercion or monetary incentives. Effective nudges utilize, rather than outsmart, the patterns in which choices are biased or influenced by contextual cues. As an example, in the context of organ donation, a government can adopt the rule that the default option is 'donate': that is, people are taken to consent to donating their organs unless they choose otherwise. They need to 'opt out' if they do not want to be organ donors. This default rule is expected to increase the number of donors by utilizing psychological inertia (i.e., the psychological bias by which people favour default options over non-default options). This default rule 'nudges' people in a socially favourable direction (because increasing organ donations saves lives) by utilizing their bias in favour of default options.

Our hope is that the discussion in our book and the sources in the philosophy of psychology that you have explored along the way will contribute to a better understanding of human cognition and agency and will change the way you think about your choices, emotions, beliefs, and actions. Knowledge (of the strengths and limitations of your mind) is power.

References

Introduction

Bargh, J. A., Chen, M., & Burrows, L. (1996). Automaticity of social behavior: Direct effects of trait construct and stereotype activation on action. *Journal of Personality and Social Psychology*, 71(2), 230–244.

Bermúdez, J. L. (2004). *Philosophy of Psychology: A Contemporary Introduction*. Routledge.

Bermúdez, J. L. (2020). *Cognitive Science: An Introduction to the Science of the Mind*, 3rd edition. Cambridge University Press.

Bloom, P. (2017). *Against Empathy: The Case for Rational Compassion*. Random House.

Cain, M. J. (2015). *The Philosophy of Cognitive Science*. Polity.

Clark, A. (2000). *Mindware: An Introduction to the Philosophy of Cognitive Science*. Oxford University Press.

Doyen, S., Klein, O., Pichon, C. L., & Cleeremans, A. (2012). Behavioral priming: It's all in the mind, but whose mind? *PloS ONE*, 7(1), e29081. URL: https://doi.org/10.1371/journal.pone.0029081.

Earp, B. D., & Trafimow, D. (2015). Replication, falsification, and the crisis of confidence in social psychology. *Frontiers in Psychology*, 6(621). URL: https://doi.org/10.3389/fpsyg.2015.00621.

Fodor, J. A. (1975). *The Language of Thought*. Harvard University Press.

Fodor, J. A. (1983). *The Modularity of Mind*. MIT Press.

Gallagher, S., & Zahavi, D. (2012). *The Phenomenological Mind*, 2nd edition. Routledge.

Gendler, T. (2011). Philosophy and the Science of Human Nature. In Open Yale Courses. URL: https://oyc.yale.edu/philosophy/phil-181.

Goldman, A. I. (2018). *Philosophical Applications of Cognitive Science*. Routledge.

Graham, G. (2013). *The Disordered Mind: An Introduction to Philosophy of Mind and Mental Illness*, 2nd edition. Routledge.

Haidt, J., Koller, S. H., & Dias, M. G. (1993). Affect, culture, and morality, or is it wrong to eat your dog? *Journal of Personality and Social Psychology*, 65(4), 613–628.

Henrich, J., Heine, S. J., & Norenzayan, A. (2010a). The weirdest people in the world? *Behavioral and Brain Sciences*, 33(2–3), 61–83.

Henrich, J., Heine, S. J., & Norenzayan, A. (2010b). Most people are not WEIRD. *Nature*, 466(7302): 29.

Kahneman, D. (2011). *Thinking, Fast and Slow*. Farrar, Straus and Giroux.

Kahneman, D., Slovic, P., & Tversky, A. (eds) (1982). *Judgment under Uncertainty: Heuristics and Biases*. Cambridge University Press.

Kihlstrom, J. F. (2004). Is there a 'People are Stupid' school in social psychology? *Behavioral and Brain Sciences*, 27(3): 348.

Loftus, E. F. (2003). Make-believe memories. *American Psychologist*, 58(11): 867–873.

Ramachandran, V. S., & Blakeslee, S. (1998). *Phantoms in the Brain: Probing the Mysteries of the Human Mind*. HarperCollins.

Schacter, D. L., & Addis, D. R. (2007). The cognitive neuroscience of constructive memory: Remembering the past and imagining the future. *Philosophical Transactions of the Royal Society B: Biological Sciences*, 362(1481), 773–786.

Schimmack, U., Heene, M., & Kesavan, K. (2017). Reconstruction of a train wreck: How priming research went off the rails. In U. Schimmack, *Replication Index: Improving the Replicability of Empirical Research*. URL: https://replicationindex.wordpress.com/2017/02/02/reconstruction-of-a-train-wreck-how-priming-research-went-of-the-rails/.

Shweder, R. A., Mahapatra, M., & Miller, J. G. (1987). Culture and moral development. In J. Kagan & S. Lamb (eds), *The Emergence of Morality in Young Children*. University of Chicago Press, 1–83.

Stone, T., & Davies, M. (1993). Cognitive neuropsychology and the philosophy of mind. *British Journal for the Philosophy of Science*, 44(4), 589–622.

Thagard, P. (2019). Cognitive science. In E. N. Zalta (ed.), *The Stanford Encyclopedia of Philosophy*. URL: https://plato.stanford.edu/archives/spr2019/entries/cognitive-science/.

Tversky, A., & Kahneman, D. (1974). Judgment under uncertainty: Heuristics and biases. *Science*, 185(4157), 1124–1131.

Weiskopf, D., & Adams, F. (2015). *An Introduction to the Philosophy of Psychology*. Cambridge University Press.

Wilson, T. D. (2002). *Strangers to Ourselves: Discovering the Adaptive Unconscious*. Harvard University Press.

Chapter 1

Aristotle (1984). *The Complete Works of Aristotle*, Volume II. Princeton University Press.

Bortolotti, L. (2014). *Irrationality*. Polity.

Bortolotti, L. (2018). Optimism, agency, and success. *Ethical Theory and Moral Practice*, 21(3), 521–535.

Brown, J. D. (2012). Understanding the better than average effect: Motives (still) matter. *Personality and Social Psychology Bulletin*, 38(2), 209–219.

Cherniak, C. (1990). *Minimal Rationality*. MIT Press.

Cohen, L. J. (1981). Can human irrationality be experimentally demonstrated? *Behavioral and Brain Sciences*, 4(3), 317–331.

Cosmides, L. (1989). The logic of social exchange: Has natural selection shaped how humans reason? Studies with the Wason selection task. *Cognition*, 31(3), 187–276.

Cosmides, L., & Tooby, J. (1992). Cognitive adaptations for social exchange. In J. H. Barkow, L. Cosmides, & J. Tooby (eds), *The Adapted Mind: Evolutionary Psychology and the Generation of Culture*. Oxford University Press, 163–228.

Davidson, D. (1982). Rational animals. *Dialectica*, 36(4), 317–327.

Descartes, R. (1985). *The Philosophical Writings of Descartes*, Volume 1. Cambridge University Press.

Fiedler, K. (1988). The dependence of the conjunction fallacy on subtle linguistic factors. *Psychological Research*, 50(2), 123–129.

Gerrans, P. (2001). Delusions as performance failures. *Cognitive Neuropsychiatry*, 6(3), 161–173.

Gigerenzer, G. (1991). How to make cognitive illusions disappear: Beyond 'heuristics and biases'. *European Review of Social Psychology*, 2(1), 83–115.

Gigerenzer, G. (1994). Why the distinction between single-event probabilities and frequencies is important for psychology (and vice versa). In G. Wright & P. Ayton (eds), *Subjective Probability*. Wiley, 129–161.

Gigerenzer, G. (1996). On narrow norms and vague heuristics: A reply to Kahneman and Tversky. *Psychological Review*, 103(3), 592–596.

Gigerenzer, G. (2007). *Gut Feelings: The Intelligence of the Unconscious*. Penguin.

Gigerenzer, G. (2008). *Rationality for Mortals: How People Cope with Uncertainty*. Oxford University Press.

Gigerenzer, G. (2012). How do smart people make smart decisions? TEDxNorrköping. URL: https://youtu.be/-Lg7G8TMe_A.

Griggs, R. A., & Cox, J. R. (1982). The elusive thematic-materials effect in Wason's selection task. *British Journal of Psychology*, 73(3), 407–420.

Hajek, A. (2019). Interpretations of probability. In E. N. Zalta (ed.), *The Stanford Encyclopedia of Philosophy*. URL: https://plato.stanford.edu/entries/probability-interpret/.

Harman, G. (1999). *Reasoning, Meaning, and Mind*. Oxford University Press.

Hume, D. (1739/2007). *A Treatise of Human Nature*, Volume 1. Oxford University Press.

Kahneman, D. (2002). Maps of bounded rationality. Nobel Prize Lecture 2002. URL: https://www.nobelprize.org/prizes/economic-sciences/2002/kahneman/lecture/.

Kahneman, D. (2011). *Thinking, Fast and Slow*. Farrar, Straus and Giroux.

Kahneman, D., & Tversky, A. (1973). On the psychology of prediction. *Psychological Review*, 80(4), 237–251.

Kahneman, D., & Tversky, A. (1996). On the reality of cognitive illusions. *Psychological Review*, 103(3), 582–591.

Kahneman, D., Slovic, P., & Tversky, A. (eds). (1982). *Judgment under Uncertainty: Heuristics and Biases*. Cambridge University Press.

Langer, E. J., & Roth, J. (1975). Heads I win, tails it's chance: The illusion of control as a function of the sequence of outcomes in a purely chance task. *Journal of Personality and Social Psychology*, 32(6), 951–955.

McKay, R. T. & Dennett, D. C. (2009). The evolution of misbelief. *Behavioral and Brain Sciences*, 32(6), 493–510.

Millikan, R. G. (1989). In defense of proper functions. *Philosophy of Science*, 56(2), 288–302.

Millikan, R. G. (2004). *Varieties of Meaning: The 2002 Jean Nicod Lectures*. MIT Press.

Millikan, R. G. (2009). It is likely misbelief never has a function. *Behavioral and Brain Sciences*, 32(6), 529–530.

Miyazono, K. (2018). *Delusions and Beliefs: A Philosophical Inquiry*. Routledge.

Neander, K. (1991). Functions as selected effects: The conceptual analyst's defense. *Philosophy of Science*, 58(2), 168–184.

Nisbett, R. E., & Borgida, E. (1975). Attribution and the psychology of prediction. *Journal of Personality and Social Psychology*, 32(5), 932–943.

Polonioli, A. (2016). Interview with Ralph Hertwig on biases, ignorance and adaptive rationality. *Imperfect Cognitions* Blog (13 October). URL: https://imperfectcognitions.blogspot.com/2016/10/interview-with-ralph-hertwig-on-biases.html.

Polonioli, A. (2017). Interview with Thomas Sturm. *Imperfect Cognitions* Blog (27 April). URL: http://imperfectcognitions.blogspot.com/2017/04/interview-with-thomas-sturm-on-science.html.

Russell, B. (1961). *The Basic Writings of Bertrand Russell*. Routledge.

Samuels, R., Stich, S., & Bishop, M. (2002). Ending the rationality wars: How to make disputes about human rationality disappear. In R. Elio (ed.), *Common Sense, Reasoning and Rationality*. Oxford University Press, 236–268.

Sharot, T. (2011). The optimism bias. *Current Biology*, 21(23), R941–R945.

Stalmeier, P. F., Wakker, P. P., & Bezembinder, T. G. (1997). Preference reversals: Violations of unidimensional procedure invariance. *Journal of*

Experimental Psychology: Human Perception and Performance, 23(4), 1196–1205.

Stanovich, K. E. (1999). *Who is Rational? Studies of Individual Differences in Reasoning*. Psychology Press.

Stanovich, K. E. (2004). *The Robot's Rebellion: Finding Meaning in the Age of Darwin*. University of Chicago Press.

Stanovich, K. E. (2009). Distinguishing the reflective, algorithmic, and autonomous minds: Is it time for a tri-process theory? In J. St B. T. Evans & K. Frankish (eds), *In Two Minds: Dual Processes and Beyond*. Oxford University Press, 55–88.

Stein, E. (1996). *Without Good Reason: The Rationality Debate in Philosophy and Cognitive Science*. Oxford University Press.

Stich, S. P. (1990). *The Fragmentation of Reason: Preface to a Pragmatic Theory of Cognitive Evaluation*. MIT Press.

Taylor, S. E. (1989). *Positive Illusions: Creative Self-Deception and the Healthy Mind*. Basic Books.

Thagard, P., & Nisbett, R. E. (1983). Rationality and charity. *Philosophy of Science*, 50(2), 250–267.

Todd, P. M., & Gigerenzer, G. (2007). Environments that make us smart: Ecological rationality. *Current Directions in Psychological Science*, 16(3), 167–171.

Trivers, R. L. (1971). The evolution of reciprocal altruism. *The Quarterly Review of Biology*, 46(1), 35–57.

Tversky, A., & Kahneman, D. (1974). Judgment under uncertainty: Heuristics and biases. *Science*, 185(4157), 1124–1131.

Tversky, A., & Kahneman, D. (1981). The framing of decisions and the psychology of choice. *Science*, 211(4481), 453–458.

Tversky, A., & Kahneman, D. (1983). Extensional versus intuitive reasoning: The conjunction fallacy in probability judgment. *Psychological Review*, 90(4), 293–315.

Tversky, A., & Kahneman, D. (1986). Rational choice and the framing of decisions. *Journal of Business*, 59(4), 251–278.

Tversky, A., & Thaler, R. H. (1990). Anomalies: Preference reversals. *Journal of Economic Perspectives*, 4(2), 201–211.

Velleman, D. (2000). *The Possibility of Practical Reason*. Oxford University Press.

Wason, P. C. (1966). Reasoning. In B. M. Foss (ed.), *New Horizons in Psychology*. Penguin, 135–151.

Wason, P. C., & Shapiro, D. (1971). Natural and contrived experience in a reasoning problem. *Quarterly Journal of Experimental Psychology*, 23(1), 63–71.

Weinstein, N. D. (1980). Unrealistic optimism about future life events. *Journal of Personality and Social Psychology*, 39(5), 806–820.

Wheeler, G. (2020). Bounded rationality. In E. N. Zalta (ed.), *The Stanford Encyclopedia of Philosophy*. URL: https://plato.stanford.edu/archives/spr2020/entries/bounded-rationality/.

Wilkins, J. S., & Griffiths, P. E. (2012). Evolutionary debunking arguments in three domains: Fact, value, and religion. In G. W. Dawes & J. Maclaurin (eds), *A New Science of Religion*. Routledge, 133–146.

Wolpe, N., Wolpert, D. M., & Rowe, J. B. (2014). Seeing what you want to see: Priors for one's own actions represent exaggerated expectations of success. *Frontiers in Behavioral Neuroscience*, 8. URL: https://doi.org/10.3389/fnbeh.2014.00232.

Chapter 2

Aronson, E. (2019). Dissonance, hypocrisy, and the self-concept. In E. Harmon-Jones (ed.), *Cognitive Dissonance: Reexamining a Pivotal Theory in Psychology*. American Psychological Association, 141–157.

Bem, D. J. (1967). Self-perception: An alternative interpretation of cognitive dissonance phenomena. *Psychological Review*, 74(3), 183–200.

Bem, D. J. (1972). Self-perception theory. *Advances in Experimental Social Psychology*, 6(1), 1–62.

Bortolotti, L. (2018a). Stranger than fiction: Costs and benefits of everyday confabulation. *Review of Philosophy and Psychology*, 9(2), 227–249.

Bortolotti, L. (2018b). Confabulation: Why telling ourselves stories makes us feel ok. *Aeon* (13 February). URL: https://aeon.co/ideas/confabulation-why-telling-ourselves-stories-makes-us-feel-ok.

Bortolotti, L., Cox, R., & Barnier, A. (2012). Can we recreate delusions in the laboratory? *Philosophical Psychology*, 25(1), 109–131.

Bortolotti, L., & Sullivan-Bissett, E. (2019). Is choice blindness a case of self-ignorance? *Synthese* (28 September). URL: https://doi.org/10.1007/s11229-019-02414-3.

Byrne, A. (2018). *Transparency and Self-Knowledge*. Oxford University Press.

Carruthers, P. (2009). How we know our own minds: The relationship between mindreading and metacognition. *Behavioral and Brain Sciences*, 32(2), 121–138.

Carruthers, P. (2011). *The Opacity of Mind: An Integrative Theory of Self-Knowledge*. Oxford University Press.

Carruthers, P. (2013). On knowing your own beliefs: A representationalist account. In N. Nottelmann (ed.), *New Essays on Belief: Constitution, Content and Structure*. Palgrave Macmillan, 145–165.

Cassam, Q. (2014). *Self-Knowledge for Humans*. Oxford University Press.

Coliva, A. (2016). *The Varieties of Self-Knowledge*. Palgrave Macmillan.

Cooper, J. (2007). *Cognitive Dissonance: 50 Years of a Classic Theory*. Sage.

Descartes, R. (1984). *The Philosophical Writings of Descartes*, Volume 2. Cambridge University Press.

Festinger, L., & Carlsmith, J. M. (1959). Cognitive consequences of forced compliance. *The Journal of Abnormal and Social Psychology*, 58(2), 203–210.

Frankish, K. (2016). Whatever you think you don't necessarily know your own mind. *Aeon* (27 May). URL: https://aeon.co/ideas/whatever-you-think-you-don-t-necessarily-know-your-own-mind.

Gazzaniga, M. S. (2000). Cerebral specialization and interhemispheric communication: Does the corpus callosum enable the human condition? *Brain*, 123(7), 1293–1326.

Gertler, B. (2020). Self-Knowledge. In E. N. Zalta (ed.), *The Stanford Encyclopedia of Philosophy*. URL: https://plato.stanford.edu/archives/spr2020/entries/self-knowledge/.

Gopnik, A. (1993). How we know our minds: The illusion of first-person knowledge of intentionality. *Behavioral and Brain Sciences*, 16(1), 1–14.

Green, M. (2019). Know thyself: The value and limits of self-knowledge. University of Edinburgh MOOC. URL: https://www.ed.ac.uk/ppls/philosophy/research/impact/free-online-courses/know-thyself.

Hall, L., Johansson, P., & Strandberg, T. (2012). Lifting the veil of morality: Choice blindness and attitude reversals on a self-transforming survey. *PLoS ONE*, 7(9): e45457. URL: https://doi.org/10.1371/journal.pone.0045457.e29081.

Hall, L., Strandberg, T., Pärnamets, P., Lind, A., Tärning, B., & Johansson, P. (2013). How the polls can be both spot on and dead wrong: Using choice blindness to shift political attitudes and voter intentions. *PLoS ONE*, 8(4), e60554. URL: https://doi.org/10.1371/journal.pone.0060554.

Hirstein, W. (2005). *Brain Fiction: Self-Deception and the Riddle of Confabulation*. MIT Press.

Hume, D. (1739/2007). *A Treatise of Human Nature*, Volume 1. Oxford University Press.

Johansson, P. (2018). Do you really know why you do what you do? TED. URL: https://www.ted.com/speakers/petter_johansson.

Johansson, P., Hall, L., Sikström, S., & Olsson, A. (2005). Failure to detect mismatches between intention and outcome in a simple decision task. *Science*, 310(5745), 116–119.

Johansson, P., Hall, L., Sikström, S., Tärning, B., & Lind, A. (2006). How something can be said about telling more than we can know: On choice blindness and introspection. *Consciousness and Cognition*, 15(4), 673–692.

Johansson, P., Hall, L., & Sikström, S. (2008). From change blindness to choice blindness. *Psychologia*, 51, 142–155.

Lawlor, K. (2003). Elusive reasons: A problem for first-person authority. *Philosophical Psychology*, 16(4), 549–564.

Lopes, D. M. I. (2014). Feckless reason. In G. Currie, M. Kieran, A. Meskin, & J. Robson (eds), *Aesthetics and the Sciences of Mind*. Oxford University Press, 21–36.

Nichols, S., & Stich, S. P. (2003). *Mindreading: An Integrated Account of Pretence, Self-awareness, and Understanding Other Minds*. Oxford University Press.

Nisbett, R. E., & Wilson, T. D. (1977). Telling more than we can know: Verbal reports on mental processes. *Psychological Review*, 84(3), 231–259.

Proust, J. (2016). How does metacognition work? *Brains* Blog (8 June). URL: http://philosophyofbrains.com/2016/06/08/how-does-metacognition-work.aspx.

Sandis, C. (2015). Verbal reports and 'real' reasons: Confabulation and conflation. *Ethical Theory and Moral Practice*, 18(2), 267–280.

Scaife, R. (2014). A problem for self-knowledge: The implications of taking confabulation seriously. *Acta Analytica*, 29(4), 469–485.

Schwitzgebel, E. (2019). Introspection. In E. N. Zalta (ed.), *The Stanford Encyclopedia of Philosophy*. URL: https://plato.stanford.edu/archives/win2019/entries/introspection/.

Strijbos, D., & de Bruin, L. (2015). Self-interpretation as first-person mindshaping: Implications for confabulation research. *Ethical Theory and Moral Practice*, 18(2), 297–307.

Turner, M., & Coltheart, M. (2010). Confabulation and delusion: A common monitoring framework. *Cognitive Neuropsychiatry*, 15(1–3), 346–376.

Wegner, D. M. (2002). *The Illusion of Conscious Will*. MIT Press.

Wilson, T. D. (2002). *Strangers to Ourselves: Discovering the Adaptive Unconscious*. Harvard University Press.

Wilson, T. D., & Kraft, D. (1993). Why do I love thee? Effects of repeated introspections about a dating relationship on attitudes toward the relationship. *Personality and Social Psychology Bulletin*, 19(4), 409–418.

Chapter 3

Boyd, R. (1991). Realism, anti-foundationalism and the enthusiasm for natural kinds. *Philosophical Studies*, 61(1–2), 127–148.

Calabretta, R., & Parisi, D. (2005). Evolutionary connectionism and mind/brain modularity. In W. Callebaut & D. Rasskin-Gutman (eds), *Modularity: Understanding the Development and Evolution of Natural Complex Systems*. MIT Press, 309–330.

Currie, G., & Ichino, A. (2012). Aliefs don't exist, though some of their relatives do. *Analysis*, 72(4), 788–798.

Davidson, D. (2004). *Problems of Rationality*. Oxford University Press.

Doggett, T. (2012). Some questions for Tamar Szabó Gendler. *Analysis*, 72(4), 764–774.

Evans, J. St B. T. (2003). In two minds: Dual-process accounts of reasoning. *Trends in Cognitive Sciences*, 7(10), 454–459.

Evans, J. St B. (2008). Dual-processing accounts of reasoning, judgment, and social cognition. *Annual Review of Psychology*, 59, 255–278.

Evans, J. St B. T. (2010). *Thinking Twice: Two Minds in One Brain*. Oxford University Press.

Evans, J. St B. T. (2011). Dual-process theories of reasoning: Contemporary issues and developmental applications. *Developmental Review*, 31(2–3), 86–102.

Evans, J. St B. T. (2012). Dual-process theories of deductive reasoning: Facts and fallacies. In K. J. Holyoak & R. G. Morrison (eds), *The Oxford Handbook of Thinking and Reasoning*. Oxford University Press, 115–133.

Evans, J. St B. T., Barston, J. L., & Pollard, P. (1983). On the conflict between logic and belief in syllogistic reasoning. *Memory & Cognition*, 11(3), 295–306.

Evans, J. St B. T., & Frankish, K. (eds) (2009). *In Two Minds: Dual Processes and Beyond*. Oxford University Press.

Evans, J. St B. T., & Over, D. E. (1996). *Rationality and Reasoning*. Psychology Press.

Evans, J. St B. T., & Stanovich, K. E. (2013a). Dual-process theories of higher cognition: Advancing the debate. *Perspectives on Psychological Science*, 8(3), 223–241.

Evans, J. St B. T., & Stanovich, K. E. (2013b). Theory and metatheory in the study of dual processing: Reply to comments. *Perspectives on Psychological Science*, 8(3), 263–271.

Fodor, J. A. (1983). *The Modularity of Mind: An Essay on Faculty Psychology*. MIT Press.

Frankish, K. (2009). Delusions: A two-level framework. In M. R. Broome & L. Bortolotti (eds), *Psychiatry as Cognitive Neuroscience: Philosophical Perspectives*. Oxford University Press, 269–284.

Frankish, K. (2010). Dual-process and dual-system theories of reasoning. *Philosophy Compass*, 5(10), 914–926.

Frankish, K., & Evans, J. St B. T. (2009). The duality of mind: An historical perspective. In J. St B. T. Evans & K. Frankish (eds), *In Two Minds: Dual Processes and Beyond*. Oxford University Press, 1–29.

Kahneman, D. (2013). Getting to the heart of the dual-system distinction. YouTube. URL: https://youtu.be/sBov_nn7TPw.

Gazzaniga, M. S. (2000). Cerebral specialization and interhemispheric communication: Does the corpus callosum enable the human condition? *Brain*, 123(7), 1293–1326.

Gendler, T. S. (2008a). Alief and belief. *The Journal of Philosophy*, 105(10), 634–663.

Gendler, T. S. (2008b). Alief in action (and reaction). *Mind & Language*, 23(5), 552–585.

Gendler, T. S. (2011). On the epistemic costs of implicit bias. *Philosophical Studies*, 156(1), 33–63.

Gendler, T. S. (2012). Between reason and reflex: Response to commentators. *Analysis*, 72(4), 799–811.

Gould, S. J. (1991). *Bully for Brontosaurus: Reflections in Natural History*. W. W. Norton & Company.

Haidt, J. (2001). The emotional dog and its rational tail: A social intuitionist approach to moral judgment. *Psychological Review*, 108(4), 814–834.

Hodges, S. D., & Wilson, T. D. (1993). Effects of analyzing reasons on attitude change: The moderating role of attitude accessibility. *Social Cognition*, 11(4), 353–366.

Kahneman, D. (2011). *Thinking, Fast and Slow*. Farrar, Straus and Giroux.

Kaufman, S. B., and Singer, J. L. (2012). The creativity of dual process 'system 1' thinking. Scientific American (17 January). URL: https://blogs.scientificamerican.com/guest-blog/the-creativity-of-dual-process-system-1-thinking/.

Kriegel, U. (2012). Moral motivation, moral phenomenology, and the alief/belief distinction. *Australasian Journal of Philosophy*, 90(3), 469–486.

Mandelbaum, E. (2017). Associationist theories of thought. In E. N. Zalta (ed.), *The Stanford Encyclopedia of Philosophy*. URL: https://plato.stanford.edu/archives/sum2017/entries/associationist-thought.

Mele, A. R. (2001). *Self-Deception Unmasked*. Princeton University Press.

Nisbett, R. E., & Wilson, T. D. (1977). Telling more than we can know: Verbal reports on mental processes. *Psychological Review*, 84(3), 231–259.

O'Brien, D. P. (1998). Mental logic and irrationality: We can put a man on the moon, so why can't we solve those logical reasoning problems? In M. D. S. Braine & D. P. O'Brien (eds), *Mental Logic*. Psychology Press, 23–44.

Plato (1995). *Phaedrus*. Hackett Publishing.

Samuels, R. (1998). Evolutionary psychology and the massive modularity hypothesis. *The British Journal for the Philosophy of Science*, 49(4), 575–602.

Samuels, R. (2009). The magical number two, plus or minus: Dual-process theory as a theory of cognitive kinds. In J. St B. T. Evans & K. Frankish (eds), In *Two Minds: Dual Processes and Beyond*. Oxford University Press, 129–146.

Schwitzgebel, E. (2001). In-between believing. *The Philosophical Quarterly*, 51(202), 76–82.

Schwitzgebel, E. (2012). Mad belief? *Neuroethics*, 5(1), 13–17.

Schwitzgebel, E. (2013). A dispositional approach to attitudes: Thinking outside of the belief box. In N. Nottelmann (ed.), *New Essays on Belief: Constitution, Content and Structure*. Palgrave Macmillan, 75–99.

Seligman, C., Fazio, R. H., & Zanna, M. P. (1980). Effects of salience of extrinsic rewards on liking and loving. *Journal of Personality and Social Psychology*, 38(3), 453–460.

Sengupta, J., & Fitzsimons, G. J. (2004). The effect of analyzing reasons on the stability of brand attitudes: A reconciliation of opposing predictions. *Journal of Consumer Research*, 31(3), 705–711.

Sloman, S. A. (1996). The empirical case for two systems of reasoning. *Psychological Bulletin*, 119(1), 3–22.

Stanovich, K. E. (1999). *Who Is Rational? Studies of Individual Differences in Reasoning*. Psychology Press.

Stanovich, K. E. (2004). *The Robot's Rebellion: Finding Meaning in the Age of Darwin*. University of Chicago Press.

Stanovich, K. E. (2011). *Rationality and the Reflective Mind*. Oxford University Press.

Stanovich, K. E., & Toplak, M. E. (2012). Defining features versus incidental correlates of Type 1 and Type 2 processing. *Mind & Society*, 11(1), 3–13.

Stanovich, K. E., & West, R. F. (2000). Individual differences in reasoning: Implications for the rationality debate? *Behavioral and Brain Sciences*, 23(5), 645–665.

Tversky, A., & Kahneman, D. (1974). Judgment under uncertainty: Heuristics and biases. *Science*, 185(4157), 1124–1131.

Wason, P. C., & Evans, J. S. B. (1974). Dual processes in reasoning? *Cognition*, 3(2), 141–154.

Wilson, T. D. (2002). *Strangers to Ourselves: Discovering the Adaptive Unconscious*. Harvard University Press.

Wilson, T. D., Dunn, D. S., Bybee, J. A., Hyman, D. B., & Rotondo, J. A. (1984). Effects of analyzing reasons on attitude–behavior consistency. *Journal of Personality and Social Psychology*, 47(1), 5–16.

Wilson, T. D., Hodges, S. D., & LaFleur, S. J. (1995). Effects of introspecting about reasons: Inferring attitudes from accessible thoughts. *Journal of Personality and Social Psychology*, 69(1), 16–28.

Wilson, T. D., & Kraft, D. (1993). Why do I love thee? Effects of repeated introspections about a dating relationship on attitudes toward the relationship. *Personality and Social Psychology Bulletin*, 19(4), 409–418.

Wilson, T. D., Lindsey, S., & Schooler, T. Y. (2000). A model of dual attitudes. *Psychological Review*, 107(1), 101–126.

Chapter 4

Bartels, D. M., & Pizarro, D. A. (2011). The mismeasure of morals: Antisocial personality traits predict utilitarian responses to moral dilemmas. *Cognition*, 121(1), 154–161.

Berker, S. (2009). The normative insignificance of neuroscience. *Philosophy & Public Affairs*, 37(4), 293–329.

Clarke, S. (2008). SIM and the city: Rationalism in psychology and philosophy and Haidt's account of moral judgment. *Philosophical Psychology*, 21(6), 799–820.

Conway, P., Goldstein-Greenwood, J., Polacek, D., & Greene, J. D. (2018). Sacrificial utilitarian judgments do reflect concern for the greater good: Clarification via process dissociation and the judgments of philosophers. *Cognition*, 179, 241–265.

Evans, J. St B. (2008). Dual-processing accounts of reasoning, judgment, and social cognition. *Annual Review of Psychology*, 59, 255–278.

Graham, J., Haidt, J., Koleva, S., Motyl, M., Iyer, R., Wojcik, S. P., & Ditto, P. H. (2013). Moral foundations theory: The pragmatic validity of moral pluralism. In P. Devine & A. Plant (eds), *Advances in Experimental Social Psychology* (Vol. 47). Academic Press, 55–130.

Graham, J., Haidt, J., & Nosek, B. A. (2009). Liberals and conservatives rely on different sets of moral foundations. *Journal of Personality and Social Psychology*, 96(5), 1029–1046.

Greene, J. (2003). From neural 'is' to moral 'ought': What are the moral implications of neuroscientific moral psychology? *Nature Reviews Neuroscience*, 4(10), 846–850.

Greene, J. D. (2008). The secret joke of Kant's soul. In W. Sinnott-Armstrong (ed.), *Moral Psychology, Vol. 3: The Neuroscience of Morality: Emotion, Brain Disorders, and Development*. MIT Press, 35–79.

Greene, J. D. (2013). *Moral Tribes: Emotion, Reason, and the Gap between Us and Them*. Penguin.

Greene, J. (2014). Moral tribes: Emotion, reason and the gap between us and them. YouTube. URL: https://youtu.be/VaoTKurm_1k.

Greene, J., & Haidt, J. (2002). How (and where) does moral judgment work? *Trends in Cognitive Sciences*, 6(12), 517–523.

Greene, J. D., Nystrom, L. E., Engell, A. D., Darley, J. M., & Cohen, J. D. (2004). The neural bases of cognitive conflict and control in moral judgment. *Neuron*, 44(2), 389–400.

Greene, J. D., Sommerville, R. B., Nystrom, L. E., Darley, J. M., & Cohen, J. D. (2001). An fMRI investigation of emotional engagement in moral judgment. *Science*, 293(5537), 2105–2108.

Haidt, J. (2001). The emotional dog and its rational tail: A social intuitionist approach to moral judgment. *Psychological Review*, 108(4), 814–834.

Haidt, J. (2007). The new synthesis in moral psychology. *Science*, 316(5827), 998–1002.

Haidt, J. (2012). *The Righteous Mind: Why Good People Are Divided by Politics and Religion*. Pantheon Books.

Haidt, J. (2013). The rationalist delusions in moral psychology. YouTube. URL: https://youtu.be/kI1wQswRVaU.

Haidt, J., Bjorklund, F., & Murphy, S. (2000). Moral dumbfounding: When intuition finds no reason. Unpublished manuscript.

Haidt, J., & Joseph, C. (2004). Intuitive ethics: How innately prepared intuitions generate culturally variable virtues. *Daedalus*, 133(4), 55–66.

Haidt, J., Koller, S. H., & Dias, M. G. (1993). Affect, culture, and morality, or is it wrong to eat your dog? *Journal of Personality and Social Psychology*, 65(4), 613–628.

Hauser, M. (2006). *Moral Minds: How Nature Designed Our Universal Sense of Right and Wrong*. Ecco.

Henrich, J., Heine, S. J., & Norenzayan, A. (2010a). The weirdest people in the world? *Behavioral and Brain Sciences*, 33(2–3), 61–83.

Henrich, J., Heine, S. J., & Norenzayan, A. (2010b). Most people are not WEIRD. *Nature*, 466(7302): 29.

Hume, D. (1739/2007). *A Treatise of Human Nature*, Volume 1. Oxford University Press.

Kahane, G. (2011). Evolutionary debunking arguments. *Noûs*, 45(1), 103–125.

Kahane, G. (2012). On the wrong track: Process and content in moral psychology. *Mind & Language*, 27(5), 519–545.

Kahane, G., Everett, J. A., Earp, B. D., Farias, M., & Savulescu, J. (2015). 'Utilitarian' judgments in sacrificial moral dilemmas do not reflect impartial concern for the greater good. *Cognition*, 134, 193–209.

Kennett, J., & Fine, C. (2009). Will the real moral judgment please stand up? *Ethical Theory and Moral Practice*, 12(1), 77–96.

Koenigs, M., Kruepke, M., Zeier, J., & Newman, J. P. (2012). Utilitarian moral judgment in psychopathy. *Social Cognitive and Affective Neuroscience*, 7(6), 708–714.

Levy, N. (2014). Neuroethics: Moral cognition. *Oxford Handbooks Online*. (doi: 10.1093/oxfordhb/9780199935314.013.003)

Liao, S. M. (2011) Bias and reasoning: Haidt's theory of moral judgment. In T. Brooks (ed.), *New Waves in Ethics*. Palgrave Macmillan, 108–127.

May, J. (2018). *Regard for Reason in the Moral Mind*. Oxford University Press.

Mikhail, J. (2007). Universal moral grammar: Theory, evidence and the future. *Trends in Cognitive Sciences*, 11(4), 143–152.

Nisbett, R. E., & Wilson, T. D. (1977). Telling more than we can know: Verbal reports on mental processes. *Psychological Review*, 84(3), 231–259.

Nucci, L. P. (2001). *Education in the Moral Domain*. Cambridge University Press.

Nucci, L. P., & Turiel, E. (1978). Social interactions and the development of social concepts in preschool children. *Child Development*, 49(2), 400–407.

Philosophy Bites (2012). Liane Young on mind and morality. URL: https://philosophybites.com/2012/10/liane-young-on-mind-and-morality.html.

Philosophy Overdose (2017). Moral judgement: Interview with Jesse Prinz. YouTube. URL: https://youtu.be/Krex1n6qVxM.

Richardson, H. S. (2018). Moral reasoning. In E. N. Zalta (ed.), *The Stanford Encyclopedia of Philosophy*. URL: https://plato.stanford.edu/archives/fall2018/entries/reasoning-moral.

Shweder, R. A., Mahapatra, M., & Miller, J. G. (1987). Culture and moral development. In J. Kagan & S. Lamb (eds), *The Emergence of Morality in Young Children*. University of Chicago Press, 1–83.

Sinnott-Armstrong, W. (ed.) (2008a). *Moral Psychology, Vol. 2: The Cognitive Science of Morality: Intuition and Diversity*. MIT Press.

Sinnott-Armstrong, W. (ed.) (2008b). *Moral Psychology, Vol. 3: The Neuroscience of Morality: Emotion, Brain Disorders, and Development*. MIT Press.

Smetana, J. G. (1981). Preschool children's conceptions of moral and social rules. *Child Development*, 52(4), 1333–1336.

Sunstein, C. R. (2005). Moral heuristics. *Behavioral and Brain Sciences*, 28(4), 531–541.

Turiel, E. (1983). *The Development of Social Knowledge: Morality and Convention*. Cambridge University Press.

Turiel, E., Killen, M., & Helwig, C. C. (1987). Morality: Its structure, functions, and vagaries. In J. Kagan & S. Lamb (eds), *The Emergence of Morality in Young Children*. University of Chicago Press, 155–243.

Wheatley, T., & Haidt, J. (2005). Hypnotic disgust makes moral judgments more severe. *Psychological Science*, 16(10), 780–784.

Chapter 5

Batson, C. D. (1991). *The Altruism Question: Toward a Social-Psychological Answer*. Psychology Press.

Batson, C. D. (2011). *Altruism in Humans*. Oxford University Press.

Batson, C. D. (2018). *A Scientific Search for Altruism: Do We Only Care About Ourselves?* Oxford University Press.

Batson, C. D., Duncan, B. D., Ackerman, P., Buckley, T., & Birch, K. (1981). Is empathic emotion a source of altruistic motivation? *Journal of Personality and Social Psychology*, 40(2), 290–302.

Batson, C. D., Klein, T. R., Highberger, L., & Shaw, L. L. (1995). Immorality from empathy-induced altruism: When compassion and justice conflict. *Journal of Personality and Social Psychology*, 68(6), 1042–1054.

Bloom, P. (2014). Forum: Against empathy. *Boston Review*. URL: http://bostonreview.net/forum/paul-bloom-against-empathy.

Bloom, P. (2015). Against empathy. YouTube. URL: https://youtu.be/WWWNUa6kmqE.

Bloom, P. (2016). *Against Empathy: The Case for Rational Compassion*. Random House.

Bloom, P. (2017). Empathy and its discontents. *Trends in Cognitive Sciences*, 21(1), 24–31.

Coke, J. S., Batson, C. D., & McDavis, K. (1978). Empathic mediation of helping: A two-stage model. *Journal of Personality and Social Psychology*, 36(7), 752–766.

Crockett, M., & Prinz, J. (2015). Is empathy important for morality? YouTube. URL: https://youtu.be/vQxp2QKYFhY.

de Dreu, C. K., Greer, L. L., Van Kleef, G. A., Shalvi, S., & Handgraaf, M. J. (2011). Oxytocin promotes human ethnocentrism. *Proceedings of the National Academy of Sciences*, 108(4), 1262–1266.

Hume, D. (1739/2007). *A Treatise of Human Nature*, Volume 1. Oxford University Press.

Insel, T. R., & Fernald, R. D. (2004). How the brain processes social information: Searching for the social brain. *Annual Review Neuroscience*, 27, 697–722.

Maibom, H. L. (2012). The many faces of empathy and their relation to prosocial action and aggression inhibition. *Wiley Interdisciplinary Reviews: Cognitive Science*, 3(2), 253–263.

Maibom, H. L. (ed.) (2014). *Empathy and Morality*. Oxford University Press.

Maibom, H. L. (2020). *Empathy*. Routledge.

Matravers, D. (2017). *Empathy*. Polity.

Mill, J. S. (1861/2015). Utilitarianism. In *On Liberty, Utilitarianism, and Other Essays*. Oxford University Press, 113–178.

Millikan, R. G. (2004). *Varieties of Meaning: The 2002 Jean Nicod Lectures*. MIT Press.

Nisbett, R. E., & Wilson, T. D. (1977). Telling more than we can know: Verbal reports on mental processes. *Psychological Review*, 84(3), 231–259.

Obama, B. (2006). Obama to graduates: Cultivate empathy. URL: https://www.northwestern.edu/newscenter/stories/2006/06/barack.html.

Persson, I., & Savulescu, J. (2012). *Unfit for the Future: The Need for Moral Enhancement*. Oxford University Press.

Persson, I., & Savulescu, J. (2018). The moral importance of reflective empathy. *Neuroethics*, 11(2), 183–193.

Prinz, J. (2011). Against empathy. *The Southern Journal of Philosophy*, 49, 214–233.

Prinz, J. (2014). Forum response: Against empathy. *Boston Review*. URL: http://bostonreview.net/forum/against-empathy/jesse-prinz-response-against-empathy-prinz.

Schelling, T. C. (1984). *Choice and Consequence*. Harvard University Press.

Sharp, F. C. (1928). *Ethics*. Century.

Slote, M. (2007). *The Ethics of Care and Empathy*. Routledge.

Slote, M. (2010). *Moral Sentimentalism*. Oxford University Press.

Smith, A. (1759/1976). *The Theory of Moral Sentiments*. Oxford University Press.

Stich, S., Doris, J. M., & Roedder, E. (2012). Altruism. In J. Doris & The Moral Psychology Research Group (eds), *The Moral Psychology Handbook*. Oxford University Press, 147–205.

Stocks, E. L., Lishner, D. A., & Decker, S. K. (2009). Altruism or psychological escape: Why does empathy promote prosocial behavior? *European Journal of Social Psychology*, 39(5), 649–665.

Chapter 6

Baer, J., Kaufman, J. C., & Baumeister, R. F. (eds). (2008). *Are We Free? Psychology and Free Will*. Oxford University Press.

Banaji, M. R., & Greenwald, A. G. (2013). *Blindspot: Hidden Biases of Good People*. Delacorte Press.

Bargh, J. (1997). The automaticity of everyday life. In R. S. Wyer (ed.), *The Automaticity of Everyday Life*. Psychology Press, 1–61.

Bayne, T. (2006). Phenomenology and the feeling of doing: Wegner on the conscious will. In S. Pockett, W. P. Banks, & S. Gallagher (eds), *Does Consciousness Cause Behavior?* MIT Press, 169–186.

BBC Radio 4. (2017). *Analysis: Implicit Bias*. URL: https://www.bbc.co.uk/programmes/b08slvk8.

Brownstein, M. (2019). Implicit biases. In E. N. Zalta (ed.), *The Stanford Encyclopedia of Philosophy*. URL: https://plato.stanford.edu/entries/implicit-bias/.

Brownstein, M., & Saul, J. M. (eds). (2016a). *Implicit Bias and Philosophy, Vol. 1: Metaphysics and Epistemology*. Oxford University Press.

Brownstein, M., & Saul, J. M. (eds). (2016b). *Implicit Bias and Philosophy*,

Vol. 2: Moral Responsibility, Structural Injustice, and Ethics. Oxford University Press.

Closer to Truth (2016). Closer to truth – Big questions in free will. YouTube. URL: https://youtu.be/9uRTjfhIf4M.

Darley, J. M., & Batson, C. D. (1973). 'From Jerusalem to Jericho': A study of situational and dispositional variables in helping behavior. *Journal of Personality and Social Psychology*, 27(1), 100–108.

Dasgupta, N., & Greenwald, A. G. (2001). On the malleability of automatic attitudes: Combating automatic prejudice with images of admired and disliked individuals. *Journal of Personality and Social Psychology*, 81(5), 800–814.

Gollwitzer, P. M., & Sheeran, P. (2006). Implementation intentions and goal achievement: A meta-analysis of effects and processes. *Advances in Experimental Social Psychology*, 38, 69–119.

Haggard, P. (2011). Neuroethics of free will. In J. Illes & B. J. Sahakian (eds), *Oxford Handbook of Neuroethics*. Oxford University Press, 219–227.

Haney, C., Banks, W. C., & Zimbardo, P. G. (1973). A study of prisoners and guards in a simulated prison. *Naval Research Reviews*, 9, 1–17.

Holroyd, J. (2012). Responsibility for implicit bias. *Journal of Social Philosophy*, 43(3), 274–306.

Holroyd, J., Scaife, R., & Stafford, T. (2017). Responsibility for implicit bias. *Philosophy Compass*, 12(3), e12410.

Kim, J. (2005). *Physicalism, or Something Near Enough*. Princeton University Press.

Latané, B., & Darley, J. M. (1968). Group inhibition of bystander intervention in emergencies. *Journal of Personality and Social Psychology*, 10(3), 215–221.

Libet, B. (1985). Unconscious cerebral initiative and the role of conscious will in voluntary action. *Behavioral and Brain Sciences*, 8(4), 529–539.

Libet, B. (1999). Do we have free will? *Journal of Consciousness Studies*, 6(8–9), 47–57.

Libet, B. (2004). *Mind Time: The Temporal Factor in Consciousness.* Harvard University Press.

Libet, B., Gleason, C. A., Wright, E. W., & Pearl, D. K. (1983). Time of conscious intention to act in relation to onset of cerebral activity (readiness-potential). *Brain*, 106(3), 623–642.

Mele, A. R. (2008). *Free Will and Luck.* Oxford University Press.

Mele, A. R. (2013). *A Dialogue on Free Will and Science.* Oxford University Press.

Mele, A. R. (2014). *Free: Why Science Hasn't Disproved Free Will.* Oxford University Press.

Milgram, S. (1963). Behavioral study of obedience. *Journal of Abnormal and Social Psychology*, 67(4), 371–378.

Milgram, S. (1974). *Obedience to Authority.* Harper & Row.

Montague, P. R. (2008). Free will. *Current Biology*, 18(14), R584–R585.

Nahmias, E. (2010). Scientific challenges to free will. In T. O'Connor

& C. Sandis (eds), *A Companion to the Philosophy of Action*. Wiley-Blackwell, 345–356.

Nisbett, R. E., & Wilson, T. D. (1977). Telling more than we can know: Verbal reports on mental processes. *Psychological Review*, 84(3), 231–259.

Oswald, F. L., Mitchell, G., Blanton, H., Jaccard, J., & Tetlock, P. E. (2013). Predicting ethnic and racial discrimination: A meta-analysis of IAT criterion studies. *Journal of Personality and Social Psychology*, 105(2), 171–192.

Roskies, A. L. (2011). Why Libet's studies don't pose a threat to free will. In W. Sinnott-Armstrong & L. Nadel (eds), *Conscious Will and Responsibility: A Tribute to Benjamin Libet*. Oxford University Press, 11–22.

Saul, J. (2013). Implicit bias, stereotype threat, and women in philosophy. In K. Hutchison & F. Jenkins (eds), *Women in Philosophy: What Needs to Change?* Oxford University Press, 39–60.

Sinnott-Armstrong, W. E. (2014). *Moral Psychology, Vol. 4: Free Will and Moral Responsibility*. MIT Press.

Soon, C. S., Brass, M., Heinze, H. J., & Haynes, J. D. (2008). Unconscious determinants of free decisions in the human brain. *Nature Neuroscience*, 11(5), 543–545.

Wegner, D. M. (2002). *The Illusion of Conscious Will*. MIT Press.

Wegner, D. M., & Wheatley, T. (1999). Apparent mental causation: Sources of the experience of will. *American Psychologist*, 54(7), 480–492.

Zimbardo, P. G. (2007). *The Lucifer Effect: Understanding How Good People Turn Evil*. Random House.

Chapter 7

3CR. (2017). Beth Matthews interviews Lisa Bortolotti on clinical delusions. *Radical Philosophy* podcast. URL: https://www.3cr.org.au/radicalphilosophy/episode-201709141530/prof-lisa-bortolotti-clinical-delusions.

Aimola Davies, A.M., & Davies, M. (2009). Explaining pathologies of belief. In M. R. Broome & L. Bortolotti (eds), *Psychiatry as Cognitive Neuroscience: Philosophical Perspectives*. Oxford University Press, 285–323.

American Psychiatric Association. (2013). *Diagnostic and Statistical Manual of Mental Disorders*, 5th edition. American Psychiatric Publishing.

Aronson, E. (2019). Dissonance, hypocrisy, and the self-concept. In E. Harmon-Jones (ed.), *Cognitive Dissonance: Reexamining a Pivotal Theory in Psychology*. American Psychological Association, 141–157.

Bayne, T., & Pacherie, E. (2005). In defence of the doxastic conception of delusions. *Mind & Language*, 20(2), 163–188.

Bentall, R. P. (1990). The syndromes and symptoms of psychosis. In

R. P. Bentall (ed.), *Reconstructing Schizophrenia*. Oxford University Press, 23–60.

Berlyne, N. (1972). Confabulation. *The British Journal of Psychiatry*, 120(554), 31–39.

Bernecker, S., & Michaelian, K. (eds). (2017). *The Routledge Handbook of Philosophy of Memory*. Routledge.

Berrios, G. E. (1991). Delusions as 'wrong beliefs': A conceptual history. *The British Journal of Psychiatry*, 159(S14), 6–13.

Bisiach, E., & Geminiani, G. (1991). Anosognosia related to hemiplegia and hemianopia. In G. P. Prigatano & D. L. Schacter (eds), *Awareness of Deficit after Brain Injury*. Oxford University Press, 17–39.

Bleuler, E. (1911). *Dementia Praecox: Or the Group of Schizophrenias*. International Universities Press.

Bortolotti, L. (2010). *Delusions and Other Irrational Beliefs*. Oxford University Press.

Bortolotti, L. (ed.). (2018). *Delusions in Context*. Palgrave Macmillan.

Bortolotti, L. (2019). Delusion. In E. N. Zalta (ed.), *The Stanford Encyclopedia of Philosophy*. URL: https://plato.stanford.edu/entries/delusion/.

Bortolotti, L., & Broome, M. R. (2012). Affective dimensions of the phenomenon of double bookkeeping in delusions. *Emotion Review*, 4(2), 187–191.

Bortolotti, L., & Miyazono, K. (2015). Recent work on the nature and development of delusions. *Philosophy Compass*, 10(9), 636–645.

Bortolotti, L., & Sullivan-Bissett, E. (2018). The epistemic innocence of clinical memory distortions. *Mind & Language*, 33(3), 263–279.

Cherry, K. (2020). What is confabulation? *Very Well Mind*. URL: https://www.verywellmind.com/confabulation-definition-examples-and-treatments-4177450.

Chinn, C.A. & Brewer, W.F. (2001). Models of data: A theory of how people evaluate data. *Cognition and Instruction*, 19(3), 323–393.

Clark, A. (2013). Whatever next? Predictive brains, situated agents, and the future of cognitive science. *Behavioral and Brain Sciences*, 36(3), 181–204.

CMAJ Podcasts. (2019). Matthew Parrott on what are delusions? *Philosophers on Medicine*. URL: https://soundcloud.com/cmajpodcasts/190048-medsoc.

Coltheart, M. (2007). Cognitive neuropsychiatry and delusional belief. *Quarterly Journal of Experimental Psychology*, 60(8), 1041–1062.

Coltheart, M., Langdon, R., & McKay, R. (2011). Delusional belief. *Annual Review of Psychology*, 62, 271–298.

Coltheart, M., Menzies, P., & Sutton, J. (2010). Abductive inference and delusional belief. *Cognitive Neuropsychiatry*, 15(1–3), 261–287.

Conway, M. (2005). Memory and the self. *Journal of Memory and Language*, 53, 594–628.

Corcoran, R., Cummins, S., Rowse, G., Moore, R., Blackwood, N., Howard, R., ... & Bentall, R. P. (2006). Reasoning under uncertainty: Heuristic judgments in patients with persecutory delusions or depression. *Psychological Medicine*, 36(8), 1109–1118.

Conway, M., & Ross, M. (1984). Getting what you want by revising what you had. *Journal of Personality and Social Psychology*, 47(4), 738–748.

Corlett, P. R., Krystal, J. H., Taylor, J. R., & Fletcher, P. C. (2009). Why do delusions persist? *Frontiers in Human Neuroscience*, 3(12). URL: https://doi.org/10.3389/neuro.09.012.2009.

Corlett, P. R., Murray, G. K., Honey, G. D., Aitken, M. R., Shanks, D. R., Robbins, T. W., ... & Fletcher, P. C. (2007). Disrupted prediction-error signal in psychosis: Evidence for an associative account of delusions. *Brain*, 130(9), 2387–2400.

Corlett, P. R., Taylor, J. R., Wang, X. J., Fletcher, P. C., & Krystal, J. H. (2010). Toward a neurobiology of delusions. *Progress in Neurobiology*, 92(3), 345–369.

Currie, G., & Ravenscroft, I. (2002). *Recreative Minds: Imagination in Philosophy and Psychology*. Oxford University Press.

Davies, M., Coltheart, M., Langdon, R., & Breen, N. (2001). Monothematic delusions: Towards a two-factor account. *Philosophy, Psychiatry, & Psychology*, 8(2), 133–158.

Dawkins, R. (2006). *The God Delusion*. Bantam Books.

Deese, J. (1959). On the prediction of occurrence of particular verbal intrusions in immediate recall. *Journal of Experimental Psychology*, 58(1), 17–22.

Egan, A. (2008). Imagination, delusion, and self-deception. In T. Bayne & J. Fernández (eds), *Delusions and Self-deception: Motivational and Affective Influences on Belief Formation*. Psychology Press, 263–280.

Ellis, H. D., & Young, A. W. (1990). Accounting for delusional misidentifications. *The British Journal of Psychiatry*, 157(2), 239–248.

Ellis, H. D., Young, A. W., Quayle, A. H., & De Pauw, K. W. (1997). Reduced autonomic responses to faces in Capgras delusion. *Proceedings of the Royal Society of London. Series B: Biological Sciences*, 264(1384), 1085–1092.

Fletcher, P. C., & Frith, C. D. (2009). Perceiving is believing: A Bayesian approach to explaining the positive symptoms of schizophrenia. *Nature Reviews Neuroscience*, 10(1), 48–58.

Fotopoulou, A. (2008). False selves in neuropsychological rehabilitation: The challenge of confabulation. *Neuropsychological Rehabilitation: An International Journal*, 18(5/6), 541–565.

Fotopoulou, A., Conway, M., Solms, M., Tyrer, S., & Kopelman, M. (2008). Self-serving confabulation in prose recall. *Neuropsychologia*, 46, 1429–1441.

Frankish, K. (2012). Delusions, levels of belief, and non-doxastic acceptances. *Neuroethics*, 5(1), 23–27.

Friston, K. (2010). The free-energy principle: A unified brain theory? *Nature Reviews Neuroscience*, 11(2), 127–138.

Gallagher, S. (2009). Delusional realities. In L. Bortolotti & M. Broome (eds), *Psychiatry as Cognitive Neuroscience: Philosophical Perspectives*. Oxford University Press, 245–268.

Garety, P. A., & Hemsley, D. R. (1997). *Delusions: Investigations into the Psychology of Delusional Reasoning*. Psychology Press.

Gerrans, P. (2014). *The Measure of Madness: Philosophy of Mind, Cognitive Neuroscience, and Delusional Thought.* MIT Press.

Gilleen, J., & David, A. S. (2005). The cognitive neuropsychiatry of delusions: From psychopathology to neuropsychology and back again. *Psychological Medicine,* 35(1), 5–12.

Hohwy, J. (2013). *The Predictive Mind.* Oxford University Press.

Hohwy, J., & Rajan, V. (2012). Delusions as forensically disturbing perceptual inferences. *Neuroethics,* 5(1), 5–11.

Huq, S. F., Garety, P. A., & Hemsley, D. R. (1988). Probabilistic judgements in deluded and non-deluded subjects. *The Quarterly Journal of Experimental Psychology Section A,* 40(4), 801–812.

Jordan, H. W., & Howe, G. (1980). De Clerambault syndrome (Erotomania): A review and case presentation. *Journal of the National Medical Association,* 72(10), 979–985.

Kopelman, M. D. (1999). Varieties of false memory. *Cognitive Neuropsychology,* 16(3–5), 197–214.

Langdon, R., & Turner, M. (eds). (2010). *Delusion and Confabulation: A Special Issue of Cognitive Neuropsychiatry.* Psychology Press.

Loftus, E. F. (2003). Make-believe memories. *American Psychologist,* 58(11), 867–873.

Maher, B. A. (1974). Delusional thinking and perceptual disorder. *Journal of Individual Psychology,* 30(1), 98–113.

Markus, G. B. (1986). Stability and change in political attitudes: Observed, recalled, and explained. *Political Behavior,* 8(1), 21–44.

McKay, R. (2012). Delusional inference. *Mind & Language,* 27(3), 330–355.

McKay, R., & Cipolotti, L. (2007). Attributional style in a case of Cotard delusion. *Consciousness and Cognition,* 16(2), 349–359.

McKenna, P. (2017). *Delusions: Understanding the Un-understandable.* Cambridge University Press.

Metcalf, K., Langdon, R., & Coltheart, M. (2007). Models of confabulation: A critical review and a new framework. *Cognitive Neuropsychology,* 24(1), 23–47.

Michaelian, K., & Sutton, J. (2017). Memory. In E.N. Zalta (ed.) *The Stanford Encyclopedia of Philosophy.* URL: https://plato.stanford.edu/entries/memory/.

Miyazono, K. (2018). *Delusions and Beliefs: A Philosophical Inquiry.* Routledge.

Miyazono, K., & McKay, R. (2019). Explaining delusional beliefs: a hybrid model. *Cognitive Neuropsychiatry,* 24(5), 335–346.

Moscovitch, M. (1995). Confabulation. In D. L. Schacter (ed.), *Memory Distortions: How Minds, Brains, and Societies Reconstruct the Past.* Harvard University Press, 226–251.

Nisbett, R. E., & Wilson, T. D. (1977). Telling more than we can know: Verbal reports on mental processes. *Psychological Review,* 84(3), 231–259.

Persaud, R. (2015). Interview with Matthew Broome. YouTube. URL: https://youtu.be/8qm0nEE9h4w.

Persaud, R. (2015). Interview with Philip Corlett. YouTube. URL: https://youtu.be/gj35UsX5LLc.

Persaud, R. (2015). Interview with Richard Bentall. YouTube. URL: https://youtu.be/5F1iEsLZzhM.

Pyszczynski, T., Greenberg, J., & Holt, K. (1985). Maintaining consistency between self-serving beliefs and available data: A bias in information evaluation. *Personality and Social Psychology Bulletin*, 11(2), 179–190.

Puddifoot, K., & Bortolotti, L. (2019). Epistemic innocence and the production of false memory beliefs. *Philosophical Studies*, 176(3), 755–780.

Radden, J. (2010). *On Delusion*. Routledge.

Rankin, K. P., Baldwin, E., Pace-Savitsky, C. E., Kramer, J. H., & Miller, B. L. (2005). Self-awareness and personality change in dementia. *Journal of Neurology, Neurosurgery, and Psychiatry*, 76(5), 632–639.

Roediger, H. L., & McDermott, K. B. (1995). Creating false memories: Remembering words not presented in lists. *Journal of Experimental Psychology. Learning, Memory, and Cognition*, 21(4), 803–814.

Rusche, S. E., & Brewster, Z. W. (2008). 'Because they tip for shit!': The social psychology of everyday racism in restaurants. *Sociology Compass*, 2(6), 2008–2029.

Salvaggio, M. (2018). The justification of reconstructive and reproductive memory beliefs. *Philosophical Studies*, 175, 649–663.

Schacter, D. L. (1999). The seven sins of memory: Insights from psychology and cognitive neuroscience. *American Psychologist*, 54(3), 182–203.

Schacter, D. L., & Addis, D. R. (2007). The cognitive neuroscience of constructive memory: Remembering the past and imagining the future. *Philosophical Transactions of the Royal Society B: Biological Sciences*, 362(1481), 773–786.

Schacter, D. L., Guerin, S. A., & St Jacques, P. L. (2011). Memory distortion: An adaptive perspective. *Trends in Cognitive Sciences*, 15, 467–474.

Schnider, A. (2003). Spontaneous confabulation and the adaptation of thought to ongoing reality. *Nature Reviews Neuroscience*, 4(8), 662–671.

Schwitzgebel, E. (2012). Mad belief? *Neuroethics*, 5(1), 13–17.

Stephens, G. L., & Graham, G. (2004). Reconceiving delusion. *International Review of Psychiatry*, 16(3), 236–241.

Stone, T., & Young, A. W. (1997). Delusions and brain injury: The philosophy and psychology of belief. *Mind & Language*, 12(3–4), 327–364.

Tranel, D., Damasio, H., & Damasio, A. R. (1995). Double dissociation between overt and covert face recognition. *Journal of Cognitive Neuroscience*, 7(4), 425–432.

Tulving, E. (2002). Episodic memory: From mind to brain. *Annual Review of Psychology*, 53(1), 1–25.

Tumulty, M. (2011). Delusions and dispositionalism about belief. *Mind & Language*, 26(5), 596–628.

Turnbull, O. H., Jenkins, S., & Rowley, M. L. (2004). The pleasantness of false beliefs: An emotion-based account of confabulation. *Neuropsychoanalysis*, 6(1), 5–16.

Tversky, A., & Kahneman, D. (1974). Judgment under uncertainty: Heuristics and biases. *Science*, 185(4157), 1124–1131.

Tversky, A., & Kahneman, D. (1983). Extensional versus intuitive reasoning: The conjunction fallacy in probability judgment. *Psychological Review*, 90(4), 293–315.

von Domarus, E. (1944). The specific laws of logic in schizophrenia. In J. S. Kasanin (ed.), *Language and Thought in Schizophrenia*. University of California Press, 104–114.

Chapter 8

Aharoni, E., Sinnott-Armstrong, W., & Kiehl, K. A. (2012). Can psychopathic offenders discern moral wrongs? A new look at the moral/conventional distinction. *Journal of Abnormal Psychology*, 121(2), 484–497.

American Psychiatric Association. (2013). *Diagnostic and Statistical Manual of Mental Disorders*, 5th edition. American Psychiatric Publishing.

Babiak, P., & Hare, R. D. (2006). *Snakes in Suits: When Psychopaths Go to Work*. HarperCollins.

Baron-Cohen, S. (1995). *Mindblindness: An Essay on Autism and Theory of Mind*. MIT Press.

Baron-Cohen, S. (2011). *Zero Degrees of Empathy: A New Theory of Human Cruelty*. Penguin.

Baron-Cohen, S., Leslie, A. M., & Frith, U. (1985). Does the autistic child have a 'theory of mind'? *Cognition*, 21(1), 37–46.

Bartels, D. M., & Pizarro, D. A. (2011). The mismeasure of morals: Antisocial personality traits predict utilitarian responses to moral dilemmas. *Cognition*, 121(1), 154–161.

Blair, R. J. R. (1995). A cognitive developmental approach to morality: Investigating the psychopath. *Cognition* 57(1), 1–29.

Currie, G. (1996). Simulation-theory, theory-theory and the evidence from autism. In P. Carruthers & P. K. Smith (eds), *Theories of Theories of Mind*. Oxford University Press, 242–256.

Dennett, D. C. (1978). Beliefs about beliefs. *Behavioral and Brain Sciences*, 1(4), 568–570.

Fletcher-Watson, S., & Happé, F. (2019). *Autism: A New Introduction to Psychological Theory and Current Debate*. Routledge.

Frith, U. (2003). *Autism: Explaining the Enigma*. Blackwell.

Frith, U. (2008). *Autism: A Very Short Introduction*. Oxford University Press.

Frith, U. (2012). Why we need cognitive explanations of autism. *The Quarterly Journal of Experimental Psychology*, 65(11), 2073–2092.

Frith, U., & Happé, F. (1995). Autism: Beyond 'theory of mind'. In J. Mehler & S. Franck (eds), *Cognition on Cognition*. MIT Press, 13–30.

Goldman, A. I. (2006). *Simulating Minds: The Philosophy, Psychology, and Neuroscience of Mindreading*. Oxford University Press.

Gopnik, A., & Wellman, H. M. (1992). Why the child's theory of mind really is a theory. *Mind & Language*, 7(1–2), 145–171.

Greene, J. D., Sommerville, R. B., Nystrom, L. E., Darley, J. M., & Cohen, J. D. (2001). An fMRI investigation of emotional engagement in moral judgment. *Science*, 293(5537), 2105–2108.

Hacking, I. (2013). Making up autism. *The British Society for the History of Science* podcast. URL: https://www.bshs.org.uk/podcast-professor-ian-hacking-making-up-autism.

Haddon, M. (2003). *The Curious Incident of the Dog in the Night-time*. Doubleday.

Haidt, J., Koller, S. H., & Dias, M. G. (1993). Affect, culture, and morality, or is it wrong to eat your dog? *Journal of Personality and Social Psychology*, 65(4), 613–628.

Happé, F. G. (1995). The role of age and verbal ability in the theory of mind task performance of subjects with autism. *Child Development*, 66(3), 843–855.

Happé, F., & Frith, U. (2006). The weak coherence account: Detail-focused cognitive style in autism spectrum disorders. *Journal of Autism and Developmental Disorders*, 36(1), 5–25.

Hare, R. D. (1993). *Without Conscience: The Disturbing World of the Psychopaths Among Us*. Guilford Press.

Hill, E. L. (2004). Executive dysfunction in autism. *Trends in Cognitive Sciences*, 8(1), 26–32.

Kahane, G., Everett, J. A., Earp, B. D., Farias, M., & Savulescu, J. (2015). 'Utilitarian' judgments in sacrificial moral dilemmas do not reflect impartial concern for the greater good. *Cognition*, 134, 193–209.

Kanner, L. (1943). Autistic disturbances of affective contact. *Nervous Child*, 2(3), 217–250.

Koenigs, M., Kruepke, M., Zeier, J., & Newman, J. P. (2012). Utilitarian moral judgment in psychopathy. *Social Cognitive and Affective Neuroscience*, 7(6), 708–714.

Levy, N. (2007). The responsibility of the psychopath revisited. *Philosophy, Psychiatry, & Psychology*, 14(2), 129–138.

Levy, N. (2013). Psychopathy and responsibility. *Practical Ethics* podcast. URL: http://blog.practicalethics.ox.ac.uk/2013/03/neil-levy-psychopaths-and-responsibility-podcast/.

Levy, N. (2014). Psychopaths and blame: The argument from content. *Philosophical Psychology*, 27(3), 351–367.

Maibom, H. L. (2012). The many faces of empathy and their relation to prosocial action and aggression inhibition. *Wiley Interdisciplinary Reviews: Cognitive Science*, 3(2), 253–263.

Maibom, H. L. (2018). What can philosophers learn from psychopathy? *European Journal of Analytic Philosophy*, 14(1), 63–78.

Nisbett, R. E., & Wilson, T. D. (1977). Telling more than we can know: Verbal reports on mental processes. *Psychological Review*, 84(3), 231–259.

Onishi, K. H., & Baillargeon, R. (2005). Do 15-month-old infants understand false beliefs? *Science*, 308(5719), 255–258.

Prinz, J. (2011). Against empathy. *The Southern Journal of Philosophy*, 49, 214–233.

Senju, A., Southgate, V., White, S., & Frith, U. (2009). Mindblind eyes: An absence of spontaneous theory of mind in Asperger syndrome. *Science*, 325(5942), 883–885.

Serious Science. (2016a). Autism: Uta Frith. YouTube. URL: https://youtu.be/2E0kvPsiUAk.

Serious Science. (2016b). Theory of mind: Uta Frith. YouTube. URL: https://youtu.be/N6ylH-LYjOM.

Serious Science. (2017). Talents in autism: Uta Frith. YouTube. URL: https://youtu.be/9mf23sL8eaI.

Sinnott-Armstrong, W. E. (2008). *Moral Psychology, Vol. 3: The Neuroscience of Morality: Emotion, Brain Disorders, and Development*. MIT Press.

Stueber, K. (2019). Empathy. In E. N. Zalta (ed.), *The Stanford Encyclopedia of Philosophy*. URL: https://plato.stanford.edu/entries/empathy/.

Talbert, M. (2019). Moral responsibility. In E. N. Zalta (ed.), *The Stanford Encyclopedia of Philosophy*. URL: https://plato.stanford.edu/entries/moral-responsibility/.

Turiel, E., Killen, M., & Helwig, C. C. (1987). Morality: Its structure, functions, and vagaries. In J. Kagan & S. Lamb (eds), *The Emergence of Morality in Young Children*. University of Chicago Press, 155–243.

Watson, G. (2013). Psychopathy and prudential deficits. *Aristotelian Society* podcast. URL: https://issuu.com/aristotelian.society/docs/watson_podcast.

Wellman, H. M., Cross, D., & Watson, J. (2001). Meta-analysis of theory-of-mind development: The truth about false belief. *Child Development*, 72(3), 655–684.

Wing, L., & Gould, J. (1979). Severe impairments of social interaction and associated abnormalities in children: Epidemiology and classification. *Journal of Autism and Developmental Disorders*, 9(1), 11–29.

Conclusion

Bloom, P. (2016). *Against Empathy: The Case for Rational Compassion*. Random House.

Kahneman, D. (2011). *Thinking, Fast and Slow*. Farrar, Straus and Giroux.

Kihlstrom, J. F. (2004). Is there a 'People are Stupid' school in social psychology? *Behavioral and Brain Sciences*, 27(3): 348.

Thaler, R. H., & Sunstein, C. R. (2009). *Nudge: Improving Decisions about Health, Wealth, and Happiness*. Penguin.

Index